FAMILY AND KINSHIP IN
CHINESE SOCIETY

Contributors

Ai-li S. Chin

Myron L. Cohen

Maurice Freedman

John McCoy

Johanna M. Meskill

John C. Pelzel

Jack M. Potter

Irene B. Taeuber

Arthur P. Wolf

Margery Wolf

FAMILY AND KINSHIP IN CHINESE SOCIETY

Edited by MAURICE FREEDMAN

Stanford University Press, Stanford, California 1970

Stanford University Press, Stanford, California
© 1970 by the Board of Trustees of the Leland Stanford Junior University
Printed in the United States of America
SBN 8047-0713-8   LC 69-18493

Preface

All but one of the essays in this book were in their original form papers written for, and discussed at, a conference on kinship in Chinese society, held at Greyston House, Riverdale, New York, September 15–18, 1966. The conference was called by the Subcommittee on Research on Chinese Society of the Joint Committee on Contemporary China of the American Council of Learned Societies and the Social Science Research Council (New York). It was the first of a series of conferences: the second, on urban society in traditional China, took place in September 1968; the third, on urban society and political development in modern China, in December–January 1968–69; and the fourth, on economic organization in Chinese society, in August 1969. The third conference was organized jointly with the Subcommittee on Chinese Government and Politics.

Fourteen papers were presented at the first conference. Five of them are, alas, missing from this book. Chen Shao-hsing sent a paper from Taiwan entitled "Family, Lineage, and Settlement Pattern in Taiwan"; he did not attend the conference because of illness, and he has since died, a tragic loss to the scholarship of his country and to the small world of sinological sociology. Arthur P. Wolf spoke at the conference on "Dynamics of the Chinese Family," but has been unable to write that contribution up for publication in this volume. Morton H. Fried presented a paper on "Some Aspects of Clan and Lineageship in a Modern Chinese City—Taipei," but he has not found it possible to publish it here. Ezra F. Vogel's "A Preliminary View of Family and Mental Health in Urban Communist China," has similarly not been available for inclusion in this book. Finally, we have not received for publication G. William Skinner's paper "Filial Sons and Their Sisters: Culture and Configuration in Chinese Families." Against these losses we are able to set Professor Wolf's paper on Chinese mourning, which he wrote after the conference and which is now printed with the remaining nine conference papers.

In addition to the paper-writers (other than Irene Taeuber, who was unable to attend the conference), the following scholars were present as discussants: Baruch Boxer, Michigan State University; Chang Kwang-chih, Yale University; Albert C. Feuerwerker, University of Michigan; Floyd G. Lounsbury, Yale University; and Barbara E. Ward, School of Oriental and African Studies, University of London. A full and edited record of the discussion, made by Elizabeth Johnson and Howard Nelson, was placed at the disposal of the contributors to help them in revising their papers; I have been able to draw on that record in the writing of my Introduction. Bryce Wood of the Social Science Research Council was responsible for the administrative work involved in organizing the conference and took a full part in its proceedings. I record my gratitude —and not as a mere formality—to the nine other authors of this book and to those whose names I have listed.

The planners of the series of conferences of which this was the first had it in mind that family, marriage, and kinship formed a suitable group of topics on which to open. A considerable amount of new work was being done on them, and there seemed to be an opportunity both to take stock of what was known and to sketch out the main lines of what research might yet usefully be done. It was our intention, of course, to draw as widely as possible on the talent available, and a number of scholars were approached in several countries of whom the final ten contributors to this volume are only some. They form a representative sample solely in respect of its necessarily heavy weighting in favor of anthropologists. Only one of the ten authors (myself) comes from a non-American institution, and only one (Ai-li S. Chin) writes against the background of a Chinese upbringing, although all of them have had firsthand acquaintance with the Chinese scene.

This book should ideally have been concerned with every major aspect of Chinese family, kinship, and marriage during the last hundred years or so, and it should of course have dealt fully with Communist China, but writers on all the necessary subjects are hard to come by. The company of sociologists and anthropologists working on China is small, and its joint competence to discuss China in the fullest sense of that noun is still further hampered by the inaccessibility of the People's Republic. But while we are in the ridiculous position of virtually ignoring Communist China in nine and a half of the ten contributions, there is nothing in the criticism (I anticipate it) that material drawn from studies made in Taiwan and Hong Kong and among Overseas Chinese is an insecure foundation for general statements about Chinese society—except, of course, in regard to the changes brought about on the mainland since 1949. Every region of China has its oddities, and if we had written this book on the basis of several studies made in, say, west China (just to argue from the poignantly impossible), we should be no better off than we are now as we work on the data from southeastern China (Taiwan, Hong Kong, and the Overseas Chinese who originate from the provinces of Fukien and Kwangtung). A constant checking of the material collected in the southeast against what we know from the literature on other parts of the country shows the sense in which it is possible to generalize about China and illuminate particular features of its social life and institutions by a close study of them in one relatively restricted area. No doubt there are valid political reasons in the minds of some people for dismissing Taiwan and Hong Kong as not being the real thing; there are no good sociological reasons. True, Hong Kong is a British colony and Taiwan was under Japanese rule for half a century. The impact of foreign government can hardly be ignored, but, at least when we write about domestic and other kinship institutions, it is not too difficult to allow for the effect of the extraneous factor and to present an account of something that is genuinely Chinese. Indeed, the objection that the parts of China open to us are peculiar by their not having been brought under the control of the Peking regime can be turned completely upside down: if we want as social scientists to get a firsthand knowledge of what certain traditional Chinese institutions were like, then Communist China is the very last place to look for them and Taiwan and Hong Kong the most obvious places.

The fortunes of selection and self-selection have led to another bias in the essays that will not go unremarked: the book leans very heavily toward the countryside. It is a great pity, because the study of Chinese society has for too long now been plagued by a prejudice in favor of rural life (the sinological bias closely following that of the Chinese who have written the record on which historians draw). The organizers of the conference were conscious of the need and did their best to redress the balance. I should remind the reader that the second and third conferences in the series have been devoted exclusively to urban life.

In the light of what has been said it will be clear that nobody will be able to pick up this book and find in it a textbook on Chinese kinship. That textbook, when it comes to be written, will have been preceded by a set of particular studies to which the present book is intended to make a contribution. Although the coverage of the book is incomplete, in the

sense that it does not deal with every significant aspect of the whole subject, it does in fact treat the main heads of the hypothetical textbook of
the future. It contains, in Mrs. Taeuber's essay, an introduction to the
demographic dimensions and problems of the Chinese family. The family is examined from different points of view by Professor Cohen, Mrs.
Wolf, Mrs. Chin, Professor Wolf, and myself. The lineage is discussed
by Professor Potter and Professor Meskill, and to some extent in my
essay. Marriage is at least touched on in every essay and is treated more
fully in the essays by Mrs. Wolf, Mrs. Chin, and me. Professor McCoy
explores Chinese kinship terminology. The economic and political implications of kinship are sketched in at various points in different essays.
Two of the essays deal with ritual implications. There should certainly
have been something substantial on the legal aspects of the subject, and
I accept responsibility for this unfortunate omission.

As I have suggested that the volume may mark a stage on the road
toward a textbook of Chinese kinship, I should like to remove the implication that the study of Chinese society marches on to a proximate destination at which a halt may be called. For, if the textbook does in fact
get to be written, it will be merely a survey of the state of knowledge at
the time it is composed and itself a preliminary to further studies and,
ultimately perhaps, a second textbook. The point, on general grounds,
is obvious and trivial, but I make it because there is a tendency, especially perhaps among young students, to think of traditional Chinese
society as something on which only so much can be said and may soon
have been entirely said, particularly in what appears to be so well-worn
a field as the family. Yet theory and experience show that the opposite
is true. We cannot now know what theoretical problems will agitate us
in the future; it is likely (indeed it is to be hoped) that they will be different from those we are concerned about at present, and that they will
require the social scientists of the future to reevaluate all the work done
in the past in the light of their new preoccupations. And it is far from
being the case that the sources for study are nearing exhaustion, a point
that will, I think, be made plain in many parts of this volume.

Marion Levy's *The Family Revolution in Modern China* (1949) and
Hu Hsien-chin's *The Common Descent Group in China and Its Functions* (1948) were admirable pioneering studies when they appeared,
and they are now admirable as classics. The topics those books dealt
with have been rethought and reassessed as the two authors themselves
recast the work of their predecessors. As long as the social sciences move
on, there will be more to be said about Chinese kinship. Indeed, there
seems to be a certain periodicity in the emergence of synthetic works on

Chinese kinship: the books by Levy and Hu, along with Olga Lang's
Chinese Family and Society (1946), represent the first postwar assess-
ment; ten years after Levy, C. K. Yang's *The Chinese Family in the
Communist Revolution* (1959) provided an evaluation of the family in
the first period of Communist rule; this book follows a decade later.
And 1979?

Our knowledge of Chinese kinship can be expanded and deepened
because we have the opportunity of studying in the field in Taiwan and
Hong Kong, and among the Overseas Chinese. But even if we were to
be cut off from these living sources (*absit omen*), there would still remain to us the vast documentation that China has both produced and
stimulated foreigners to produce. It is for the sinologues to say how far
the Chinese (and Japanese) documents would take us; I would venture
the opinion, based on my indirect knowledge of them and on my acquaintance with the Western writings, that there is today no shortage
of data on China—that the shortage from which we suffer is one of ideas.
I have been struck time and time again by the experience of going back
to old sources that I thought I knew thoroughly and finding for the first
time what some fresh notion had inspired me to seek out. Social scientists are easily persuaded that what they will discover in the field will
depend on the apparatus of ideas they carry to it; they do not so readily
apply the moral to their reading.

The value of mixing the field study of China with the study of the
older literature is one of the great lessons learned by the social scientists
in recent times, and they have learned it partly in the course of the
seminars and conferences sponsored by the Subcommittee on Research
on Chinese Society. The importance attached to the use of the store of
published knowledge may be gauged by the gigantic effort that has been
put into the preparation, under Professor Skinner's guidance and by his
labors, of bibliographies to lead scholars to their necessary reading on
China. But there is another important kind of intellectual traffic ex-
emplified in this book by Professor Pelzel's essay on Japanese kinship.
China, we are discovering more and more, can be profitably studied
within the context of the group of societies with which it shares a clas-
sical tradition. We are only at the beginning of what I am convinced
will be a chief feature of the social science work on China in the years
immediately ahead of us: the systematic comparative study of China in
the company of Japan, Korea, and Vietnam. The amount of sociological
knowledge about the last two of those countries is so small that the first
benefit to be derived from comparative East Asian studies will be the
light cast on them from China. But it seems to me certain that our

understanding of China itself will stand to gain from a close examination of the variants of "Chinese" institutions and cultural expressions as we find them in this larger world.

Of the contributors to the volume all but Professor Meskill, the historian, Mrs. Chin, the sociologist, and Mrs. Taeuber, the demographer, are anthropologists (although Professor McCoy is also a linguist and Professor and Mrs. Wolf can lay claim to the status of social psychologist). In designing the conference we were concerned to bring together people from a variety of disciplines; although as things turned out, three of the discussants were anthropologists (Professors Chang and Lounsbury and Miss Ward), we had a historian in Professor Feuerwerker and a geographer in Professor Boxer. One can make too much of interdisciplinary research and discussion, but in the study of so complex a civilization as that of China the anthropologists (who so far as the sociological group of disciplines is concerned are in the majority) would be the losers by talking only to one another. The Joint Committee on Contemporary China is to be congratulated on providing institutional settings within which people of several disciplines may come together.

M.F.

London, September 1969

Contents

Contributors

AI-LI S. CHIN grew up in China and came to the United States to study at Wellesley College for her B.A. and at Radcliffe for her Ph.D. in sociology. She did research at Harvard's East Asian Research Center from 1961 to 1965. In 1963, she went with her husband to Taiwan, where under a Fulbright Research Grant they collaborated on a study of college youth. She and her husband are co-authors of *Psychological Research in Communist China*, 1969. At present she is a Research Associate at the Center for International Studies, M.I.T., working on a project concerning the Chinese in the United States.

MYRON L. COHEN received his Ph.D. in 1967 from Columbia University, where he is now Assistant Professor in the Department of Anthropology and the East Asian Institute. Between 1963 and 1965 he did library and field research in Taiwan on a predoctoral research fellowship from the Social Science Research Council. He is the author of various articles on Chinese social organization, and is presently completing a monograph based on his field study.

MAURICE FREEDMAN has been Professor of Anthropology in the University of London at the London School of Economics and Political Science since 1965; he has taught there since 1951. He has served as a visiting professor at Yale and Cornell universities and at the University of Malaya. He was Chairman of the London Committee of the London–Cornell Project for East and Southeast Asian Studies from its foundation in 1962 until 1969. He was President of the Royal Anthropological Institute of Great Britain and Ireland from 1967 to 1969. He has made field studies in Singapore, Indonesia, and Hong Kong. His publications in the Chinese field include *Chinese Family and Marriage in Singapore*, 1957; *Lineage Organization in Southeastern China*, 1958; *Chinese Lineage and Society: Fukien and Kwangtung*, 1966.

JOHN MCCOY received his Ph.D. from Cornell University, where he is now Associate Professor of Linguistics and Chinese Literature. After wartime service in South China with a Chinese army unit, he returned for graduate work at the University of Chicago and Harvard. For the next eleven years he served with the United States Government, chiefly in Tokyo and Hong Kong. At Cornell his training and research has been focused on linguistics and anthropological linguistics of Southeast China with publications on Szeyap and Boat People dialects. At present he is in Asia working on linguistic and literary aspects of early Chinese folk poetry.

JOHANNA M. MESKILL studied at the University of Frankfurt, at Columbia, and at the University of Chicago, where she received a Ph.D. in history. She held postdoctoral fellowships for study and research in Taiwan. Her interest is in Chinese social history, especially of the Ch'ing period, and in Taiwanese local history. A book-length study of a Taiwanese gentry family is in preparation. She edited, under her maiden name, Menzel, *The Chinese Civil Service: Career Open to Talent?*, 1963, and is contributing to the forthcoming *Taiwan: A Case Study in Chinese Local History*. From 1956 to 1968 she taught at Vassar College, and she is now Associate Professor of History at Lehman College in the City University of New York.

JOHN PELZEL, who is Professor of Anthropology at Harvard University and Director of the Harvard-Yenching Institute, received his Ph.D at Harvard in 1949. During World War II he was with the United States Marine Corps in the Pacific, and from 1947 to 1949 he was associated with the Civil Information and Education Section, SCAP, Tokyo, where he worked on revision of the writing system of Japanese, supervised a national sample survey of literacy, and did fieldwork on social organization. In line with his interest in comparative social organization of China and Japan, he has done fieldwork in Hong Kong and has served as a visiting professor at the University of Tokyo. He has edited *Nihonjin no yomi-kaki nōryoku*, 1951, and co-edited *A Selected List of Books and Articles on Japan*, 1954.

JACK M. POTTER received his Ph.D. from the University of California, Berkeley, where he is now Associate Professor of Anthropology. His research has been primarily in the fields of traditional Chinese rural society and comparative peasant studies. He is the author of *Capitalism and the Chinese Peasant: Social and Economic Change in a Hong Kong Village*, 1968, and co-editor of *Peasant Society: A Reader*, 1967.

IRENE B. TAEUBER is Senior Research Demographer, Office of Population Research, Princeton University. She is a past president of the Population Association of America, a past vice-president of the International Union for the Scientific Study of Population, and a member of the Subcommittee on Chinese Society of the Joint Committee on Contemporary China of the American Council of Learned Societies and the Social Science Research Council. She is co-author of the Rockefeller Foundation report on *Public Health and Demography in the Far East*, 1950, and author of *The Population of Japan*, 1958,

Nihon jinko, 1965, and numerous articles on China and Chinese populations. She is presently working on a monograph on the population of the Chinese cultural area.

ARTHUR P. WOLF received his Ph.D. from Cornell University in 1964 and taught there for five years. He is now an Associate Professor of Anthropology at Stanford University. His present interest is in Chinese family organization and its relationship to personality processes and population problems in northern Taiwan.

MARGERY WOLF, the wife of Arthur Wolf, is the author of *The House of Lim,* 1968, a book describing the farm family with whom she lived during her first field trip to Taiwan. She is currently working on a study of the life of women in rural northern Taiwan.

FAMILY AND KINSHIP IN
CHINESE SOCIETY

Introduction

MAURICE FREEDMAN

This book opens with two essays on the family. Both are based on recent field work in Taiwan, one dealing with Hakka-speakers and the other with Hokkien-speakers. I should like to suggest some of the ways in which the two contributions advance our knowledge of the subject, carrying it on to a stage from which further progress may be made. If we take the two papers together, we shall see that they raise, either directly or by implication, all the problems that students of the Chinese family have so far confronted. One of the writers concentrates on the constitution of the family and the nature of its economic organization, the other on the quality and properties of interpersonal relations as seen through the study of child rearing.

The heart of Professor Cohen's argument is that the Chinese word *chia* is ambiguous, for he says that it can mean a group, an estate (of property), or an economy (a set of economic activities). The term has more usually been treated as the Chinese equivalent of the English "family," and we see that we are already in deep water, for "family" and *chia* each have variable meanings within the context of the societies in which they are used; and they are certainly not simply to be translated into each other. Indeed, one cannot get very far into Professor Cohen's paper without being brought up sharp by the realization that "family," as a term of art in sociology and anthropology, must be one of the vaguest words in a vocabulary already well furnished with vague words.

In the study of China it has become traditional to start from the connection between family and residence and to construct four main forms of the family when marriage is of the standard kind that transfers women from their natal houses to the houses of their husbands. The first of these

forms is the unit of spouses and their children, commonly termed an elementary or nuclear family. If we follow out the potential development
of such a small family, we can see how the other three forms may emerge
from it. Assume that the parents marry out their daughters and bring in
wives for their sons. Those sons have children; a third generation has
appeared. If all the people so far mentioned, less the married-out daughters in the middle generation, live in one unit, we have what is conven-
tionally called a joint family. If, on the other hand, there is only one
married son (other sons, if any, having left the house), we have what is
usually referred to as a stem family. The terminology seems to have been
fixed by Lang (1946);* we shall consider later how appropriate it is.
Finally, if a joint family is denuded of its senior generation, so that the
family unit consists of two or more married brothers with their wives
and children, we have what some would call a fraternal joint family.

Much of the earlier argument on the Chinese family centered on the
statistical frequency of these forms (or variants of them); and it was
soon established that joint and fraternal joint families were a minority.
In the next stage of the discussion an attempt was made to see the various forms as aspects of the cycle of development of the Chinese domestic
family, the more complex forms growing out of the simpler and the
simpler resulting from the combined effects of death and partition (*fen-
chia*, division of the family). Yet the introduction of the last element
complicated the analysis by compromising the exclusive preoccupation
with residence, and at the same time it drew attention to an ambiguity
in the very word "residence." On the formal partition of a family—
assume a fraternal joint family for the sake of simplicity—a given estate
of property was divided up among the brothers, each then establishing
his own household with its separate cooking place. But it does not automatically follow that these new units were in all respects residentially
segregated, for they might continue to share the main hall of the house
(the other rooms of which they had parceled out among themselves),
there jointly to congregate for ritual and other purposes. Here, then, was
a family composed of several households each with its own estate.

Professor Cohen takes the discussion a step further when he intro-
duces the idea of a *chia* economy: a *chia* group with a *chia* estate par-
ticipates in economic activities of which the exploitation of the estate
may be only one element. But the relationship in real life among these
three manifestations of *chia* may be complex. The group may not all
live in one place; they may not all derive benefit from the estate; they
may not all be involved in one set of economic activities. A family occu-

* Full references are listed on pp. 249–57. The characters for Chinese and Japanese terms used in the text will be found on pp. 259–61.

pying one building or complex of buildings, then, may include more than one *chia*, in the sense of a group associated with an estate. On the other hand, such a *chia* may be residentially dispersed and its members may operate independently of one another in their economic life. No wonder Professor Cohen has to say "that there may be more to domestic units than meets the demographer's eye." All investigators of Chinese domestic institutions need to be aware that the units they set out to count and analyze have protean forms; to put the matter another way, that they can enumerate different classes of unit depending on the criteria they adopt. A set of statistics that simply counts units occupying discrete dwellings says less than enough—in a way it says too much—about the families it lists.

At the end of his essay Professor Cohen glances at past attempts to correlate differences in *chia* complexity with differences in social and economic standing: the convention has been to say that the rich and high-status families are relatively complex (they appear as joint families) and the poor and low-status families are relatively simple (appearing as elementary or stem families). Quite rightly, Professor Cohen suggests that there may be many different sets of economic and social circumstances that will affect the constitution of families. Yet, while I agree with the point he is making, and accept the criticism that models of "rich-large" and "poor-small" families are far too crude, I think that we may go a bit too far toward ruling out the possibility that there is a very general pattern in Chinese society by which wealth and social standing are associated with family complexity. In time we shall see; the debate is open.

The reader will note that Professor Cohen has gone back to and made good use of older evidence in the light of the analysis he has conducted on his own field material. He has a general point to make about China as a whole. In Mrs. Wolf we find an author who is less willing to move outside her Taiwan field data; she justifies her reluctance by saying that "the data on socialization in other areas of China are so limited, and our assumptions about uniformity of customs across such a vast country have in the past proved so erroneous." She is certainly right on the first point; I am not so sure about the second. I shall follow her in caution but shift the emphasis: what Mrs. Wolf writes about child rearing and personal relationships in the families in "her" Taiwan village seems to me to fit in general what we know about families everywhere in China; and on the assumption that her account furnishes us with a generalizable model, I shall assert that she makes clear in her precise and sensitive analysis much that has hitherto been obscure.

Consider, for example, the case of the relations between brothers, one of the most fragile bonds in Chinese society, Confucian moralizing not-withstanding. The evidence is all about us for saying that brothers compete for scarce resources when they are members of one domestic unit and keep one another at arm's length when they no longer share a common residence. We see the rivalry in the ordinary run of domestic affairs, in fraternal behavior when the family is partitioned, and in the brothers' resort to *feng-shui* (geomancy) to exploit the fortune-inducing properties of a parental grave (see p. 178 below). Again, we know that a joint family does not usually survive for long the death of the senior generation; when that focus of unity is removed, the resulting fraternal joint family has great difficulty in holding together.

Mrs. Wolf's contribution to our understanding of the matter lies in what she has to say about the foundation of the rivalry in the experience of childhood. "As children," she writes, "the elder is required to yield to his younger brother's demands in all things, some of which are outrageous when the younger is still small." But once they grow up, "the younger is expected to yield to his older brother's decisions and guidance, a situation for which he has been poorly prepared." And she later adds: "Had the younger brother been trained from infancy to submit to the elder, the Chinese joint family might be less of a myth." But Mrs. Wolf also shows how the behavior of the wives of the brothers bears on the difficulty in the fraternal bond, noting the "comparative ease with which sisters-in-law can manipulate the brittle relationship between their husbands." And if anyone doubts the general validity of her observations, let him consider the first chapter of the popular version (eighteenth century) of K'ang Hsi's *Sacred Edict*, where he will find ample confirmation that the minds of the moralizers were not closed to the evidence that their precepts were difficult of achievement:

But forsooth, you love to listen to what your wives have to say, and perceiving that there is some reason in their talk, you listen until before you are aware of it you believe them. The wife of the elder brother says to him, "How lazy, how prodigal, your young brother is! You laboriously make money to keep him, and he still finds fault: are we his sons and daughter-in-law, that we ought to yield him the respect due to a parent?"

The wife of the younger brother will also say to him, "Even if your elder brother knows how to make money, you have made money too; you do as much as he does in the home. . . . But *his* children forsooth, they *are* children, buying this, that and the other to eat,—can it be that our children are not fit to live?"

A little to-day and a little to-morrow of such talk as this, and thenceforth the brothers' affections will all have grown cold, and at length they begin to quarrel in consequence. (Baller 1892: 12f.)

I should like to draw attention to one other family relationship on which Mrs. Wolf's account throws special light, that between father and son. A reviewer of my *Chinese Lineage and Society* said that I had cut the Chinese father down to size; I am in good company, for Mrs. Wolf does the very same. She shows how the paternal aloofness and discipline give way in late life to a state in which the father is threatened with domestic impotence by the maturing and assertiveness of his sons. Indeed, by the time a man is a grandfather, he is well on the road to being a marginal member of the family so far as authority and decision-making are concerned. Now, I think that this crucial point has a bearing on at least two problems in analysis.

The first is our judgment of the viability of joint families. The systematic strains built into them and the conflicts expressed or engendered by the processes of socialization (see the last paragraph of Mrs. Wolf's essay) seem on the whole to be containable as long as the father can hold on to his authority; at the point his grip loosens, the family splits. To come back to a matter arising from Professor Cohen's essay, one may speculate that a father's authority will be exercised more forcefully and for a longer time when the family enjoys wealth and high social standing, i.e. when his authority is buttressed by economic power and influence derived from the extra-domestic sphere. Once again, this time starting from the relationship between father and son, we are considering the possibility that richer and higher-status families tend to be more complex in structure.

The second point is the connection between the gradual abdication of parental authority and the nature of domestic ancestor worship. The ancestors are, with some important qualification, benign (see p. 174 below); and it may be that the Chinese case can be taken to support a hypothesis that fearsome ancestors are to be found only in systems where men retain their authority and control over their juniors until they die. Certainly, it would be worth examining forms of ancestor worship throughout the "Chinese" world to see whether paternal authority and the harshness of ancestral behavior vary together. China itself and Japan show mild ancestors and the retirement of men from domestic power (see Freedman 1967: 93–99); on Korea and Vietnam I am not well enough informed, but we may want to interpret some recent data contained in an important study of Okinawa (Lebra 1966: 196) as meaning that the maintenance of paternal control is connected there with a generally harsher version of the Sino-Japanese ancestors.

One of the many advantages of Mrs. Wolf's essay is that it contains a section ("Variations") devoted to the family when it is constructed about other than the "standard" form of marriage. It is easy enough to forget that the taking of "little daughters-in-law" and the marriage-in of sons-in-law are institutions with a very wide distribution and high incidence in China; and Mrs. Wolf's analysis of the domestic consequences of the "unorthodox" forms is a basis for a more general study of them, for the existing literature is not silent on the subject.*

I shall say finally of Mrs. Wolf's essay that it suggests most eloquently how the study of the dense and intertwined personal relationships in the family may afford us some insight into the manner in which Chinese behave outside the context of domestic life. A good deal has been said in the past, usually in a simple-minded way, about the Chinese family as a model of its society. That it certainly is not, but it would be profitable to explore the consequences for general social behavior of the kind of domestic training for social relationships that Mrs. Wolf describes and analyzes.

We come now to Mrs. Taeuber's paper, for many aspects of which the previous essays have prepared the way. Here we are given the opportunity of reflecting on the significance of the only comprehensive body of statistical population data to have been collected in continental China; and while this material is technically deficient in a number of ways, and defective in comparison with what is ideally available from Japanese sources in Taiwan and British sources in Hong Kong, it is distributed over the mass of China and contains clues to regional variations in family structure. It is a tragedy that the schedules and the machine cards of the Buck population survey of 1929–31 no longer exist; they would have furnished Mrs. Taeuber with better data than those she has had in fact to work on. But luckily for us, her long experience in the handling of demographic data on China has enabled her to extract some extraordinarily valuable conclusions from what was at her disposal. It is not the least important aspect of her study that it forms part of a re-examination of other existing data.

The data used in the essay refer to families of farm operators. We need not be unduly concerned about the limitation of the study to people whose lives are bound up with agriculture, for they form the great bulk of China's population. It would have been a great advantage to have comparable material on nonfarming families in the countryside, not to mention urban families; but at least the farming people on their own form a large and useful class for the study of variation. On the other

* Arthur P. Wolf's forthcoming paper, "Adopt a Daughter-in-Law, Marry a Sister: A Chinese Solution to the Problem of the Incest Taboo," *inter alia* surveys the evidence on "little daughters-in-law."

hand, we shall certainly have to worry about the word "families." The units counted in this census-type survey are in reality individuals and households. True, the households are overwhelmingly composed of people closely related by kinship and marriage, but the domestic units enumerated are defined by their co-residence and commensality. That is to say, we cannot know anything about the family links between the units (some of them may in fact be members of residential groups not forming single cooking-and-eating units) or about people not resident in the household but who are nonetheless members of the *chia* in relation to their property and general economic activities.

There is a further difficulty. The heads of households are taken to be the farm operators; that may account for the absence of female heads. It is a fair guess from what we know in general about China that some widows will have been the heads of their households. (Note that in Table 13 10.2 per cent of the females in the line of the head are mothers of the heads.) Again, there is no way of knowing what significance to attach to the percentage of 1.2 given in Table 13 for fathers of heads. Does the figure mean that very few old men stand back from leadership, or that nearly all the senior men have been returned as heads even when many of them were in fact more or less retired? Mrs. Taeuber says that the man who was returned as the head of a family usually remained so until he died. That is factually wrong as a description of Chinese society, being true only in the sense that when investigators ask their questions the senior man is put forward as a matter of form. The sociological categories within which the data were collected were taken from Western procedure and are open to question for China.

Yet once we are alert to the ambiguities we are able to see that Mrs. Taeuber's analysis takes us a long way toward understanding the constitution of the peasant family as household. It is of course no surprise that nuclear families are in the majority (more than three-fifths) and that just over three-quarters of all family members in the sample are heads, their wives, and their children. Mortality will to some degree account for the simplicity of structure, for great numbers of men are unlikely to live long enough to preside over the families of their married sons. On the other hand, the simplicity will also have been due to the moving out of some of the family's male members in pursuit of work. (If a man left home to take up residence with his wife's father, he was presumably counted as his father-in-law's son in the statistics.)

But perhaps the most interesting part of the analysis of structure can be approached through what Mrs. Taeuber says about family size. There is a relationship among family size, land worked, and kind of land tenure. At least in the rice regions, nuclear families tend to be found among tenants, and larger families among owners and owner-tenants. There is clearly some adaptation of family size (and with it family structure) to primary economic resources, but of course one has to be cautious in interpreting a correlation between size of family and size of landholding. Given a more or less fixed per capita distribution of land, for example, small families would necessarily have less land than larger ones; in other words, the process of family partition would inevitably lead to there being some families small and "poor" and others, just before partition, big and "rich." I suspect, however, that that is by no means the whole story; there may in fact be a tendency for the per capita distribution of land in larger families to be bigger than in the smaller, so that the former are in reality the richer. (See the evidence on Ting Hsien in Gamble 1954: 25, 66, 84.) We have returned to the recurrent debate on the greater viability of complex family structure among the well-to-do and the prominent.

The data are arranged by climatic region, and Mrs. Taeuber is concerned to see what differences among the regions may emerge. She shows, for example, that larger families characterize the South, the Red Basin, and the Northern Plain and Northern Highlands (as against the Southeastern Hills, the Southwestern Plateau, and the Lower Yangtze regions). She says that the regional differences in family size in relation to land seem to be more adaptive in the Southeastern Hills and the Southwestern Plateau, these being frontier areas of advancing settlement, and in the lower Yangtze, an area of intensive agriculture. And at other places she draws attention to differences between "traditional" and "adaptive" regions. We may ask, what precisely are the factors that produce the regional variations? Are they environmental-economic—crops, irrigation, soil fertility, and so on? If that is the case, then indeed there may be very important variations within as well as between regions, and even from one small area to the next. On the other hand, the differences may (also) be the result of some gross structural differences in the extra-domestic social life of each region or area. We shall find when we turn to Professor Potter's essay on the lineage that regional differences are again explored, and we may be stirred to consider the possibility of linking up differences in distinct forms of kinship grouping with one another and with variations in social and economic environment. It is to important questions such as these that Mrs. Taeuber's analysis tends, yet I am reluctant to leave her essay without stressing that, for all the variations to which it draws our attention, it also seems to establish for the whole of continental China a kind of family-household system that is uniformly Chinese in its principles and numerical properties.

We have seen that the vocabulary for forms of the Chinese family seems to have been established in its present shape by Lang's study of 1946. It may be worth arguing against one element in it, lest some confusion be bred or maintained by the language used. Lang (1946: 14n) writes that the term "joint family" is most commonly used in the anthropological literature in describing this "type" in India. As I have said elsewhere (Freedman 1966: 49), the "joint" character of the Hindu family as a property-owning unit has been muddled up by the sociologists and anthropologists with its morphology. In China, as in India, a joint family exists when two or more men jointly hold a family estate; the presence of several married sons has nothing to do with it. To go back to Professor Cohen's paper, we may say that the *chia* is a joint family whatever its precise composition. What are called joint families in the literature on China (and in the essays in this book and earlier in the Introduction) would be better described as something else—I have suggested "grand families." If it were just a question of words, there would be no point in arguing; but the issue is in fact one of keeping matters of morphology distinct from those of property. I hope that my fellow contributors will forgive me the pedantry.

In the last of the group of four papers dealing exclusively with the family we have a comparative study of family relationships in Taiwan and the mainland, based on what is said or implied about those relationships in short stories. The results of Mrs. Chin's exercise in the sociology of literature will surprise most readers, for even if they are not taken aback by the desperate sadness of the stories from Taiwan, they will be jolted by the traditionalism—one might almost say conservatism—of the Communist stories. Mrs. Chin explains how the paradox comes about. Starting from the revolutionary literature of the 1920's and 1930's, in which family ideals were called in question, if not flouted, she traces one development to the early 1960's in Taiwan and another to a similar period on the mainland. In the former case we find a literature written by a young urbanized elite, which deals with the themes of love and family against the background of a society where the family revolution has been suspended while the official ideology encourages a return to tradition. The writers do not any longer attack the family; they concentrate on portraying the uneasiness of personal relationships and the problems of the isolated individual. It is a very special section of society in Taiwan that is illuminated by the stories. In contrast, in mainland China on the eve of the Cultural Revolution official policy appears to have brought the story writers round, after a period during which attention was turned away from the family, to endowing it with many of the virtues ascribed to it before the early revolutionary assault had begun. In the group of Communist stories examined by Mrs. Chin, we are given the illusion that we are seeing up and down the Chinese countryside a rather jolly society in which Communist ideals and standards of behavior fit comfortably into a more or less traditional pattern of domestic relationships. It seems odd on the face of it that the Taiwan stories recognize only nuclear families and in general ignore the traditional apparatus of kinship and marriage, while the stories from the mainland describe three generations in the family, women with their daughters-in-law, and a kind of cheerful domestic bustle.

To put the matter bluntly, the Communist stories give us the party line for the years 1962 to mid-1966. Yet for all that, they cannot be taken as mere ideology, for even if they rest on no observation whatever of real life (which is doubtful), what they hold out as ideal presumably exerts some influence on reality. At the very least, what they propose to the Chinese common reader is likely to be more congenial than the models offered in earlier years. (One wonders what the model has been since the Cultural Revolution began in 1966.) Mrs. Chin is persuasive when she writes, "The Chineseness of these stories is beyond question." The characters speak like Chinese. They act in ways we readily recognize from our experience of their fellow-countrymen elsewhere. By contrast, the people who appear in the Taiwan stories do not seem particularly Chinese, although within the limited world portrayed in the stories they may in fact be more genuine than their mainland counterparts.

This essay underlines the precariousness of our position as students of modern China. Mrs. Chin with her knowledge of the society can stand the Taiwan stories against their social background. We are left wondering what it is that moves like a shadow on the mainland. Of course, Mrs. Chin does not offer us the Communist stories as a substitute for portraits from real life; she has more complicated sociological aims. But inevitably she arouses in us a half-suspicion that through her work we have caught a glimpse of some real thing, and we may well feel frustrated as a result. She must accept that feeling as a compliment to her skill.

With Professor Potter's essay we make the transition from the family to wider forms of kinship. That essay and Professor Meskill's, which follows it, deal with the lineage, a subject that comes up for some further discussion in my own essay. But before commenting on the treatment of this form of agnatic kinship I have to make the point that the volume lacks a full enough consideration of non-agnatic kinship outside the domestic sphere. My essay tries to show some of the problems that arise in the analysis of the relations that flow through mothers and sisters, but the whole question of matrilateral kinship, and with it affinity, deserves the kind of wide-ranging inquiry so far made only of the family and the lineage. Obviously, the place given to matrilateral kinship in any local system will depend on the extent to which agnation accounts for the composition of the community (see Gallin 1960: 632f), while it will vary with the nature of political ties between lineages.

The deep segmentary lineage is by no means found everywhere in China—it is part of Professor Potter's purpose to account for the uneven distribution—and in the regions where it is to be discovered it achieves different degrees of elaboration. In this connection the corner of mainland China still under British rule has proved to be of crucial importance, for it has afforded us the opportunity of examining the whole range of lineage complexity, from the height reached by the lineage of Cantonese-speakers studied by Professor Potter in his pioneering field work to the relative simplicity of the forms found predominantly among the Hakka population (see Aijmer 1967: 53–59, and Pratt 1960). Potter's work on Ping Shan has been reinforced by Baker's study (1968) of Sheung Shui, another New Territories lineage of traditional power and riches.

Three aspects of Professor Potter's discussion call for some comment. The first is the careful documentation of the asymmetrical structure of a lineage in which wealth is unevenly accumulated at different points. Ping Shan is assuredly an extreme case in the degree to which segment holdings of land have been built up at the expense of family holdings, but it is precisely to that extent illuminating. With the additional evidence from Dr. Baker's study of Sheung Shui and from other less detailed data coming from other inquiries in the New Territories, it is now clear that we have a satisfactory model of the Chinese lineage with which to evaluate the facts available for China as a whole. The second aspect is tightly connected with the first. In Professor Potter's study, as again in Dr. Baker's, the precise relationship between the segmentary system, land tenure, higher-level ancestor worship, and the maintenance of tombs is spelled out. I can think of no more striking evocation of the persistence in the New Territories of certain links in that complex than the photograph in Dr. Baker's book that shows, in the front rank of a group worshiping at a tomb, a row of young men arrayed in the academic robes of graduates of the University of Hong Kong. Tradition is alive with modernity.

The third aspect is Professor Potter's approach to the problem of what constellation of factors need to be taken into account in the attempt to explain the development of deep and complex lineages in some places only. A good deal of the New Territories evidence having now been supplied, we may well think that the time has come both for a more ambitious effort to comb the literature on mainland China and for a concerted set of studies in Taiwan to test the important hypotheses that Professor Potter advances. It happens that the paper written for the conference by the late Chen Shao-hsing referred to data from Taiwan that bear directly on the problem. These data (on the history of Chinese settlement of the island in the frontier period, on the emergence of some influential lineages and their control under both Ch'ing and the Japanese rule, on the surname composition of various communities, and on the holding of land by lineages) were drawn from a variety of Chinese and Japanese official and academic sources. They demonstrate the possibility of bringing together the resources of the rich documentation on the past, some of it painstakingly culled from unpublished land and population registers, with material from field studies. (There have recently appeared a few important papers that bring evidence to bear on problems of lineage formation and structure: Cohen 1969; Pasternak 1968a, 1968b, 1969.)

Professor Meskill's essay is a splendid demonstration of precisely that dual form of study. It is not to be wondered at that a historian of China should feel compelled to comment (some might say with unnecessary brevity and politeness) on the failure of anthropological students of Chinese society to make use of the written evidence. Professor Meskill has done what anthropologists should certainly have done before her. Her use of a combination of sources (genealogies, historical documents, administrative records, and the data from her own field work) is a bold and original application of method. Happily, other people have since undertaken like studies in both Taiwan and Hong Kong.

The written genealogy, in manuscript or print, is the obvious document to turn to when one is studying Chinese kinship organization, although not every student in the field will be lucky enough to find one. Many such genealogies have been gathered up and stored outside China, as Professor Meskill explains, and it is of the first importance to discover what social facts and inferences may be drawn from them. It was necessary for Professor Meskill to carry out her field study in order to establish the relationship between the document and social reality. How fortunate we are now to have been put on our guard by her researches.

Perhaps the first thing that strikes us as we read her essay is that written genealogies may exist in the absence of any organized lineage group, or perhaps in anticipation of it. That is to say, a genealogy is an attempt to place on record a given amount of information, of both a biographical and kinship nature, on a set of individuals; it is another matter whether that set is a formally constituted group. And when it is, the data recorded may mislead the unwary scholar either by omissions due to ignorance or censorship or by imaginative reconstruction of the past. If, for example, different groups of agnates are to be brought together within the framework of a single genealogy, there may be difficulty in "splicing" the different strands, and the strands once spliced will make a shaky premise for a historical argument. There is an entertaining illustration of an abortive attempt at such an operation to be found in Dr. Han Suyin's autobiography: the written genealogy of her family in Szechwan was a cause of worry to her father's younger brother because it appeared to have mislaid six generations; he instituted inquiries among "another branch of the clan," but in the end was forced to give up the search for a satisfactory solution (Han 1965: 33–35).

But Professor Meskill points all her own morals, and I shall comment on only one more matter in her essay. She says that a survey and classification of written genealogies can help us "clarify further the problem of an adequate vocabulary and typology for the whole range of agnatic kinship groups." I leave it to her, as the expert, to decide how far the study of genealogies will in fact aid us in understanding the differential morphology of groups; we have by no means heard the end of the story of that morphology. That we have not yet been able to arrive at an agreed language for describing Chinese agnatic groups of various kinds is by itself no tragedy, although it sometimes impedes communication; the absence of a set vocabulary shows our uncertain grasp of the social phenomena we are striving to interpret.

The chief difficulty turns upon the pair of terms "clan" and "lineage." As for "lineage," writers in English have now generally opted for that term when they discuss local units of men all of whom trace patrilineal descent from one ancestor. (For an exception, see Hsu 1963.) But in fact some segment or segments of such a unit may be distant from where the lineage is based, while two or more such local lineages may be grouped into a higher-order agnatic unit centered on a common ancestral hall or tomb. (An example of such a unit will be found in Professor Potter's data on the Tang local lineages in the New Territories.) That situation, in my view, still keeps us within the context of lineage organization, for the larger unit is basically of the same nature as the smaller, which are its segments. But a problem arises from the fact that, with or without the aid of written genealogies, two or more local or higher-order lineages may in some circumstances organize themselves for common action on the basis of their common descent, which in the first place may be marked by nothing more than their having the same surname. I would argue that if the action endures and the new grouping establishes itself by setting up some focus of its unity, typically an ancestral hall or endowed tomb, then a lineage of (still) higher order has come into being. But if the action is transitory, then the cooperating lineages are still linked by bonds of mere clanship. That is to say, I am proposing that the word "lineage" be confined to permanent organized groups and that other and temporary groupings based on agnation be described as clans.

My own essay appears next in the series. It was originally the only one devoted to ritual matters, but, as I have explained in the Preface, Professor Wolf later submitted his ingenious paper on mourning costume to strengthen the analysis of kinship and marriage by examining them through their symbolic representations. Although Professor Wolf's essay was written after the conference, at which the question of mourning dress was barely discussed, it brings out clearly and reinforces some of the analytical points that emerged from the symposium as a whole.

Note, in the first place, how Professor Wolf's treatment demonstrates the marked change brought to fraternal relationships when brothers become members of different households, and how it underlines the essential equality of the fraternal tie. When, as he puts it, brothers have domestic property rights in common they cannot wear red in their mourning for one another; once they have ceased to hold common membership of the domestic unit they don "prophylactic" red, for their lives are now independent, and the mourning brother's fortunes may be put at risk by attending his late brother's funeral. The point is germane to the argument that the structure of Chinese kinship forces brothers into separate paths and makes them jealous of their several rights and chances. In my essay I draw attention to the fact that in *feng-shui* the competition between agnates is to be seen most dramatically in the behavior of brothers, among whom "there is a built-in tendency to be rivalrous when they are adult."

The color red shows us, Professor Wolf argues, one aspect of the fraternal relationship; in his analysis of the use made of "white cloth" he arrives at another aspect. Brothers are now seen to fall into a single category with friends and affines; what these three classes of people have in common is that in relation to the man for whom they mourn they have "the essential quality" of being his peers. "White cloth" is therefore a mark of equality, and so far as brothers are concerned, we are back at the question treated in Mrs. Wolf's paper and, within the context of ancestor worship, in my own: "Despite the ritual primacy of the oldest son . . . there is, in real life, equality between brothers and no transfer from father to son of a power to control the other mature sons."

What Professor Wolf says about the equality of affines may perhaps serve as a corrective to a view put forward in the part of my essay dealing with marriage rites. I say there that marrying off a daughter puts the girl's family "ritually and socially in a relationship of inferiority with the boy's." Professor Wolf writes: "One family may be wealthier or more powerful than the other, but in the realm of kinship they stand on the same plane. Marriage itself does not create a hierarchy of wife-givers and wife-receivers." I think the evidence is in favor of a view that the bride's kin stand ritually inferior to the groom's, but Professor Wolf is undoubtedly right in stressing the "essential equality" contained within the affinal relationship, just as he is right in seeing the "essential equality" in the fraternal bond, where it may be masked by the etiquette of deference due from junior to senior.

Professor Wolf's treatment of mourning costume and mine of marriage rites bring us to exactly similar conclusions about the status of the married woman vis-à-vis her own kin, although the ambiguity of her status is made in my analysis to form part of a more general ambiguity of affinal ties. Professor Wolf shows in a striking manner how his informants in the Taiwan town of Sanhsia gave uniquely conflicting versions of the mourning attire to be worn by daughters; the problem is that nobody is certain where a married woman stands. Just because the language of Chinese mourning costume is precise, there must be contradictory formulations of the correct wear for persons who stand in ambiguous relationships. The marriage rites "pose a problem and leave it unresolved. How is a woman to reconcile her duties as wife and daughter-in-law with those she has as sister and daughter?" The analysis of mourning attire shows the same problem and the same lack of resolution; it is a conflict built into the system.

Toward the end of his essay Professor Wolf contrasts junior-senior distinctions made in mourning costume with those made in kinship terms of address. The former distinctions he sees as the symbolic expression of property rights, the latter as the symbolic expression of "daily patterns of authority." We are thus encouraged to think about the ways in which different symbolic systems in Chinese society may express different facets and properties of the institutions of kinship and marriage.

What can we learn by a study of kinship terminology? Professor McCoy's essay represents for us in the Chinese context a convergence of modern linguistics and anthropology. It is by no means the first attempt to analyze the Chinese system of kinship terminology; to Professor McCoy's own list of past studies I would add those by Fei (1936–37) and Hsu (1942; 1947). But in the study that appears here we have a pioneer application to the Chinese data of the sharp tools made by linguists and linguistically inclined anthropologists in recent years.

In an exercise of this sort we have to be very clear about the assumptions made and about the objectives and their limitations; I think Professor McCoy sets them out very clearly. In approaching the study of kin terms we assume, to begin with, that we can in fact isolate a part of the total language that we may legitimately call "the kinship terminology." Languages differ among themselves in the extent to which "words" applied to kin are also used to mark other relationships—between persons, between persons and things, and sometimes between things. The Chinese vocabulary of kinship is not completely confined to the relationships of kinship and marriage, but within that context it forms a system that can be set off, for one kind of analysis, from other systems. The aim of Professor McCoy's analysis is to isolate its components. Although some of them, as we are shown, lie on or near the surface of the language, others have to be imported by the analyst; and there is accordingly no guarantee that the final classification of kin and affines corresponds exactly with what native speakers of the language think.

But even if the resulting classification is not "thought" in this fashion, it may yet be demonstrated to fit with some of the arrangements of social life. And far from being a mere linguistic exercise—an elegant formal account of a specialized vocabulary—Professor McCoy's account shows his eagerness to link discriminations made in the language with properties of kinship groupings and behavior. It is for that reason that the essay is important to the whole collection; it reinforces our understanding of certain social properties and suggests others of which we may be only dimly aware.

For example, Professor McCoy decides to analyze the relationships between an individual and persons in or attached to his line into three categories: lineal, collateral, and affinal. He suggests at the same time that the main benefit of the classification "appears when the three-way split also concides with such secondary structuring of kin as are found in mourning grades, ceremonial participation, and inheritance." The tripartite division by itself does not segregate agnatic from non-agnatic collaterals, but when the first three elements in the codes for the reference terms are read together, we can see that all the codes beginning $F_1D_1R_1$ and $F_1D_1R_2$ are applied to agnates and all those beginning $F_1D_2R_1$ and $F_1D_2R_2$ are applied to persons related through the mother or the sister. (There is, however, the inconvenience that the codes for the sister terms begin $F_1D_2R_2$; sisters are of course agnates.) Professor McCoy mentions the connection between this classification and the mourning grades (*wu fu*), which play a very important role in the ideal grouping of kinsmen, marking out close agnates in the first place and proceeding to groups composed of the mother's close agnates, the children of her sisters, and the children of certain female agnates (a male ego being assumed). Affines are accommodated by wives being placed alongside their husbands in the agnatic group and the group of the mother's agnates. There are separate groups defined in relation to married women and for men in regard to their married-out female agnates. (See Freedman 1958: 40ff, 101 ff.)

These mourning grades are in reality a code for assigning graded legal obligations among kinsmen and affines, and their history is bound up with that of kinship terminology in a manner indicated by Fêng (1948: 41):

Using the family and sib [lineage] as the bases for their ideological structure, these [Confucian] literati elaborated the mourning system with a view to the maintenance of sib solidarity. In the course of the elaboration of the mourning system they also standardized its basis, the kinship [terminology] system, for a carefully graded system of mourning rites requires a highly differentiated kinship nomenclature, lest an awkward incommensurability ensue.

But the official mourning grades are not fully reflected in the systems of mourning that we can actually observe being practiced. Apart from anything else, since the official grades have to define legal relationships, they prescribe reciprocal mourning obligations between seniors and juniors, whereas in real systems juniors mourn for seniors but not vice versa. With what mourning grades, then, is the system of kinship terminology connected? Do the terms reflect (that is, are they based on the same code as) the official system of mourning or some real system? And if the latter, are the variations in real systems expressed in the varieties of kinship terminology to be found among those who practice those systems? It is, of course, one of the big questions in the study of Chinese kinship whether all the "vernacular" systems of terminology bear a similar relation to the official (dictionary) system.

It would be foolish to assume that from the study of Chinese kin terms will emerge a classification of kinsmen and affines that fits at all points either some abstract official model of the society, some ideal in the minds of speakers, or the practical arrangement of people on the ground. Professor McCoy has made a start with Toishan data to work out the nature of the implied classification and its institutional connections; his careful example will have to be followed many times before the linguistic and sociological properties of Chinese kinship terminology as a whole are fully within our grasp.

In the Preface I referred to the importance of studying China within an East Asian setting. Professor Pelzel's summary of the Japanese kinship system, with which the book closes, demonstrates what is to be gained by confronting China with a civilization which, though it has taken over much from its western neighbor, is based sociologically on very different principles. As one reads Professor Pelzel's essay many of the features of Chinese family and kinship that one tends to take for granted (and perhaps also to ascribe unthinkingly to Confucius's other islands) suddenly jump out of the context where they had been quietly resting and demand to be treated as problems.

It is bound to strike us that the Japanese *ie* belongs to a different world of structure from that of the Chinese *chia*, even though the two terms are written with the same ideograph, and that the larger assemblages of kin in Japan lack the form and significance we have learned to associate with the Chinese lineage. A first conclusion from the contrast between the two societies may well be that we had not before realized the transitoriness of the Chinese family. In a strict Mainean sense, the *ie* is a corporate group: it never (in principle) dies. But the *chia* is in a perpetual state of dissolution, for when the partition of a family takes place, none of the resulting units retains the precise identity of the unit from which it springs. True, there is a ritual primogeniture in China, and by keeping the family's stock of ancestor tablets the oldest son could be said to carry on the family; but the stock changes its composition every generation, and the links with the past are regularly severed. The family estate is unlikely to be maintained as an entity over the generations except when there is only one son in each of them.

In order to achieve permanence the Chinese family must convert some of its property into impartible "trusts"; but in so doing it initiates a group that soon will have nothing to do with the family, for it will have become an extra-domestic segment of a lineage. Consider these facts with what Professor Pelzel says about Japanese genealogies: they pertain to *ie*, families that cross the generations with their identity intact. In China, families (as distinct from lineages) may sometimes keep up genealogies, but they are, so to say, part of the machinery for linking individuals to the wider descent system that takes its origin from an ancestor standing well outside the family sphere. In a nutshell, it seems that the perduring units of kinship structure are in Japan the *ie* and in China the lineage; the "lineage" in Japan and the *chia* in China are passing phenomena. If we now consider Professor Pelzel's statement that for Japanese the "genetic legitimacy is racial or ethnic, not subsocietal," we shall begin to ask ourselves what systematic social, economic, and political differences between China and Japan we may associate with the fact that Chinese society is segmented into agnatic communities, each with its distinct point of origin, whereas the members of Japanese society trace their ancestry to a common source.

Professor Pelzel hints at the founding of Chinese political life on the tension between loyalty to kin and loyalty to the state—the "conflict between the purposes of kin and non-kin that Confucius failed to resolve for Chinese ideology." The Japanese did not face the same dilemma: organizations that fall somewhere between family and nation, in China include very few viable task-oriented groupings, but in Japan are numerous. It will not be long before we are wondering how the differences between the two kinship systems bear on the great debate on why Japan was able to turn itself into a mature industrial society and China failed. (See Jacobs 1958: 149ff, and Levy 1953.) By extension, the inquiry is bound to lead (if we assume for the moment that there are enough facts to go on) to an examination of what Communist policy has sought to do in the realm of kinship to shape China for its modern destiny. (See Yang 1959.)

The essay on Japan discusses the institutionalization of emotion in the family and the correlative neglect of what Professor Pelzel calls "the social personality of the individual member." Different kinds of family system provide for different modes of personal interaction, different styles of family behavior, and different conceptions of the person. It is a theme we have already seen tackled for China in Mrs. Wolf's essay and in Mrs. Chin's; and the contrast set up by Professor Pelzel between the Japanese and Chinese systems should certainly force us to look beyond what has already been done to a fuller social psychology of the Chinese domestic way of life. It is a pleasing paradox that a book on China should come to a climax in an essay on Japan.

Developmental Process in the Chinese Domestic Group

MYRON L. COHEN

The notion that most Chinese lived in "joint" or "large" families has been thoroughly discredited by now. Certainly, it is not necessary to again confirm the point here. But if we agree, using Lang's definitions (1946: 13), that simple and stem families greatly outnumbered those of the joint type, we may add that the discussion as it has been presented so far has obscured aspects of Chinese domestic organization that are both intrinsically interesting and relevant to the study of family size and complexity. In this paper I argue that the property-holding unit known in Chinese as the *chia*—which has generally been identified as the "family"—was actually a kin group that could display a great deal of variation in residential arrangements as well as in the economic ties that bound its members together. These variations could appear within the history of a given *chia* in such a way as to make it equivalent at certain times to what is usually regarded as a family; but the *chia* could also exist as a social unit in the absence of a single family-like arrangement of all its members.

Some of the material introduced in this essay was provided by sixteen months of fieldwork during 1964–65 in a southern Taiwan Hakka-speaking community, which I will call Yen-liao. With a resident population of 746 in May 1965, Yen-liao is located in the *chen* (township) of Mei-nung, which in turn forms one of the administrative subdivisions of the *hsien* (county) of Kaohsiung. The argument that I develop in this paper derives for the most part from my interpretation of the Yen-liao data. Nevertheless, I also use evidence from other parts of China, in the hope that my remarks and conclusions may be more generally applicable.

The *fang* and the *chia* are the smallest units defined within the Chinese kinship system. Though the term *fang* may be used in reference to patrilineal groupings of varying size and genealogical depth below the lineage level, it is also used to designate the conjugal unit consisting of husband, wife, and children. (For the use of the term *fang*, see Hu 1948: 18; Fried 1953: 31.) As for the *chia*, it has been defined as "the economic family, i.e., a unit consisting of members related to each other by blood, marriage, or adoption and having a common budget and common property" (Lang 1946: 13). A *chia*, of course, may vary in size, in generational depth, and in the degree to which there is extension (more than one *fang*) in each generation. It is only when there is more than one *fang* within the *chia* that the *fang/chia* differentiation has force. Thus it is obvious that if a multi-*fang chia* is localized to the extent that at least two *fang* are co-resident in the same household, an "extended family" of one sort or another is visible to the observer.

A *fang*, however, is more than a unit of reference. In many, if not most, cases the marriage that established the *fang* also made it an autonomous unit with respect to property rights and economic resources. In theory, the bride had exclusive rights over parts of her dowry, which might have included cash; this confirmed her as an independent property-holder. (See McAleavy 1955; Cohen 1968.) In fact, her husband as well as she might use these rights to develop an economic subsystem on a *fang* basis distinct from the larger system of the *chia*. (The custom of adopting a "little daughter-in-law" into the household to eventually marry the son may have produced modifications in the position of the *fang* vis-à-vis the *chia*; see Fei 1939: 54f.) Elsewhere (Cohen 1968), the *chia* has been treated primarily as a unit localized within one household, and the *fang* has been viewed from that perspective. For our present purposes the existence of the *fang* and its distinguishing features, by and large, may be taken for granted; I will, however, refer to a few situations in which the distribution of *fang* members sheds light on the organization of the *chia*.

Like *fang*, *chia* is a term of many uses. In the course of my own fieldwork I often heard agnates who shared a common ancestor many generations removed refer to each other as "people of the same *chia* (*t'ung chia jen*)." Even people with identical surnames who were in no position to trace their actual genealogical ties (if such existed), would use similar phraseology. Needless to say, closer agnates would not hesitate to count themselves as members of the same *chia*. I do not know the extent to which this wide range of usage was found in most of China. Certainly it has been most common to think of the *chia* as a family arrangement of some sort, although there has been some confusion over the term, as was noted in a recent summary of work on the subject: "At the base of our hierarchy is the family or *chia*. Exactly what the term means has never been agreed upon and perhaps it is a variable which is subject to local variations" (Osgood 1963: 355).

It is of some interest that one of the earliest efforts to identify and describe the *chia* involved the use of data gathered in a community that had sent many of its members abroad. Within Phenix Village, Kulp distinguished four kinds of "families" (Kulp 1925: 142f). Of these, two—the "conventional-family" and the "religious-family"—are of no concern here, for they refer to agnatic groupings not at the domestic level. (See Freedman 1958: 33.) The "natural-family," which consists of "father, mother (wife or concubines), and children" (Kulp 1925: 142), clearly refers to the *fang*. One or more "natural-families" may be found within the "economic family," which "is a group of people who on the basis of blood or marriage connection live together as an economic unit. It may be a natural-family or a number of natural-families which have not divided the ancestral inheritance" (Kulp 1925: 148). But Kulp on the same page then indicates that the "economic-family" may not necessarily be a co-residing unit:

Members of the economic-family may all live under one roof, under several roofs joining one another, in houses somewhat separated in the village, or far apart as in Chaochow, Swatow, or the South Seas [Southeast Asia]. So long as there is no distinction between the income and outgo of funds and so long as the whole group is administered by a certain head or *chia-chang*, the persons living under these arrangements belong to an economic-family.

Kulp's "economic-family," then, is defined on the basis of both a common estate and a common budget. This, surely, is a *chia*; he refers to its leader as a *chia-chang*. But the terminological looseness I noted in Yenliao must also have been found in Phenix Village: the "religious-family" also has its *chia-chang* (Kulp 1925: 149). There is yet another difficulty in Kulp's description; according to his account, the only way a new "economic-family" is created is "by the division of property and the declaration of separate finances" (Kulp 1925: 149). To what extent was the considerable out-migration from Phenix Village tied in with the formation of new "economic-families" in this fashion? Though Kulp provides no direct answer to this question, he indicates in his description that some "economic-families" might very well include persons who had departed for Southeast Asia. So if at least some of the out-migration did not involve the formation of new "economic-families," can it be that in such circumstances the migrants remained in a situation where there was "no distinction between the income and outgo of funds" and where the entire "economic-family" was still "administered by a certain head or *chia-chang*"? The answer seems to be no. Those who had left, Kulp tells us (1925: 50), accounted for "as many as one-third of the total men in the village population."

[Yet] not more than one-tenth of the emigrants return successful. Many of them, while in foreign lands, are barely able to send back enough money to keep their families alive. Not a few persons are forced to live from hand to mouth, finally returning broken in productive efficiency, a charge upon their families, or dying miserable deaths away from home with none to burn the candles. (Kulp 1925: 53.)

What emerges from Kulp's description is a sociological no-man's-land found between the establishment of discrete "economic-families" on the one hand, and the existence of an integrated economic unit (perhaps spanning the ocean) on the other. Ch'en Ta, in the English edition of his book, refers to the latter arrangement as the "dual family system" (Ch'en 1940: 121). However, he really means one "family" residentially separated into two (or more?) units, and in the earlier Chinese text he uses the phrase " 'dual family-head' system," i.e., *"liang t'ou-chia"* *chih-tu* (Ch'en 1938: 126). The circumstances leading to the *"liang t'ou-chia"* *chih-tu* are similar to those described by Kulp. From Ch'en's book it can clearly be seen that emigration is often an aspect of "family" activity rather than a process to create new families. Referring to one sample of emigrants, Ch'en (1940: 136f) noted that "at least two-thirds, and more probably three-fourths, of the emigrants leave home at an age when . . . they are not heads of households, though many of them may be married." Furthermore, the young emigrant "remains subject to the head of the family" (Ch'en 1940: 137). New "families" are formed through the division of property (Ch'en 1940: 130f).

Neither Kulp nor Ch'en explicitly states what I suggest can be drawn from their writings: that the "family" or "economic-family" might continue to exist as a unit in the face of both the physical and economic disengagement of its members. The way the emigrant ultimately related to the group he left behind depended, in addition to other factors, on his achievements, or lack of them, overseas. From Kulp and Ch'en it can be gathered that although there were various possible relationships, all were encompassed by the "family" unit. The migration to Southeast Asia is but a better-known example of a process that occurred over wide areas of China. I say "better-known" because physical dispersion is more pronounced in the context of migration from one country to another and the Overseas Chinese presumably had a greater chance to succeed than did persons who sought their fortunes within China. Furthermore, the overseas migration of the Chinese became an object of great interest in itself, so the role played by the "family" in the process received a commensurate share of attention.

Some of the problems encountered in dealing with "family" units might be clarified if first the corporate and developmental features of the *chia* as such are understood. Having said this, I must add that it is easier to deal with the partition of a *chia* than with its development. The *chia* is a group of persons who not only have kin ties to each other, but also have a series of claims of one sort or another on the *chia* as an estate. I have already noted that use of the term *chia* may vary in scope of reference. Nevertheless, its meaning in at least one terminological context is quite precise: it applies to a specific, bounded, kin group acting in terms of an equally well delineated body of holdings. This type of action is referred to in *fen-chia*, "to divide the *chia*." There is nothing vague about this; *fen-chia* has or has not taken place. If it has, two or more *chia* exist where before there was only one, and the estate of the original *chia* is distributed accordingly.

There are thus at least two broad areas of inquiry regarding the development of the *chia*. The first concerns the variety of arrangements to be found within the pre-*fen-chia* context; the second deals with pre-*fen-chia*/post-*fen-chia* contrasts. The tendency among scholars has been to lump these two together by viewing the development cycle only as culminating in the dismemberment of previously integrated households. But there are indications that the life and death of a *chia* might involve much more. If Levy's generalizations about Chinese "family" type in "traditional" times are accepted, then the movement of Chinese abroad may be seen as an extension of a very common pattern. During that period, he states, "the average Chinese" must have lived in the *famille souche*, "a family in which one of the sons marries and continues to live with the parents, while the other sons and daughters marry and go out of the family unit" (Levy 1949: 55f). How did the *famille souche* operate in the face of the equal rights to the *chia* estate held by brothers? These rights, he says,

could not have been meaningful to peasants living in areas where the average family's land was just sufficient to support life. Under such circumstances . . . only one son could feasibly remain. Whether given a cash settlement or not, the other sons had to go elsewhere or find alternative employment in the locality. . . . When holdings had reached a bare subsistence level, the assumption by one son of the total responsibility for the support of the parents . . . would often be accepted by the other sons as adequate reimbursement. (Levy 1949: 56f.)

According to Levy, then, there were ways by which claims to *chia* holdings could be adjusted. He cannot be sure, however, to what extent such adjustments, which the Chinese call *fen-chia*, actually took place. He does briefly indicate one alternative: "These excess sons sometimes left the family only temporarily and sent their wages back home for the economic betterment of the family. . . . Such sons were at best only peripheral family members" (Levy 1949: 52n).

Lang presents evidence that alternatives to *fen-chia* were quite common. Speaking of traditional China, she notes that "sons . . . seldom left their homes. If they did so without formally separating themselves from their family, they sent their earnings to their parents" (Lang 1946: 17). At the time of her research, members of the "working class and lower middle class in Peiping" were still part of the "tradition bound group," and this was reflected in their family life: "They send money to their rural homes, leave their wives and children with their old folks, and regard their sojourn in the city as temporary, even when they spend their entire lives there" (Lang 1946: 82).

As a contrast to the Peiping group with traditional occupations, Lang (1946: 86) also discusses the "new industrial workers" found in Shanghai. In spite of certain differences, the Shanghai workers still seem to be very much involved in traditional *chia* arrangements:

Thus 28 textile workers (out of 44) and 13 employees of public utilities (out of 43) still owned land. With the majority of them this ownership was purely formal: they derived no income from it (they left the land to their brothers and other near relatives), only retaining title as security against possible unemployment. Some of them rented their land. Several workers expected to inherit land from their fathers. (Lang 1946: 87.)

I would suggest that differences between the Peiping and the Shanghai workers may have involved something more than tradition and modernization. Unfortunately, the extent to which the ties of the Shanghai workers to their home regions were qualified by *fen-chia* or the lack of it is not clear. Lang's problem, like Kulp's, is that she is talking about families but dealing with *chia*. Her solution, also identical to Kulp's, is to use the concept of the "economic-family" to sort out what she regards as functional domestic units (Lang 1946: 13). Yet Lang is fully aware of the existence of the *chia* in the sense in which I have been using the term, and she must grapple with the problem in the part of her research that involves the enumeration of families on the basis of type and size. What seems to be the cause of concern is that the "economic-family," like the *chia*, can display variations in the distribution of its members:

One cannot . . . refuse to regard as family members those who do not reside with the family. . . . A young man may work at a place very distant from his family's residence, yet remain a member of his father's or brother's family. For example, he may send money home, he may return to marry a girl his parents or brothers have chosen for him, and later may leave his wife and children with them. (Lang 1946: 135.)

Lang's solution is to incorporate features of both the "economic-family" and the *chia* in the demarcation of family units. Residence is considered the paramount criterion, however, if the dispersion of a *chia* is on a *fang* basis, regardless, apparently, of the *fang's* possible inclusion in a larger "economic-family." A son is taken to have established a new family if he lives with his wife and children apart from his father (Lang 1946: 136).

If the sources I have cited above indicate nothing else, they certainly show that there may be more to domestic units than meets the demographer's eye. In the face of both the *famille souche*, which may have been quite prevalent, and the dispersion of conjugal units, the *chia* could survive. Before discussing the extent to which this survival could have significance in terms of the interaction of *chia* members, we must pay attention to the variety of forms the *chia* could assume.

Dealing with the structural variability of the *chia* is both a descriptive and an analytic task. For descriptive purposes, I first discuss the *chia* as it could be found at a moment in time. To simplify matters somewhat, I reduce the relevant components of the *chia* to three: the *chia* estate, the *chia* group, and the *chia* economy. The *chia* estate is that body of holdings to which the process of *fen-chia* is applicable. The *chia* group is made up of those persons who have rights of one sort or another to the *chia* estate at the time of *fen-chia*. Division, of course, is on the basis of male members of the *chia* group; but the process may also be conceptualized as division on the basis of the *fang* or *fang* segments (surviving members of a *fang*) found in each of the generational levels comprising the *chia* group. The *chia* economy refers to the exploitation of the *chia* estate (and the benefits derived therefrom) as well as to other income-producing activities linked to its exploitation through remittances and a common budgetary arrangement.

The connections between the three components can assume a variety of forms. To simplify matters once more, I assign each component only two possible alternative characteristics. The *chia* estate is either concentrated or dispersed; if concentrated, the members of the *chia* group exploiting it are from one household only; if dispersed, exploitation is by members of the *chia* group residing in two or more households. Similarly the *chia* group may be either concentrated in one household or dispersed in more than one. The *chia* economy is either inclusive or non-inclusive. An inclusive economy is one in which all members of the *chia* group participate. Participation need not necessarily be productive: dependents (the aged, the ill or disabled, children, students) may also be involved. If some members of the *chia* group do not participate in the *chia* economy, it is non-inclusive.

The Chinese family has by and large been described in terms involving or assuming the existence of a *chia* in which the estate is concentrated, the group is concentrated, and the economy is inclusive. (To anticipate later remarks, it can be noted that such an arrangement of the three components can occur at varying times during the history of a given *chia*.) I will choose, somewhat arbitrarily, to view a *chia* newly formed through division. The new *chia* consists of a man, his wife, and some unmarried children. They derive their income from land they own or rent. All live together in one household, and if there are secondary sources of income, these are combined with that derived from working the land. Let it be further assumed that the estate remains sufficient to provide for the rearing and livelihood of the younger generation. These children, all still at home, enter their adulthood; the daughters marry out and the elder of the sons—there are two of them—obtains a wife. Shortly thereafter, the second son also marries. The sons' wives are absorbed into the economy and contribute labor in the performance of domestic and productive tasks, and they also have children of their own. The group is now complex, consisting of two *fang* in the second generation. The parents die, but the two *fang* continue to live together for a period of time. Finally, each demands complete control over its share of the estate, and the *chia* divides.

The above, of course, is a sketch of the maximal developmental cycle of the Chinese family as it has been frequently described. (See Freedman 1961–62: 327.) A simple family develops into one that is stem, as that term has been defined by Lang (1946: 14), which definition does not necessarily imply the existence of the *famille souche* pattern described by Levy (1949: 55–56); and after the marriage of the second son the family becomes joint and then, with the death of the parents, fraternal-joint. For the purposes of this discussion it is essential to note that the three components have remained in unchanging relationship with each other throughout the developmental history of this *chia*.

However, the connections between the components can vary. An inclusive economy can be found in association with a dispersed estate and, of necessity, a dispersed group. In *The Golden Wing* (1948), Lin Yueh-hwa describes at one point in the story how Dunglin entered into a partnership with his sister's husband and established a shop in a town near his home village. Dunglin's share of the shop actually belonged to his *chia* as a whole, as did some land in the village. Though Dunglin lived and worked in the shop (frequently coming home), his wife lived in the village with his mother and the *fang* composed of Dunglin's brother, his brother's wife, and their children (Lin 1948: 11f). The economy certainly was inclusive: "As the family had not been officially divided, the capital and money income of the store, as well as family lands and their produce, were still common property, belonging to both brothers. Thus the two men took an interest in each other's work and planned together for the good of the whole family" (Lin 1948: 13).

Dispersion on a somewhat greater scale was found in a group distributed between the village of Nanching and the nearby city of Canton:

Wong Han was a wealthy landlord with considerable landholdings in the village and an import and export firm in the city of Canton. A man in his early sixties, he lived with his wife, two concubines, two married sons and their wives, one unmarried son and two unmarried daughters, and three grandchildren, all as one household with common property. Although the married sons and their wives spent most of the time in their common city residence, family unity was effectively maintained among the fourteen members. (C. K. Yang 1959b: 17.)

For a final example of this particular *chia* form, I turn to my own field data. The case I describe is extreme in regard to the size of the group and the extent of its dispersion. The group was one of the largest (and wealthiest) in the region where the study was carried out. Yet it is one of a kind with the previous cases cited.

In May 1965, the group of which Lin Shang-yung was the *chia-chang* consisted of forty-two persons. In the oldest generation only Lin himself survived. In the second generation the marriage of each of his three sons had led to the formation of as many *fang*. The first of these had twenty-two members: in addition to the father and mother it included five sons and two daughters, the wife and seven children of the first son, and the wife and four children of the second. The second *fang*—twelve persons in all—consisted of a father, a mother, four sons, four daughters, and the wife and child of the first son. In the third *fang*, with the father and mother there were five young children. The Lin *chia* had established four households, each associated with a part of the estate. There were the buildings and fields that had been obtained (and later expanded) by Shang-yung when he separated from his brother. In an adjoining village (Yen-liao) the *chia* owned a rice mill, and in yet another nearby settlement it operated a shop selling fertilizers and animal feed. About twenty-five miles to the south, additional land and buildings had been purchased. In the management of all these holdings, a common budget was maintained. Funds and goods were transferred as needed, and expenditure by the manager of a given enterprise was scrutinized by other group members. Shang-yung continued to live at the site of the original holdings. With him were some members of the first and second *fang*: the two daughters of the first *fang*, the oldest married son, and two of his children, the father and mother of the second *fang*, their seven unmarried children, and their married son's wife and child. The married son had lived there prior to his induction into the army (and even he still participated in the economy, for he continued to receive money from home to supplement very low soldier's pay). Part of the first *fang* —the second married son, his wife and four children, and the two youngest unmarried sons—resided at the rice mill. Living in the south was another unmarried son of the first *fang*, and the wife and remaining children of the first married son. The mother of the first *fang* also lived there, and the father divided his time between the south and the rice mill. The entire third *fang* was quartered at the shop.

So far we have described situations in which the *chia* economy is inclusive and the group and the estate are either both concentrated or both dispersed. But an inclusive economy and a dispersed group can also be found together with a concentrated estate. In such a case only group members in one of the households exploit the estate; other members of the group receive remittances from or send them to the estate. Most of those receiving money from the estate were, in traditional times, dependents such as students studying for the examinations or a small minority of apprentices who might pay their masters some sort of "tuition" or who might continue to get additional spending money from home. Remittances to the estate by officials, merchants, craftsmen, salaried workers, etc., were much more common. In his description of the rise and fall of gentry families, Ho gives many examples of the remittance system among the gentry and wealthy merchants (Ho 1962: 292, 312). For less prestigious groups, relevant data from Lang have already been cited. I am unable to find much evidence from mainland China about the residential variations that were possible in such circumstances, but generalizing from observations made in Taiwan, I can say that although remittances were commonly from single men or married men whose wives and children were still residing with the other members of the group, there were also cases of remittances being forthcoming when dispersion was along *fang* lines.

Though this discussion has not covered the entire range of variations possible within the inclusive economy, the main patterns have been set forth, and we now turn to the non-inclusive economy. It is, of course, always associated with a dispersed group; one or more members of the group are economically independent and residentially separated from the rest. The remaining members can exhibit varied residential and economic connections with the estate identical to those found in the context of an inclusive economy.

Though examples of such situations could be cited here, these may be left to the reader's imagination or experience, for it is now pertinent to ask if a *chia* group with a non-inclusive economy is, indeed, worthy of consideration as a discrete social unit. As a group of kinsmen is it any different from one constituted along identical genealogical lines in which *fen-chia* has taken place one or more times?

The very fact that all members have claims to the estate gives the group at the very least a sort of terminal cohesion. It can be expected that the group will either reassemble or in some fashion have dealings with each other at the time of *fen-chia*, or even prior to *fen-chia* if the death of a member leads to a realignment of the rights to the estate enjoyed by the survivors. The existence of a dispersed group with a non-inclusive economy has been observed by Moench among the Overseas Chinese (mainly Hakka) in Tahiti. This unit he calls the "dispersed family": "The dispersed family is that group of persons who maintain residual claims to shares of an undivided patrimony. This dispersed family is seldom a production group and is thus irrelevant in a discussion of production: its relevance is to problems of exchange, succession and family division" (Moench 1963: 72).

Although under the conditions of life in Tahiti the "dispersed family" may have been the end of the line as far as significant interaction among members of the group was concerned, this was not necessarily the case in China. The connections between the components of the *chia* could change. To see this requires that they be considered diachronically and developmentally. In a post-*fen-chia* situation similar to that described earlier, in which the estate and group are concentrated and the economy is inclusive, the possibilities for various kinds of development were many. Simon's account of the history of Ouang-Ming-Tse's "family" illustrates some of these (Simon 1887: 209f; this source was used by

Freedman 1958: 23f). Simon records Ming-Tse's description of the successful development of the *chia* headed by his paternal grandfather:

At that time my grandfather was far from rich. . . . When the number of children was found to be on the increase, it was decided that the boys should learn trades, and go to town to add to the common weal. My father was the one to begin. He had six brothers and sisters younger than himself, and chose the trade of carpenter. His apprentice fees were paid for three years, and his wants provided for until he was able to maintain himself. He was soon, however, able to save something to bring home to the fortnightly meetings. Three other sons followed his example, and my father increased the size of his field with their savings, pushing back the boundaries, and as soon as he could give employment to one of them, he recalled him. Only one, the youngest, remained at Fou-Cheou, and became one of the first merchants in the town. (Simon 1887: 226f.)

Of his father's two older brothers, one was already established as a mandarin, and the other had remained on the farm throughout (Simon 1887: 226). How the mandarin achieved his success is not made clear, nor is it indicated why the youngest brother never returned. During many of the years that it existed, then, this group was dispersed. While they were apprentices, the boys remained *chia* dependents. Next came a period of self-support, which meant exclusion from the economy, followed by a re-inclusion into the economy, first through remittances sent home and then through participation once more in the exploitation of the estate. No information is provided about the presence or absence of economic ties between the estate, on the one hand, and the mandarin and the merchant, on the other. If there were no such ties, these two remained members of the group only insofar as they demanded their shares at time of division (Simon 1887: 230).

Though this is a success story not duplicated by the majority of *chia* in China, it does illustrate some of the more important junctures that must have characterized the development of many of them. The first of these is the initial dispersion of the group, most often occurring on the basis of managerial decisions taken by the senior generation—usually in the person of the *chia-chang*—and affecting the junior members of the group. In situations where there was one son only—and this may have been quite common (see Lang 1946: 10)—dispersion might occur only in the face of extreme poverty (see Fei and Chang 1949: 272), natural calamities, or war, for in ordinary circumstances, the primary concern was the continued exploitation of the estate. For the poor with more than one son, dispersion was often a grim necessity forced on them by the inability of their land to support many people. Nevertheless, dispersion was tied in with the notion that diversification of the economy into nonagricultural activities was one means of achieving success, and there are good indications that the advantages in such an arrangement were recognized by poor and rich alike. The poor often made the attempt, or wished they could, and the rich frequently owed their favorable position to successful implementation of diversification schemes. (See Cohen 1967 for a brief discussion of economic diversification within the traditional framework of Chinese society, and its carry-over into contemporary Yen-liao.) In a rural setting an effort to diversify often, if not usually, meant leaving one's parents and home community for a length of time (Fei and Chang 1949: 271f; Chow 1967: 117). The physical mobility associated with such attempts to diversify the *chia* economy must be kept distinct from that possibly resulting from *fen-chia*. My own work in Yen-liao brought to light several cases of brothers at the time of *fen-chia* converting their portion of the estate into cash and leaving the village to seek their fortunes elsewhere. These men had participated in the dismemberment of the *chia*; those who leave while still belonging to the original *chia* group might very well be concerned with promoting *chia* survival and advancement.

Following the dispersion of the group, the issue then became one of success or failure. Here, of course, the rich had advantages over the poor, for unless he was supported by a lineage or some other source of non-*chia* funds, a youth leaving the farm was unlikely to get a chance to compete in the examinations. For the very rich, even if a career outside officialdom were intended, the influence that could be brought to bear by powerful members of a group would probably assure success in most cases. Apprenticeship was a common means of effecting the dispersion of the group. Within this category some positions were more desirable than others, so here prior ties and influence also played a part. (See Fried 1953: 165f.)

In terms of the *chia* economy, success meant the onset of remittances, and there are good reasons to believe that most persons did send home a portion of their earnings. Yang has spoken of this in general terms:

Most of the villagers who seek work in the city . . . send their earnings back to their homes to be used to buy land and build houses for the family. If they are married, the wives and children remain in the family home. If they were single when they left the village, they usually return to marry a girl chosen by the family. (M. Yang 1945: 228.)

Though this passage perhaps overstates the case, it does provide some clues about why this tendency could be so prevalent. A son could and did sometimes establish economic independence (*fen-chia*) from his parents as well as from his brothers. (Fei 1939: 66f provides one of many examples.) However, this rarely, if ever, occurred before his marriage. In all probability, most sons who went out to work did so at an early age; if they were apprenticed, they certainly did. In general, the younger the son was, the greater the managerial authority exercised over him by the *chia-chang* (C. K. Yang 1959a: 139). Yet when he left, he still had the support of the *chia*: to the extent that the value of its holdings permitted, the *chia* economy was geared to ensuring that the son be provided a wife (C. K. Yang 1959a: 25). Furthermore, he still had rights to the estate.

Before marriage, paternal authority might in itself be sufficient to ensure that a young man working outside faithfully remit home a portion of his earnings. And there were compelling reasons for the *chia-chang* to see that the youth living away from home turn over to him as much of his earnings as possible. Matters of support aside, if the *chia-chang*'s son had married brothers working the estate, there was already the possibility of *fen-chia*. The sons remaining at home also were quite anxious that the *chia-chang* continue to obtain remittances from their younger brother, for if these did not enable them to expand the estate, at least it would reduce the burden of rents or other expenses. The additional source of income, contributing to the maintenance of the estate as a whole, served to counter divisive tendencies that might develop between the *fang*.

After marriage, the situation would be somewhat different. The person working outside was now in a position to assert his own rights to the estate. The situation was now one of cooperation among equals, for if the man living outside was earning money for the estate, his brothers were exploiting it for all. Although it is certainly true that in general and ultimately "the rights of brothers to more or less equal shares of property ... entailed a constant pressure against unity'" (Freedman 1958: 27), in the context of the diversified *chia* economy this pressure could be lessened. (See Cohen 1967, 1968. M. Yang 1945: 238 gives an example of a highly interdependent *chia* economy.)

Finally, with increasing wealth a dispersed group might be formed (or maintained) by the expansion of the estate to different locales. In effect, the *chia* group might follow the estate and set up new households. Ouang-Ming-Tse noted that his younger brother living in Foochow had bought some land in the village, "which is cultivated by his eldest son." He added that "when he gives up his business to two of his sons, as he soon will do, he will return here" (Simon 1887: 227). It cannot be determined from the text if this simply meant a shift from one to the other of the two households containing the *chia* group, or if *fen-chia* is implied. Similar dispersed estates and their associated households were observed in Taiwan, where mobility was pronounced. In Lin Shang-yung's *chia*, discussed earlier, there were from 1949 to 1965 four different conjugal units that occupied the rice mill sequentially for periods ranging from three to five years. In such *chia*, it may be added, the interdependence of the various *fang* is so complex as to present real obstacles to early *fen-chia*.

Of course, it is probable that a great many, if not most, of the persons who went out looking for work were failures. Failure did not necessarily mean an inability to survive. The critical standard was whether survival was accompanied by remittances. Failure, indeed, might sometimes have the same result as success—a return to the original *chia* household. (See Lang 1946:16.) This could also occur during times of war or other disturbances. In Nanching, before 1933 for instance, there were about one hundred "families" with "long-term" emigrants. By 1948–51, war and economic depression had forced many of the emigrants to return, so the number of such "families" had been reduced to forty or fifty (C. K. Yang 1959b: 71).

The *chia* group, then, was distinguished by the potential of its membership to rejoin the *chia* economy, as well as by the possession of an estate. The circumstances through which *chia* members might once again come to participate in a common residential or budgetary arrangement were varied, as were those associated with the development of the economy in its non-inclusive form. The possibility arises that a good deal of the movement of persons in Chinese society, movement connected with "horizontal" or "vertical" social and economic mobility (Ho 1962), or with efforts to achieve such mobility, in fact occurred within a *chia* framework. To be sure, there were obvious exceptions. The number of potential *fang* within a *chia* could be reduced through the sale or adoption out of children, or through a man's marrying into his bride's *chia*; marriage in any event involved transfer of a person, in most cases a woman, from one *chia* to another. Again, as I have noted, men leaving their natal homes might do so following *fen-chia*. Nevertheless, it is likely that most men seeking employment and opportunities away from their birthplace remained members of their original *chia* group. *Fen-chia* was a very different matter. It was a jural act of fragmentation; together with partition of property there was termination of many kinds of actual or potential cooperation and mutual support. On the other hand, *fen-chia* also meant ending the obligations that tied *chia* members together. In the final analysis, the responsibilities of kinship in a post-*fen-chia* situation were quite contingent: the separate *chia* headed by brothers could suffer or enjoy very different fates. (See Smith 1900: 328.)

Factors leading to early *fen-chia* were associated mainly with membership in a common household. It was under one roof that conflicts of interest were likely to emerge quickly; when members of a *chia* group lived together, dissatisfaction over distribution of *chia* resources or other situations increasing tension between the *fang* could appear most rapidly and with greatest force. In general, it may be that *fen-chia* was delayed by circumstances involving an inclusive or non-inclusive economy associated with a dispersed *chia* group. Such situations, perhaps, also increased the chances of success (an improvement in economic circumstances) or prolonged its enjoyment.

The *chia* was the crucial domestic unit in China, one in which ties between persons were associated with common ties to an estate. The estate could vary in size and value; at one extreme it could consist of a humble home, a few agricultural tools, and a small area of farming land, rights to which might only be those of tenancy. Although great poverty could deprive the *chia* of the minimum endowment for corporate cohesion, what evidence there is suggests that even in comparatively recent times such a situation prevailed only in a minority of cases. (See Tawney 1932: 33f.) In any event, a contrast stressing the presence or absence of a *chia* estate is more useful than one emphasizing gross differences in domestic organization, as between wealthy and poor or gentry and peasant, for at least prior to the establishment of the present government on the mainland, the bulk of China's population was organized on a *chia* basis, and it is precisely in the *chia*'s adjustment to many different social and economic situations that the variability of arrangements possible within the *chia* framework can be seen.

The relationships among *chia* members, then, were quite flexible; one might even say that the *chia* as a social group was highly adaptable. Likely parallels in other aspects of Chinese social structure provide an area for future investigations that may considerably increase our understanding of Chinese society and behavior.

Child Training and the Chinese Family

MARGERY WOLF

The Chinese family has been examined in many contexts—from its place in the economy to its role in ancestor worship. Only in passing has it been considered in terms of the family's basic function: the training of future adult members. The accumulation of data about socialization processes is essential to our understanding of human behavior and personality development, but even the researcher whose interests are confined to more specific problems may find that such information yields unexpected insights into areas of culture seemingly unrelated to children. The cooperation, or at least interaction, of the entire domestic group is required to one degree or another in the preparation of the family's children for future responsibilities. Adult attitudes and approaches to the job of socialization suggest a great deal about their attitudes toward one another and their evaluation of their own positions in the family.

Generalizations about the Chinese family in this essay are drawn from the experience of a two-and-a-half-year field study of child-training practices in a small village of Hokkien-speakers in northern Taiwan. The research, designed by my husband, Arthur Wolf, had a dual purpose: to carry out a conventional anthropological village study and to replicate the work of the Six Culture Project. The Six Culture Project, under the direction of its senior members, John W. M. Whiting, Irvin L. Child, and William W. Lambert, sent field teams to six different societies to collect systematic information on child rearing, carefully timed observations of child behavior, child interviews, and comparable ethnographic data (Whiting *et al.* 1966). Their methodology included techniques traditional to anthropology as well as those confined until then to psychological laboratories. To their elegant design we added, among other things, some homemade projective tests, informal parent observations and interviews, questionnaires administered in local schools, and, in collaboration with W. W. Lambert, a biochemical analysis of the epinephrine and norepinephrine levels of our sample of 64 children.

In the process of observing and interviewing parents, we found that we were being given information beyond that asked for in our specific questions—information that told us much about the dynamics of the family. A Chinese woman's assumptions about the behavior of close kinsmen, assumptions she may be neither willing nor, in many cases, able to express, were often clearly delineated in her responses to questions about who was responsible for feeding and disciplining her child. Although our questioning was nearly always directed toward adult interactions with the family's children, the responses frequently contained spontaneous information about adult interaction with other adults in the family, a type of information, incidentally, that is extremely difficult to elicit by direct questioning. In a sense, our study of child-training practices produced quite accidentally a projective test of the dynamics of the Chinese family. More simply, it provided another perspective from which to examine the Chinese family and the nature of the interactions of its members.

In Taiwan there remains an old and stable laboratory of traditional Chinese culture. Between 1895 and 1945 Taiwan was under the control of a Japanese colonial government, but Japanese influence over such institutions as the family was superficial at most, and in many rural areas nonexistent. Moreover, the isolation Japan imposed on her colony protected the traditional culture from the Western influences that provoked so much of the social upheaval in China during the 1920's and 1930's. The comments made by Wusih factory girls interviewed by Olga Lang in the 1930's (Lang 1946: 266ff), so full of uncertainty about their new status and new rights, are strikingly similar to those made now by the girls working in Taiwan's factories. Change is coming to Taiwan and will continue with increasing speed as the younger people declare their independence and use it to experiment with new ideas and new ways.

The village of Peihotien (a fictitious name) is located on the edge of the Taipei basin, a fifteen minute walk from the railroad and a half hour from there by train to the city of Taipei. Although the majority of the families in the village own land, few obtain their sole income from the land. Nearly every family has one member who brings in wages from a job outside the village. Peihotien's proximity to an urban center seems to strengthen rather than to weaken family ties. The market town of

Tapu (a fictitious name) has, besides a railway station, several small factories that can and do employ the young people of Peihotien. From Tapu it is only fifteen minutes by train to a small city with many employment opportunities. It is feasible in terms of time and it is economically advantageous for the young men and women of the village to remain a part of their parents' domestic units and commute to employment elsewhere. Few young people, including those without obligations to parents in Peihotien, leave the village to be closer to work opportunities.

Although my observations are based on information obtained from Hokkien-speakers in Taiwan, I refer to my informants as Chinese or as Taiwanese, both of which they are. I am nonetheless aware of the dangers of implying uniformity across a culture that is so full of variation. Strictly speaking, the term "Taiwanese" includes the Hakka, about whose family life I know very little, and the term "Chinese" includes people as disparate as the wealthy bureaucrat in Peking and the poor peasant living hundreds of miles away on the Yunnan plateau. It is tempting but dangerous to generalize that the family tensions reflected in the child-training practices of Peihotien are found within other social classes and linguistic groups. It is tempting because many of the conclusions reached in the following analysis are familiar to those who have observed the Chinese family in other provinces, centuries, and social classes; it is dangerous because the data on socialization in other areas of China are so limited, and our assumptions about uniformity of customs across such a vast country have in the past proved so erroneous. I will, however, venture a conservative assertion: as long as power is vested in the senior generations of a family (i.e., the grandparents) child-training practices will change more slowly than other aspects of culture. Older people, in particular older females, are less exposed to and less vulnerable to innovative ideas. And, until the Communist movement, new ideas were both less available and less appealing to the lower classes. Given the strong tendency toward hypergamy in Chinese marriage, the conservative attitudes of lower-class women probably travel fairly high up into the social hierarchy. In other words, it seems reasonable to assume that child-training practices among the Chinese are not particularly open to Western influences and are likely to accurately reflect traditional goals and values—as long as those goals and values are maintained. In Taiwan, the authority is just beginning to pass from the hands of the grandparents to those of the parents.

Just as current research has made us aware of the unexpected frequency and broad geographic distribution of alternative forms of mar-

riage in China, it is probable that further research will find more variation in the nature of relationships within the family. It would be foolish
to assume that the particular tensions and the particular socialization
techniques discussed in this paper are typical of China as a whole. The
variations that occur in conjunction with alternative forms of marriage
in Peihotien are enough to discount this. Undoubtedly the economic
base of a community, the status of its women, the importance of matrilateral kin ties, and any number of other factors can affect the style of
interaction among family members *and* the techniques they use to train
their children. The child-training practices in a remote village in
Kwangsi province may vary greatly from those of Peihotien, but they
will nonetheless be related to the tensions afflicting the families of that
particular village.

Mothers and Fathers

Both the mother and the father of a Taiwanese child share the same
broad goals in the training of their son. They want him to become a
strong healthy adult who is obedient, respectful, and capable of supporting them in their old age. They want a son who will not embarrass or
impoverish them by his excesses, who will maintain if not increase their
standing in the community, who will handle relations with outsiders
skillfully but at the same time keep them at a polite distance. No matter
how alienated man and wife may be from each other, they nonetheless
share these common aims in regard to their children. The techniques
they use to implement these goals differ considerably and, more importantly, so does the intensity of their desire for any particular result in
their sons.

A father's relationship with his son is both affectionate and informal
until the boy reaches the age of six or seven. In the evenings the small
boy accompanies his father on errands about the village, and falls asleep
on his father's lap as the older man chats with neighbors and friends.
Although fathers do not play games with their children, they are apt to
play with them in the manner that an American adult plays with a kit-
ten or puppy. Fathers of young children are usually fairly well prepared
with the sweets or pennies that dry the tears resulting from scraped
knees and bumped heads. In return a father expects very little. A toddler
is too young to understand what his father wants when he asks the child
to bring him a packet of cigarettes, and a four-year-old is too young to
understand that he must obey his father's command. The child's disobedience is treated with either amusement or tolerance, depending on
his age and his father's mood. If the child's infantile behavior becomes

annoying, or if, as so often happens with Chinese children, he falls into a kicking, screaming rage over some small (though conclusive) frustration, he is simply turned over to his mother or older sister with little or no paternal comment.

The age of reason has been established by Taiwanese parents at about six years, coinciding in modern times with the child's beginning school. Since this age is unmarked by any ceremony (other than that of starting school), the father's subsequent change in behavior must seem to the child abrupt, bewildering, and drastic. Social pressure and the father's own understanding of "what is right" force him to create a social distance between himself and his son. The sleepy child no longer finds a haven on his father's lap but is told to go to bed. If he decides to shoot one more marble before complying with his father's request to fetch him cigarettes, he hears his name called in the stern, icy voice of the feared schoolmaster. He may still accompany his father about the village for a while, but the behavior expected of him in his father's presence tends to turn the outing into an ordeal not to be repeated if avoidable. As their interaction becomes more and more formal and their conversation deteriorates into paternal lectures, the father's dignity becomes more impressive and more impregnable.

Taiwanese fathers say that it is only from this aloof distance that they can engender in their sons the proper behavior of a good adult. "You cannot be your son's friend and correct his behavior." A child will not take seriously the friendly suggestions of an obviously loving adult, but he will obey the commands of a stern feared parent. This philosophy, of course, reflects (or is reflected in) the educational techniques of Chinese schools even today. Be it unintentional or simply concomitant, this remoteness also builds the supports necessary to maintain the senior male's position of authority over his adult sons. The weakening powers of an aging father, both mental and physical, provide the all-important social justification for a young man desiring independence and/or control of the family destiny. The increasing indecision and faltering that might be revealed in the camaraderie of an informal relationship can be concealed for a considerably longer time when the son is faced with an austere, aloof figure of authority toward whom society demands he show respect and obedience. All fathers are aware of this potential problem, but whether it actually motivates their behavior is another question, and one not within the scope of this paper. For whatever reason, fathers believe that if they are to teach their sons at all, they must first teach them obedience and respect.

Long before they have learned to fear their father, children are aware of his power in the family. On several occasions I have heard a three- or four-year-old imperiously warn his mother to stop interfering with his (usually dangerous) activity lest he summon his father to beat her. Although the father's wrath may not yet have been directed toward him, the child has observed its effect on his mother or his elder siblings. Children with older siblings may not find their father's change of behavior toward them as abrupt or as unexpected as do first- and second-borns. The mother, intentionally or not, provides considerable assistance to her husband in building his image of authority. The recalcitrant child, or the child who has committed a serious misdeed, may be threatened with all sorts of dire punishments, but if he has reached the "age of reason," or has siblings who are six years of age and older, the threat of paternal punishment is one of the most effective. If the mother's threat is actually carried out and the father beats his son, the strokes may be far lighter than the mother's would have been, since the punishment is administered with cool forethought; but perhaps for the same reason the emotional effect on the child is far stronger.

A male is born into a community and grows up there, learning almost unconsciously the idiosyncrasies of his physical environment and of the temperaments of his neighbors and relatives. By the time he reaches adulthood, there is little in his everyday social world that is so surprising or uncertain that he cannot deal with it automatically. His own peculiarities of temperament or behavior have long been accepted (or rejected) by his neighbors and are hardly worthy of comment. He is a member of a family that considers all non-kin as outsiders and of a community that similarly considers all non-residents. Not so the wife of this man. Growing up in a similar social environment in a distant village, she enters a community of outsiders to live with a family that until the day of her marriage has been classified by her as outsiders. Whereas security and familiarity are givens to her husband, to her they are completely absent and may be for many years to come, if not (in her frightened young eyes) forever. In her first few years of marriage, her own children will seem more a part of this new community than she can ever hope to be. Under these conditions, it is not at all surprising that she should give precedence over the inculcation of respect and respectability in her sons to a different set of values. Her concern in her isolation is more with her own personal well-being than with the vague expectations of the somewhat alien world of her husband and his family. To them, her infant son is the next link in a long chain of descendants carrying their name and their future. To her, he is the source of the first bit of security she has felt since she entered the family. He is her defense against her mother-in-law and her sisters-in-law. His birth, providing an object of shared concern, may change her somewhat ambiguous relationship with her husband into a more satisfactory commitment, but if it does not, the dissatisfactions of that relationship will not matter as much. She may simply endure her present situation and build toward a future family environment that will not be hampered by mothers-in-law or be dependent on husbands. No matter what is involved in her current status, the whole quality of her future life depends on the strength of the ties she develops with her son.

The salient difference between what a Chinese mother and a Chinese father hope for in their relations with their sons can best be described in slightly exaggerated terms. A Chinese father wants respect and obedience even at the price of fear or dislike. If he is to maintain his authority over the household when his sons are themselves adults, he must have their respect if not their admiration, their obedience if not their affection. He is aided in his endeavors by the sanctions of his culture, the example of his neighbors, and the teachings of the schools. A Chinese mother would certainly appreciate her son's respect and obedience, but not at the price of his affection. Her marriage into a family of strangers has forced her to depend entirely on herself in constructing working relationships. The degree to which she can depend on those ties is less related to the sanctions of society, the examples of neighbors, or the teachings in the local school than to the intangibles of affection, spontaneous gratitude, and goodwill. Chinese culture extracts from a son the obligation of supporting his mother and showing her a minimum degree of respect; but a woman's experience with social sanctions has usually been that they have operated against her position rather than in any way promoting it. Far more dependable are the ties of affection and gratitude that she weaves in the years of her son's childhood.

Chinese society has given a father both the power and the authority to manage his adult sons. A mother's authority is not so clearly stated, and so she must establish her power in a more subtle fashion. For her, the father's method of withdrawal into formality would be both difficult and dangerous. When her son is six years old, she may expect more of him in terms of obedience and chores, but her menial services to him are still a necessity and will be for some time. These services are often extended considerably longer than is necessary, and are referred to again and again when the child is being punished. "Why are you so bad? Do you want me to die? Then who will feed you and take care of you?" Mothers seem to be as convinced as fathers that learning does not take place without physical punishment, but mothers administer beatings in a very different atmosphere. The father's beating is usually preceded by a stern lecture on the expectations of the family and administered with a cool temper; the mother's beating usually grows out of the frustrations of the day and is administered in fury (and often as not interrupted by a relative or neighbor). Once her anger has passed, she may comfort the crying child, explaining why she *had* to punish him, or if he has run away before she managed to strike him, she may just let the whole matter go with a few words of warning when he returns. Impending punishments by a father do not blow over. Paternal punishment of a child or of his siblings occurs just often enough to make it a useful threat, one which mothers employ frequently. As mentioned previously, this threat serves to establish more firmly the father's position of familial superiority, but it also has an interesting side effect on the mother's position. She appears in the role of go-between. Each time she makes the threat and does not carry it out, she becomes the child's go-between rather than the father's, the child's ally rather than the father's. An adult son fuming under the continued dominance of his father is far more likely to recall these "interventions" by his mother than the beatings he received at her hands.

Village mothers state, as do the fathers, that you must not let a child know you love him or you will not be able to correct his behavior, assuming of course that if you love him you will forgive anything. The open expression of affection toward an older child is considered not only in bad taste but bad for the child. One must not praise children for accomplishments or they will feel they have done well enough and will stop trying to do better. Superficially these dicta do seem to be observed. Upon presenting an essay or school report to his father for his chop (to assure the teacher that it has been seen by the parent), a child who has placed second in the class is admonished to reach first place by next year, and if he has placed first he is warned to do as well the following year or expect a beating. The father may swell with pride as he discusses the matter later with the child's grandmother or mother, but he will show no pleasure in the child's presence. If other adults comment on the achievement, the father counters with deprecating remarks about the child's other, bad, characteristics, concealing his pride from no one, except perhaps the child. The mother's reaction to the child's accomplishment will be somewhat the same, but her pleasure will be less carefully concealed from the child; the extra ten cents to buy sweets or the choice piece of food swiftly stuffed into his mouth before the dish goes on the table will not go unrelated to her pride in him. Like his father, his mother rarely pets or hugs him, but unlike the father, she has many other means available to her for expressing her affection: cooking his favorite dishes, granting privileges, or simply listening to childish prattle about the day's happenings at school. The constant interaction between mother and child provides far more opportunity for the mother to influence her child's attitudes than does the briefer more formal interaction of father and son. Most mothers make good use of their opportunities.

The inferior status of female children is not as pronounced in times of prosperity (the present situation in Taiwan) as it is during periods of economic hardship. Sons are of course preferred, but most families want at least one daughter if they can afford her. In general, the treatment of a girl is not dramatically different from that of her brothers. The attitudes her parents hold toward her, however, are quite different. The expectations and consequent behavior of father and mother toward their son are almost reversed when they deal with their daughter. As an adult the daughter will be nearly irrelevant to her father. Very little of his future prestige or his physical comfort in his declining years will depend on anything she does or does not do. The rigid standards of respect and obedience her brother must adhere to as an adult are of less value in her, since she will be in another household. As long as she does not become wantonly immoral while a member of her father's household, she is a luxury he can enjoy. Fathers who are acting against their natural propensities in the treatment of their sons, find considerable satisfaction in a relaxed informal exchange with their daughters. As long as he maintains the general rules of propriety (i.e., does not openly express his affection for her or allow her publicly to disobey him), he is safe from the criticism of his neighbors. Should she turn out to be a poor wife and daughter-in-law, criticism would not be directed at him, her father, but rather at her mother as the person responsible for her training in the domestic arts. Ultimately, the hardship would fall on the girl herself.

An adult daughter will have no more opportunity to add to her mother's comfort or status than she will to her father's. If she turns out to be an excellent mother and daughter-in-law, she will by definition see less of her mother and relegate her to a position of minor importance in the demands on her time and affection. Publicly, or even privately, the mother will receive little credit for having trained her so well. Should the daughter fall short of adult standards, criticism will eventually be directed at her mother's laxness and incompetence. This potential criticism, however, has little influence on the mother's everyday attitude toward training her daughter. Until one of her sons marries and provides her with a daughter-in-law, the services of her daughter are needed.

She can afford to smile on the disobedience and arrogance of her son as on interest accumulating on a loan, but the misbehavior of her daughter threatens daily operating expenses. If she has a family of any size at all, she must have someone to help her wash the vegetables, mind the younger children, hang out the clothes. If the mother does not establish early at least the minimum standards of obedience in her daughter, she will suffer for it several times each day. If some degree of responsibility has not been internalized, the mother will not dare leave the girl in charge of infants and toddlers, send her on errands, or depend on her to have the rice washed in time for dinner.

Taiwanese mothers believe that no children can be expected to understand much during their first six years of life. This is not to say that all training is delayed until their sixth birthday, but rather that not much is expected to result from it until after that age. Nonetheless, by the time they are five, most little girls are doing a few chores regularly and certainly are minding their slightly younger siblings. Before this time, the mother's treatment of her sons and daughters is not noticeably different except in one aspect. The techniques the mother employs throughout are essentially the same, but the intensity of the training for girls is considerably stronger. I doubt that there is any conscious intent involved in this; the girls as potential errand-runners and baby-sitters are kept closer to home and thereby receive a larger dose of the medicine administered. Even in behavior not immediately relevant to their mother's requirements for helpers, girls are found to socialize earlier and better than boys. Their performance on a variety of quantitatively measured variables is usually more consistent with the stated adult values at a considerably earlier age.

The warm intimate relationship that mothers desire with their sons they more frequently achieve with their daughters. As the daughter begins to worry about how she herself will fare at the hands of an unknown husband and mother-in-law, her mother's complaints about the behavior of her husband and his relatives fall on a more sympathetic ear. Her father's indulgence does little to increase his stature in his daughter's eyes, and often serves to damage it, since he is unlikely to defend to her his usually harsher public behavior toward her mother. She may retain a real though slightly cynical affection for her father, but the more frequent interaction plus their increasing similarity of interests and anxieties will involve her sympathies more deeply with her mother. The contrast between her mother's worried fretful questioning of the matchmakers and her father's calmer financial evaluations of a proposed match cements the emotional ties between the women. Her father may be, and often is, even more concerned than his wife about the treatment his daughter will receive at the hands of her husband's family, but as a man he must pretend to consider it irrelevant, and never having experienced this traumatic change himself, he truly is unaware of many of its more painful aspects. It is on her mother's good judgment that the girl must depend. The tears ritually required of bride and mother when the former leaves the home on her wedding day may fall for different reasons, but they rarely are forced.

As young men sons may fear their fathers, but they nonetheless emulate them, rejecting the open intimacy desired by their mothers in favor of a more manly stance. Even so, the mothers' efforts have not, in most cases, been in vain. As age gradually erodes and reverses the relationship between son and father, that existing between son and mother erodes little and reverses only in the way the mother desires. Should her relationship with her husband be antagonistic, the mother may begin early to isolate him by referring decisions about the household economy to her son rather than to the head of the household. As her son's earning capacity increases and his wages come to her for the purchase of daily requirements, she may also discuss with him the advisability of this or that major purchase or the advantages of joining this or that cooperative loan association. This show of trust and increasing dependence both strengthens their relationship and erases any lingering resentment the young man may have of the punishments received at her hands in his youth. Should, on the other hand, the relationship between husband and wife be a happy one, the wife can act as peacemaker between the older man, fearful of losing his hard-won authority, and the younger, impatient to test his own abilities. She can flatter and in many ways train the younger man by referring to him the minor domestic decisions (decisions she might have made herself without consulting her husband) and by discussing the larger decisions with both men, allowing each to feel that his was the decision acted upon. Eventually, however, the two must meet head-on in conflicts outside her domestic sphere, and the inevitable change in authority will proceed either speedily or gradually, depending on the personalities and abilities of the two men. The external pressures of his world demand that the son treat his aging father with respect, but the internal pressures of his socialization demand that he repay his mother with more than respect.

Grandparents

By the time she is a grandmother, a Chinese woman usually has come to regard her husband's family and community as her own. To her

daughter-in-law it is inconceivable that the older woman was ever anything but a representative of the interests of that family. Most women
are delighted when their son marries and a daughter-in-law enters their
home. Unless the marriage is a love-match, the older woman has chosen
the girl herself and investigated her qualities and faults as carefully as
possible. Because of the exaggerations of go-betweens, she expects a
great deal of her daughter-in-law. The girl's mother, her peers, and her
own observations have taught the bride what is expected of a daughter-
in-law, and she usually enters her husband's family determined to do her
best to fulfill these expectations. For the first few months, or perhaps
only weeks, after the marriage, there exists between mother-in-law and
daughter-in-law that amiable relationship that in the West is supposed
to exist between husband and wife during what is called the honeymoon
period. Village women laugh at new mothers-in-law singing the praises
of their sons' wives, saying, "We'll wait a while and then see." Indeed,
they usually have a very short period to wait. The two women's good
feelings quickly sour after a series of disagreements about how to pickle
radishes, when to wash clothes, how much to spend on excursions, and
when to have the evening meal on the table. Regardless of the merits of
her position, the older woman is likely to be the victor in any conflict
for a good many years to come.

No matter how antagonistic the young wife may feel toward her
mother-in-law or how confident in her own abilities, at the birth of her
first child she finds herself in need of the older woman as she will at no
other time. The child should be born in its father's home, but if this
proves impossible, almost anywhere would be preferable to the natal
home of its mother. The young woman's mother is sometimes called to
be with her during her first delivery, but even if she should arrive in time
to help her daughter during her travail, propriety and her own responsibilities prevent her from staying longer than a day or two. During those
first few weeks when the infant seems so fragile to the new mother and
each act in its care so fraught with disaster, it is to her mother-in-law
that she must turn for reassurance and advice. In the months and years
that follow, the young mother may come to regret this early dependence
and to resent her mother-in-law's continuing advice, but by then the pattern is set. Even with later births, she will need assistance if not advice, and the two seem to be indivisibly joined in the aging Taiwanese
female.

I suspect that the influence the grandmother exercises over the child-
training practices of her daughter-in-law with her first two or three
children makes this area of culture highly resistant to change. Young
women, particularly with the increased literacy of modern times, may

approach motherhood with some new notions about the proper way to care for and train children. Their attempts to implement these notions are likely to find little support from their mothers-in-law. The older woman's resistance may not be directed against change in and of itself but simply against taking chances with something so valuable as her grandchild. If she has been fortunate enough to raise several children to a respectable adulthood, she will be convinced of the splendid efficacy of her methods; if she has had the misfortune of losing a number of children, she will be convinced that raising children is far too hazardous an enterprise to allow unknown techniques introduced by an inexperienced young woman. Considering the lowly status she occupies in the household and the absence of friends or supporters in the community, it would be a rare young woman who could maintain enough independence to raise her children in an unconventional way. She could not expect much support from her husband, who would likely look to his mother as the family expert in this area of life. At best the young mother must compromise, and since she is usually only one of many caretakers, her efforts at innovation are likely to be wasted or so watered down as to be unnoticeable. By the birth of her third or fourth child, when she is more apt to have a freer hand in its upbringing, she will be far too busy to start something new and her zeal may well have faded anyway.

A grandmother may wish to supervise her daughter-in-law in the care of her son's child and may even feel required to intervene when the job is not being done in a way she deems proper, but in general she would prefer to enjoy her grandchildren without any of the painful responsibility of molding them into good sons and responsible daughters. Of course, she does not want them to grow up in such a way as to disgrace the family that has now become *her* family, but when she sees an exasperated mother disciplining her grandson more harshly than she thinks necessary, she has no qualms about interfering and moderating the punishment. Nor need she feel any anxiety about granting what the mother has denied, giving money for sweets that the mother has refused, ignoring misdemeanors that the mother judges crimes. A grandmother's physical comfort and security depend on the strength of the relationship she has built with her son, but her grandsons need only exist to fulfill her hopes in regard to them. She can enjoy their affection without any restraint, and cherish the knowledge that there will be at least two generations to follow her coffin to the grave and burn incense before her tablet.

In the first few years of her grandchildren's lives, the grandmother may be regarded by her son as the final authority and the expert on raising children, but as she begins to enjoy the children more, and as her

daughter-in-law gains confidence in herself and in the eyes of her husband, the grandmother's position as expert weakens. For many Taiwanese women this shift to the side is graceful and happy, the grandmother
finding she takes more pleasure in nurturing and spoiling her grandchildren than in competing with their mother. Depending on her age,
the grandmother may at the same time be turning over more and more
of the household responsibilities to her daughter-in-law, but more likely
she still has quite a few more years of power to control the domestic
organization. If, however, the older woman feels really threatened by
her daughter-in-law, fearing, for example, that her son may be induced
to move to the city for employment or set up a separate household, the
tension between the women is felt in all their interactions. The poor
grandmother must again take up arms in the battle she thought she had
won—the battle for the prime position in the affections of her son. Both
grandmother and mother then compete for the children's loyalty and affection, the former to tighten her ties to her son and the latter to build
toward her own future security. Both set up incidents in which the ad-
versary appears in the worst possible light to the bedeviled son-husband,
and in which, incidentally, the children are given sound practical training in manipulating human relationships. Most of the children in Peihotien could tell us which adult in the family particularly favored him and
who favored each of his siblings, parental favoritism being freely discussed by the family in the children's presence. It is not too farfetched
to suggest that in those families in which favoritism follows lines of
factionalism in the family, the seeds of antagonism between adult brothers are sown.

No matter how well fought the battle, the outcome of any long conflict
between mother- and daughter-in-law is as inevitable as the shifting of
authority from a father to his son. If she has raised her son well, he will
not desert her, but with age her influence in the kitchen and over the
family budget will gradually diminish and eventually disappear. If she
has not treated the daughter-in-law more outrageously than is considered normal in village life, the position of the aged mother in the family
of her children is usually enviable compared with that of the aged father.
The life expectancy of women on Taiwan, as in most other countries, is
considerably longer than that of men, but from the situation of the few
elderly men we observed in the village, it is clear that the women's efforts to ensure a comfortable secure old age are more effective than
those of their spouses. To be sure, a few old women spend their last years
being shuffled from the home of one son to another, never allowed to
stay longer than a prescribed period; more commonly they live qui-

etly in the home of the son who stays on the land or who is financially more capable of caring for a larger family.

By the time their first grandchildren have reached the age of reason, most grandfathers are beginning to feel serious threats to their authority in their sons' growing competence and income. By the time the last-born grandchildren reach this age, the grandfather's authority in the family is either completely gone or in a state of sham. Either the old man decides, as did his wife, to forget the forms and enjoy this next generation, or he realizes the futility of assuming the mask of aloof dignity in order to correct behavior. To the children, he is a source of pennies for sweets, an occasional place of solace when the rest of the childhood world turns against them, and a good place for stories when nothing else is doing. The truly aged man no longer able to work at much of anything in the midst of a busy household is a pitiful sight. His physical needs are usually met (although some old men complain that they are not), but busy mothers cannot prevent children from teasing and cannot or will not punish children for disobeying even simple commands an old man might issue. His son sees that all the forms of filiality are observed for the public eye, but his ambivalence toward his aged father often allows for little more. Old women, however, even those who made the lives of their daughters-in-law miserable in earlier years, usually find life considerably more comfortable. Until completely senile or physically incapacitated, they can perform functions in the household that even a revengeful daughter-in-law finds valuable. Sewing, nursing sick children, rocking fussy infants to sleep—these are minor but time-consuming occupations not suitable to old men or half-grown children, but they suit an old woman very well. And when she is beyond even this, if she has trained her son well, his affection will see to it that his wife cares for her with a gentleness that an old man might never experience. The funeral of the father will, nonetheless, be more elaborate than that of the mother.

Sisters-in-law

Rural Taiwanese children, particularly those born early in their mother's child-bearing career, enter a world teeming with adult relatives. Theoretically, these adults should consist of the father's parents, his brothers, and his brothers' wives—adults toward whom and from whom certain behavior is expected by tradition. Father's older brother should be like father only a bit more awesome; father's younger brother should be like father only a little less formal; the wives of both these men should be like second mothers. Actually, few children grow up with a paternal uncle and his family in their home, although many children do

have such relatives in their immediate neighborhood. Moreover, few children consider their father's brother's wife in any way similar to their own mother, and very few women would, under any circumstances, consider treating their husband's brother's children in the way they would treat their own children. If the brothers and their wives are on good terms, they do not want to endanger these good relations by disciplining one another's children; and if, as is more common, their relationship is brittle but still operative, nothing could more quickly open (or reopen) hostilities than a fracas between the wives over the misbehavior of a child. During the few years that the two couples are members of the same joint family and during the briefer period in which the family property is divided, all manner of antagonisms and jealousies are raised that will color their relations with one another for many years to come.*
The exact role played by the wives during these trying years varies with their personalities and with the quality of their relations with other family members, but it is almost never that of peacemaker. It would seem reasonable to expect a daughter-in-law to welcome her husband's younger brother's new wife into the family as an ally against their traditional foe, the mother-in-law, but other factors seem to operate against this. For one thing, the first daughter-in-law and her children have undergone the financial strain and parental tension that exists in a household accumulating the money and negotiating a marriage settlement for a son. Moreover, when this expensive troublesome commodity arrives, she is often given preferential treatment for a period of time or, if nothing else, is the source of much attention and interest. When the household settles down again, the older daughter-in-law is likely to take advantage of the younger's inexperience in the family's routines to shift both duties and blame for errors onto her head, at the same time, of course, shifting the mother-in-law's hostility. This behavior does little to endear older brother's wife to younger brother's wife, and though deposing the mother-in-law might have some advantages for the older daughter-in-law, it would have little for the younger, producing merely an exchange of tyrants. Nevertheless, the sisters-in-law have and work toward, albeit separately, a common goal, that of separate *chia*. Their husbands are fully and emotionally informed of each incident of preferential treatment from the senior generation, the bad habits one man's children are learning from his brother's poorly trained wretches, and the opportunities his children will surely miss because he is forced to make up the deficit in the family budget caused by his brother's insufficient income.

* In my book (Wolf 1968) I have described in considerable detail the difficult years that precede the division of a joint family.

The fact that very few joint families in Peihotien survive the marriage and fatherhood of a second son indicates the success of the sisters-in-law. The relationship between brothers in Taiwanese society is both weak and strained by inconsistent dicta concerning proper behavior toward each other. As children, the elder is required to yield to his younger brother's demands in all things, some of which are outrageous when the younger is still small. If the younger child desires some prize possession of the older and when denied it proceeds to beat the older boy with a stick or rock, the elder has no choice but either to give him the object or to leave the scene with it before adult attention is attracted. If, out of a mixture of pain and frustration, he slaps his younger brother, he can expect punishment for himself and special favor for his little brother. As they grow older and the elder brother is no longer a caretaker but still responsible for his younger brother, the latter continues to hold the strings of power. If elder brother does not like his behavior, in a particular instance, the younger can easily and often does provoke a quarrel, knowing full well that the parents will punish the elder automatically without giving him a chance to explain his actions as an attempt to correct younger brother's aberrant behavior. Younger brothers learn very early and very concretely that older brothers yield to younger brothers, and yet as adults the expectation is exactly the reverse—the younger is expected to yield to his older brother's decisions and guidance, a situation for which he has been poorly prepared. The comparative ease with which sisters-in-law can manipulate the brittle relationship between their husbands is not difficult to understand. Although some students of Chinese society suggest that the wives merely capitalize on the brothers' competition for the parental wealth or property, this seems quite a minor factor in their conflict, since the equality of their shares is clearly prescribed by the culture. Far more explosive is the emotional content of their relationship and the inadequacy of their training, in particular the younger brother's, for their adult roles of dominance and submission. Unless he is extraordinarily tolerant, the elder will retain some degree of resentment over the troubles his younger brother has caused him for so many years, and he may be just a bit heavy-handed in wielding his at last consistently approved authority; unless he is exceptionally adaptable, the younger brother will find his position untenable. If left to themselves, adult brothers might be able to overcome the strains built into their relations with one another, but most men marry before any compromise can be reached and often before the conflict between them has become fully apparent. Their wives are not motivated toward effecting such a compromise. In view of the fact that the brothers are given wives during the same period of time that they are adjusting their adult roles toward one another, it is understandable that the Taiwanese so often place the blame for the break-up of the family on "the narrow hearts of women" rather than on the contradictory demands the society makes upon their husbands.

The intensity of the hostility between brothers and brothers' wives lessens considerably after the family property is divided and each unit is established as a separate household, but their mutual distrust never disappears completely. Much as they might like to pursue a policy of complete noninvolvement, their housing usually makes this difficult. In many cases they will continue to share the same courtyard and the same guest hall, and their children will grow up playing more often with one another than with other village children. To prevent trouble or perhaps just for spite, a mother will warn her children not to go into the other part of the house or even not to play with their father's brother's children, but it is not a very practical order. The children nonetheless are influenced by their parents' distrust and are more wary around these adults than around others—less cheeky and somewhat more self-conscious.

The adults' attitude toward aggressive behavior in their children and their handling of fights between children reflect quite sharply the tensions within the family and the weight the various family members give to relations with one another and with other adults in their environment. All adults state emphatically that a child must not aggress against another no matter what the provocation, even if it is to defend himself or his property. Fathers point out that quarrels between children can draw in adults and endanger the good relations between relatives whose economic or social assistance may one day be essential. A grandmother condemns aggressive behavior because of its disruptive influence within the family. The escalation of a squabble among the children can be the final act that precipitates the family division. With time the perimeters of her world draw in, and the activities within the family become more significant to her than ever before. Even after her sons set up separate homes, a grandmother will want their relations at least to appear harmonious, since they are the source of her prestige and her pleasure. Her daughters-in-law are just as eager to prevent children's quarrels. During her first years as a resident outsider in the community, the young mother's only relief from the pressures of her husband's relatives is in the casual friendships developed with unrelated village women in like situations. These friendships, both because they develop in a time of great need and because they continue to provide a channel through which any injustice can be placed before the social jury of the village, are too important to a young woman to risk in a children's quarrel. Quarrels amongst her own children will be handled with a severity that depends much on her tolerance for noise and turmoil, but quarrels with unrelated children will not be countenanced. To a certain extent, the mother will also share her husband's attitude toward quarrels involving the children of relatives, but her handling of these children may well depend on just who the parents are. If her child reports that a village child struck him, she may scold or spank her own child for even being in a situation that led to aggression, studiously ignoring the actual transgressor or making light of his act should it come to his parents' attention. If, however, her child reports that his cousin attacked him, she is more likely to let his grandmother, the cousin's mother, the men of the family, and most of the village know that her sister-in-law's children are slyly dangerous and likely to strike at any time. Her own child could expect at least a cursory scolding for playing with undesirable companions. If her own child is clearly and obviously responsible for a fracas with a cousin, woe be unto him because his mother will be overconscientious about letting the family and the larger world know that she will not stand for such behavior on the part of her children, punishing the child with a severity that he may have neither expected nor deserved.

Village children have developed a technique for taking revenge on an attacker that is both safe and rewarding. They report the transgressor to his parent, a strategy obviously safer than reporting to their own. The mother of the naughty child then either beats her own child in the presence of his victim or promises to do so when she finds him. If the offending child has his wits about him and avoids his home for a few hours, the beating may never take place, his mother either having forgotten about the matter or having decided to settle for a scolding, since the victim is no longer there to observe the outcome. It seems quite likely that this ingenious technique of retaliation is first learned and most consistently reinforced in the context of the family. By reporting a cousin's misdeeds to his mother, a child places her in a situation in which she can do nothing but punish her child severely, no matter how long he stays away from home, since she is under the constant critical observation of the family of his victim.

Taiwanese children are aware almost from birth of the latent or perhaps active hostility between their parents and their father's brothers' families. That these people and their children must be treated with more circumspection than others they learn early and, as we have just seen, painfully. Their paternal cousins, nonetheless, will be their most frequent playmates. It is here, long before they are old enough to conceive

of it in the abstract, that they learn the intricacies of kin behavior—
the obligations it imposes and the penalties it extracts. As adults these
paternal cousins will be the very people to whom a man turns when he
needs a peacemaker, emergency funds, a job for his son, an introduction
or letter of credit, or sympathetic advice in the quarrels between his
brothers and himself. It will be to preserve their goodwill that he pun-
ishes his own children harshly for aggression. Yet in his childhood his
parents will have ingrained the proper style for their interactions for
almost the opposite reasons, reasons ostensibly relevant only to their
own generation.

Variations

The preceding generalizations have assumed, as do most studies of
the Chinese family, a "typical" family in which wives for the sons are
brought in from "outside" as adults, and adult daughters are married
into other "outside" families. This is undoubtedly the most common situation in China, but there is a large body of evidence from all over
China indicating that these are not the only means of providing men
with wives and ancestors with descendants. A sizeable proportion of the
marriages arranged in Peihotien before 1930 departed from the normal
pattern. Some families chose for one reason or another to bring adult
males of another surname into their families as husbands for their daughters and fathers of their grandchildren; other families chose to adopt and
raise female children who would become their sons' wives upon adulthood. The children resulting from these marriages grew up with a set of
family relationships quite different from those of children born into more
"typical" families. Since many of these differences provide contrasts to
some of the relationships previously discussed, it may be useful to examine them briefly.

In the past, a good many families on Taiwan, both poor and wealthy,
solved the social and financial problem of providing their sons with
wives by adopting an infant girl (*sim-pua*, little daughter-in-law) who
was raised as a sibling but married to the son when the two reached an
appropriate age. For a variety of reasons this custom has almost completely disappeared in the past generation, at least on Taiwan. There
are still, however, many adult *sim-pua* and many children and adults
who grew up in families with *sim-pua*. In theory, a *sim-pua* was to be
treated as a daughter of the family until the time of her marriage, but
in practice she was often treated as something slightly lower than a
daughter. She was expected to do more work earlier and was frequently
the victim of harsh punishments, punishments resulting more often from
her adoptive mother's unhappiness at her own lot in life than from the

sim-pua's behavior. By the time she was married to her brother, she and her adoptive mother had worked together in the house for many years. Her training in the domestic arts was far more thorough than that of a daughter. If a daughter proved inept in some task, the mother would simply push her aside and do it herself. Not so the *sim-pua*. Even though still a child, her adoptive mother would be conscious of the fact that this was not a daughter she was training for someone else, but a daughter-in-law with whom she herself would have to live. In some families, the relations between the two were almost as warm and as affectionate as that between any mother and daughter, but even in those where they were not, the *sim-pua* was habituated to submission, both as a means of avoiding pain and as behavior appropriate to her status. No matter how personally distasteful she might find the physical aspects of her marriage to a former brother, she was at least spared the many adjustments required of other newly married women. Her loyalties to the family in which she was reared were not disrupted, and her obedience and respect continued to be to the parents of her former brother and now husband. Nothing new outside her husband's bed was required of her. From the mother's point of view, the situation must have been a comfortable one. The young woman in her son's bed was more completely under her control than her son would ever be. There was no need for the older woman to assert her authority over a newcomer and no risk that her grandchildren would be raised in any way other than as she wished. The girl carried no threat to her security and had been, moreover, carefully trained over the years to make her mother-in-law's old age even more comfortable.

Unfortunately, for the purposes of this study, parents were no longer adopting *sim-pua* when we were in Taiwan, and I had no opportunity to evaluate any differences the presence of such a girl might have made on the parents' general child-training practices. It is possible that a young mother with a son and a *sim-pua* might feel more confident about her future security and be less consistent in her attempts to weave the complex emotional ties with her son that other Taiwanese mothers feel essential to their future well-being. This seems unlikely, though, in terms of the general orientation toward males; ultimately, it is the son on whom the mother must depend. Until recently sons have dutifully married the *sim-pua* their parents raised for that purpose, but there is considerable evidence that they find these marriages unsatisfactory, at least sexually. Men who married *sim-pua* are much more likely to visit prostitutes regularly and to arrange a semipermanent source of sexual satisfaction outside the family with a female over whom the mother has no control whatsoever.

From comments made by adult *sim-pua*, it seems that the adoptive father's behavior toward *sim-pua* was more similar to his behavior toward his sons than to his behavior toward his daughters. Rather than enjoying informality and affection in his relations with her, he tended either to ignore the girl or treat her with the distance and reserve that was his son's lot. This seems reasonable in view of the fact that her future behavior and her loyalty are more relevant to his future and the family's than those of his own daughter who leaves the family to marry. Although we were assured repeatedly that *sim-pua* were just like daughters until their marriage, it may well be that the relationship was nonetheless tinged in the father's mind with the semi-avoidance behavior expected toward a daughter-in-law. Whatever the cause, *sim-pua* tended to speak of their father/father-in-law with great respect but little warmth.

It is also unfortunate that at the time of our visit to Peihotien there were no families that contained two or more brothers married to *sim-pua* and in which all partners were living. (There were cases in which remnants of their families were living together and others in which they lived in the same compound, but we neglected to inquire whether the former had recombined after a crucial death or in which generation the latter had set up separate households.) I think it is safe to assume that the presence of *sim-pua* would have little effect on the development of the brothers' relationship with one another. As adults, however, the brothers marry women whose primary loyalty is to their joint family and parents—women who are also joined (presumably) in the warm relationship of sisters. A few well-documented cases of more than one *sim-pua* marriage in a sibling order might well provide a crucial test of the relative weight of the internal strains within a family that leads to its division.

Not a few families on Taiwan have found themselves required to make an uxorilocal marriage for one of their daughters, either because of the lack of an adult son when an urgent need is felt for additional income or because the complete absence of sons in a generation threatens the line of descent. Like the *sim-pua*, the young woman who marries uxorilocally is not required to leave the family in which she has been raised and toward whom her loyalties have been due up to the time of her marriage. There the similarity ends. During her childhood her parents are unlikely to consider the possibility that *she* might be their source of support and the family's source of continuance, constantly hoping that a son would either be born or adopted to fulfill the family's needs. As such she would be raised like any other daughter: less used to submission than a *sim-pua*, less belabored about her reasons to be grateful and loyal to her parents, and certainly less well trained in the domestic arts. Since uxorilocal marriages are more common amongst girls high in the sibling order, she probably had special consideration from her grandparents simply by being first on hand. She may for the same reason, although with less certainty, also be a favorite of her father. Compared with a *sim-pua* of her age, she may seem arrogant, willful, and unfilial; compared with a daughter born later in the sibling order she may seem slightly more assertive and somewhat more inclined toward independent attitudes.

The man who makes an uxorilocal marriage could be of the highest moral standards, of unusual intelligence and strength, and have an exceptional earning capacity. He would be nonetheless not quite the equal of other men, by virtue of his willingness to enter his wife's family. All girls are aware to some degree of the traumatic adjustments they must make when they leave their natal families at the time of their marriage, but they are also aware of the propriety and respectability of this move. No matter how delighted a girl may be to avoid these trying experiences, few young women who are party to uxorilocal marriages feel that its advantages in comfort are worth the disadvantage of being married to a man who is by definition inferior. Such a woman will comply, having little other choice, but both she and her parents are aware that they have done slightly less than right by her. The socialization process she has experienced increases the likelihood of her dissatisfaction and the likelihood of its being communicated to her parents.

Parents are even more thorough in the investigation of the qualities and capacities of an uxorilocal groom than they are with a prospective daughter-in-law, but when the man enters his future home, he is greeted with far more suspicion. His mother-in-law is constantly on the watch for any signs of growing intimacy with her daughter which might lead her to suspect that he is trying to "take her away from the family." His father-in-law is in the extremely ambiguous position of being suspicious, dependent, and, if the daughter happens to be a favorite, suffering from a mixture of guilt at forcing her into a "bad" marriage, delight at keeping her at home, and perhaps a tinge of Freudian jealousy. When grandchildren are born, the family often becomes more strained, not less. The grandmother, perhaps in collusion with her daughter, consciously undermines her son-in-law's position with his children, interfering with any discipline he may impose, and encouraging his children to believe that their primary loyalty is to the family of their mother. The young father finds himself in a position strikingly similar to that of the young mother in the customary form of marriage. His authority over his children is not clearly stated, and he must use exceptional means to establish it. He cannot use the father's traditional tool of aloof dignity, or his children will be lost to him forever. Because of this, and perhaps also because of their own isolation in the family and the village, men who have made an uxorilocal marriage seem to spend considerably more time in their children's company than do fathers in a normal family. Grandmothers of children from uxorilocal marriages are careful to make even fewer demands on their grandchildren than other grandmothers, but they have far fewer chances to relax and enjoy them.

If in time the daughter's loyalties do shift to her husband, or, as is so often the case in recent times, she chose the man herself, the parents' worst fear may come true—the younger couple leaves the family. The social reproach, although present, is never as strongly voiced against a daughter's abandonment as against a son's, and the break is consequently less difficult to make. Few daughters literally abandon their parents but simply put some geographic distance between them, continuing to provide financial support and insisting that at least one of the children bear the maternal grandfather's surname. If the uxorilocal marriage was simply a stopgap until a younger brother was old enough to assume responsibility for the family, the break is a natural one and may even have been formally arranged in the marriage contract. Whatever the circumstances of their departure, if the children are of school age, their father is going to have a ticklish resocialization job to do if he hopes to insure his future and found a normal family. His success may depend as much on the quality of his relations with his wife as on his own capacities. Needless to say, there are families in which uxorilocal marriages are very successful. One family in Peihotien was a model of domestic harmony, with the son-in-law behaving and treated as an unusually filial son rather than as a doubtful son-in-law. There was another family in Peihotien, equally atypical, who had maintained themselves for three generations without ever having a permanent adult male in residence. It is interesting to note that this family has in the present generation of women finally managed to produce a son by way of a long since dismissed son-in-law. At the age of sixteen, the boy is so utterly lacking in the virtues of filial respect and obedience as to have kicked his crippled grandmother. From the experiences of this family, the establishment of a successful matriarchy seems highly unlikely.

Conclusion

In the preceding pages the Chinese family has been examined in terms of the basic function of families everywhere: the raising of children. The attitudes various family members bring to the job of socialization throw a new light on familiar problems. The husband-wife relationship has been deemed of secondary importance both by the Chinese and by the scholars who study their customs. Insofar as the interaction between husband and wife is not overly charged with either positive or negative emotions, it is indeed a secondary relationship in the context of the family. The wife who does not despise her husband is not likely to raise her children to treat him as an outsider in his own family; the husband who does not reveal an unusual attachment to his wife is not likely to motivate his mother to an anxious competition with the younger woman for the loyalty of his children. When either the personalities or the behavior of husband and wife threaten to intensify the relationship with extra warmth or extra tension, it becomes disruptive to the more important parent-child relationship—in one generation or the next. This disruption, whichever direction it takes, is reflected in the attitudes of various members of the family toward the children of the family.

The brittle relationship between adult brothers is an important facet of Chinese kinship, from its role in the dissolution of joint families to the inherent weakness it brings to the lineages. When such a crucial relationship is also such a fragile one, when the society values a close relationship, and when its fracture causes intense and lasting hostility, it cannot be explained simply in terms of adult problems. A review of child-training practices suggests that the failure of the relationship originates in the inconsistent preparation of the brothers for their adult roles. This background makes credible the sudden disintegration of their relationship when they come into conflict over income and property. Had the younger brother been trained from infancy to submit to the elder, the Chinese joint family might be less of a myth.

The subtly different definitions of filiality that seem to be held by mothers and by fathers, and the strikingly different techniques they use to realize their definitions, say a great deal about the anxieties and the defenses of women in an androcentric society. They also give us a useful basis for comparison between families continuing their descent through the patrilocal form of marriage and those coping with a lack of male heirs by "marrying in" a son-in-law. The young man who makes an uxorilocal marriage finds himself in a situation quite similar to that of his sister. His rights over his children, like his sister's rights over hers, are not clearly stated, and, again like his sister, he forms ties with them that are individualistic and not dependent on the children's acceptances of cultural mores and values.

It would be satisfying to be able to conclude this paper with an outline for the systematic use of socialization techniques as predictive instruments in the study of the Chinese family. Obviously, that is out of the question. One of the thoughts selected for restatement in this concluding section suggests that the socialization process *reflects* a set of tensions within the family; another argues that child training seems to be the *source* of tension; the third example points out that a particular pattern of socialization is found useful as a basis for comparing two marriage types. There *is* an intimate relationship between the way in which a family trains its children and the dynamics of that family, but the exact nature of that relationship and its predictive value, if any, are yet to be discovered. In time the social sciences may reach a level of sophistication that will allow a quantitative analysis of small groups such as the family. Until that time, those of us interested in things Chinese would do well to cast a speculative eye at the way Chinese are raised. We may find evidence of change, of conflict, or of an error in analysis; at the very least, we will gain further evidence of what the Chinese want of family life.

The Families of Chinese Farmers

IRENE B. TAEUBER

Why did the Han Chinese among all peoples become and remain the world's largest cohesive ethnic group? What features of their culture resulted in the development and maintenance of a large population? How were these features different from those of the Thai, the Hindus, or others? Clearly, a distinctive pattern of mortality, fertility, and migration would explain the increase and expansion of the Chinese population, for the growth of a population at specific times and over time is a cultural as well as a biological process. The culture was such that it eased and perhaps stimulated the migration and adaptation of people to distant places. As Chinese men married native women or had children by them, the rates of Han population increase rose, and economies and societies over wider and wider areas were Sinicized.

The questions we raise remain for scientists of many disciplines to answer. Our approach to the study of diversity and change in the Chinese population is demographic. Although only fragmented and dispersed records and surveys are available, Chinese populations that have been studied, whether in China or abroad, show marked similarities, even though within China there is great regional diversity. These patterns of demographic behavior suggest that among the Chinese there are certain common motivations and responses relevant to population dynamics. One way to learn more of these responses is to study them as they are illustrated on the level of the family. The continuity and the mobility of a family are affected by social and economic as well as demographic factors. A person's life cycle involves transitions in family roles as well as in economic and social roles. Marriage, birth, and death are processes of the family, and the migrations of persons are related to family structure and function.

Our knowledge of the Chinese population, though limited, is now far advanced in comparison with what was known through national records between the 1850's and the 1930's. Attempted censuses in 1909–11, in 1915, and in 1928 were abortive. In the early years, the study of population was confined to the universities, but in the 1920's and 1930's, when increased political, economic, and social activities suggested a China in forward motion, the problems of demographic ignorance were no longer just academic, and a knowledge of population became one of the essential bases for the tasks of modernization.

The data that are analyzed here were collected in a field survey of families of farm operators in selected areas of China in the years 1929 to 1931.* The survey covered 16,786 farms in 168 localities and 38,256 farm families in twenty-two provinces in China during the years 1929–33. Local records were examined, interviews were conducted with responsible people, detailed farm schedules were collected, agricultural and related questionnaires were administered to farm operator households, and population and vital statistics schedules were secured from larger numbers of households. Because of limited funds, the state of China in the late 1920's and early 1930's, and the specific goals of the study, areas to be examined were purposively selected. Students from the areas supervised the activities. Thus neither the areas nor the families interviewed can be assumed to be representatives of the regions or of all farm families in China, for villages with students in the University of Nanking had at least one family at an economic level that permitted the maintenance of the student; and the areas where students did the interviewing were concentrated on major transportation and communication routes. The interviews were selective, too, because they were given during periods of peace, stability, and relative normality: if there was famine, epidemic, or disaster, there could be no interviewing; banditry would preclude the survey, too. Although the measurements of these biases is impossible in the absence of data from probability samples of the population, it is apparent that the families of the farm operators included in the survey were disproportionately high in economic status. The areas were unduly

* This pioneering attempt to study the diverse regions of China was the China Land Utilization Study (Buck 1937a). Under the direction of J. Lossing Buck, a population survey was conducted with the cooperation of the Milbank Memorial Fund as part of the China Land Utilization Survey of the University of Nanking and the China Council of the Institute of Pacific Relations. The population and vital statistics data were processed and analyzed by or in association with the Milbank Memorial Fund. Edgar Sydenstricker and Frank W. Notestein were responsible successively for the direction of the study (Chiao 1933–34; Notestein 1937, 1938). Various tabulations and processed data were made available by the Milbank Memorial Fund and Frank Notestein for use in a comparative demographic study of peoples of Chinese and related cultures. The schedules and machine cards are no longer available.

representative of those accessible to the great cities and the developing commercial and industrial sectors. The population dynamics were those of periods of peace, relatively adequate nutrition, and relative freedom from epidemics.

The Regions

The selection of areas to study was designed to provide information for regions of China, but the delineation of regions had to proceed after the collection of the data. The agricultural regions as finally determined were based mainly on crop type, the primary division being between the wheat region of the north and the rice region of the south.

CLIMATIC REGIONS OF CHINA*

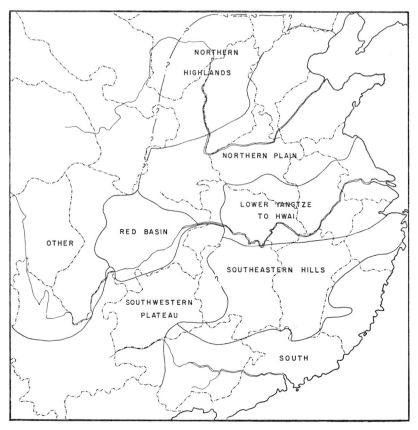

* University of Nanking–Milbank Memorial Fund Study of Population and Vital Statistics, Households of Farm Operators, 1929–31.

The population survey was conducted separately from the agricultural surveys, and larger numbers of households were contacted. The data were tabulated for eight climatic regions rather than for the eight agricultural regions of the land utilization studies. Five of the climatic regions considered together (the South, the Southeastern Hills, the Southwestern Plateau, the Red Basin, the Lower Yangtze to the Hwai) and the Szechwan-Yunnan areas are roughly equivalent to South China or the rice region of the agricultural surveys. Two of the climatic regions (the Northern Plain and the Northern Highlands) are roughly equivalent to North China, the wheat region. The areas included in the population survey are listed in Table 1, along with the province, the agricultural region, the number of households, and the population of each area.

Households and families were the units for collection and analysis in many substantive aspects of the Land Utilization Survey. By definition, the farm operator was the head of the household, defined as the co-living unit that ate together (Buck 1937a: 475). Information on household size was obtained in all surveys from local records. Information on precise relationship to head of household was secured in the population survey.

The characteristics of the agricultural population in the years around 1930 reflected the geographic, climatic, subcultural, and developmental histories of the people. Informants recalled an average of three famines

TABLE 1. STUDY AREAS OF THE POPULATION SURVEY BY CLIMATIC REGION,
PROVINCE, AGRICULTURAL REGION, HOUSEHOLDS, AND POPULATION

Study areas by climatic region	Province	Crop code*	Number	
			Families	Population
All areas			38,256	202,617
1. *South*			1,905	11,107
Chaoan	Kwangtung	1	100	646
Kaikiang	Kwangtung	1	600	3,219
Kityang	Kwangtung	1	404	3,320
Lungki I	Fukien	1	610	2,935
Lungki II	Fukien	1	81	396
Minhou	Fukien	2	110	591
2. *Southeastern Hills*			1,641	7,680
Kinhwa	Chekiang	2	290	1,459
Tuchang	Kiangsi	2	616	3,205

* Crop code: 1. Double-cropping rice; 2. Rice-tea; 3. Southwest rice; 4. Szechwan rice; 5. Yangtze rice-wheat; 6. Winter wheat–kaoliang; 7. Winter wheat–millet; 8. Winter wheat.

Study areas by climatic region	Province	Crop code	Number Families	Number Population
Tungyang	Chekiang	2	534	2,261
Yin	Chekiang	2	201	755
3. *Southwestern Plateau*			1,856	9,404
Kunming	Yunnan	3	621	3,133
Kweiyang	Kweichow	3	613	3,025
Tsunyi	Kweichow	3	622	3,246
4. *Red Basin*			2,562	14,124
Chungking	Szechwan	4	299	1,801
Fowling	Szechwan	4	333	1,653
Jenshow	Szechwan	4	103	605
Jung	Szechwan	4	100	637
Jungchang	Szechwan	4	100	574
Kiakiang	Szechwan	4	98	420
Kienchow	Szechwan	4	105	585
Kienwei	Szechwan	4	102	552
Lushan	Szechwan	4	100	463
Mienyang	Szechwan	4	319	1,545
Nanki	Szechwan	4	100	551
Pishan	Szechwan	4	269	1,796
Suining	Szechwan	4	224	1,292
Tzechung	Szechwan	4	207	1,140
Yaan	Szechwan	4	103	510
5. *Lower Yangtze to Hwai*			11,786	58,168
Changsu	Kiangsu	5	220	952
Chenkiang	Kiangsu	5	586	2,322
Chu	Anhwei	5	202	1,067
Chungsiang	Hupeh	5	224	1,506
Funing I	Kiangsu	5	301	1,564
Funing II	Kiangsu	5	86	511
Hwaining	Anhwei	5	379	1,774
Hanchwan	Hupeh	5	603	2,946
Ho	Anhwei	5	788	4,280
Hwangpei	Hupeh	5	295	1,807
Kiangying	Kiangsu	5	515	2,756
Kunshan I	Kiangsu	5	609	2,622
Kunshan II	Kiangsu	5	806	3,853
Liuan	Anhwei	5	601	3,471
Shih	Anhwei	5	620	2,497
Shunan	Chekiang	5	101	445
Tai	Kiangsu	5	588	3,222
Taihu	Anhwei	5	240	1,245
Tehtsing I	Chekiang	5	500	2,255
Tehtsing II	Chekiang	5	202	1,027
Tungin	Chekiang	5	1,009	4,026
Wuchin	Kiangsu	5	255	1,320
Yencheng I	Kiangsu	5	125	589
Yencheng II	Kiangsu	5	600	3,439

Study areas by climatic region	Province	Crop code	Number	
			Families	Population
Yencheng III	Kiangsu	5	625	3,191
Yencheng IV	Kiangsu	5	100	629
Yunmeng	Hupeh	5	606	2,852
6. *Northern Plain*			15,643	86,511
Anyi	Shansi	7	304	1,419
Changli I	Hopeh	6	199	1,446
Changli II	Hopeh	6	163	1,116
Chanhwa	Shantung	6	603	3,616
Cheng	Honan	6	1,124	6,260
Chengting	Hopeh	6	100	624
Chi	Honan	6	301	1,693
Chowchih	Shensi	7	584	2,723
Fuping	Hopeh	7	101	629
Hancheng	Shensi	7	601	3,272
Hokian	Hopeh	6	595	3,481
Hweimen	Shantung	6	101	645
Ishih	Shensi	7	1,000	4,097
Ishui	Shantung	6	236	1,400
Kaifeng	Honan	6	588	3,330
Licheng	Shantung	6	597	3,251
Linchang	Honan	6	458	2,337
Lingpao	Honan	7	602	3,071
Mien	Shensi	7	590	3,859
Nankung	Hopeh	6	630	3,712
Nanyang	Honan	6	609	2,845
Su I	Anhwei	6	598	3,339
Su II	Anhwei	6	120	678
Suhsui	Hopeh	6	300	1,759
Taian	Shantung	6	135	903
Tangyi	Shantung	6	123	682
Tsang	Hopeh	6	360	2,280
Tsincheng	Shansi	7	300	1,627
Tsing	Hopeh	6	198	1,366
Tsining	Shantung	6	250	1,379
Tsiyuan	Honan	7	300	2,221
Tung	Hopeh	6	170	840
Wei I	Shantung	6	368	2,081
Wei II	Shantung	6	784	4,217
Weinan	Shensi	7	331	1,685
Yencheng	Honan	6	621	3,192
Yenshan	Hopeh	6	599	3,436
7. *Northern Highlands*			1,938	11,000
Paotow	Suiyuan	8	201	895
Shouyang	Shansi	7	308	1,570
Taiku	Shansi	7	250	1,074
Tingpien	Shensi	8	300	1,920
Tsinglo	Shansi	8	259	1,877
Tsingyuan	Shansi	7	320	1,875
Yulin	Shensi	8	300	1,789
8. *Other*			925	4,623
Lifan	Szechwan	4	310	1,457
Tali	Yunnan	3	615	3,166

and 16 lesser calamities per *hsien* (Buck 1937a: 124–26). All areas that were studied were remote from economic and social modernization. The agriculture was basically efficient, the nutrition, mostly derived from grain or potatoes, was adequate. However, the interviews occurred in good years, the households studied were those of farm operators, and the informants were obviously only those who survived the calamities. In addition, the households and populations of the southern regions were under-represented in the villages studied, and those of the lower Yangtze and the northern wheat region were over-represented. The impact of these biases on the data may be great, but there are no simple indicators of how great.

The People

Summary data on occupations and education are given for all areas and the climatic regions in Table 2. Agriculture was the full- or part-time occupation for 75 per cent to 90 per cent of the men; 40 to 50 per cent of the men reported that they had had some schooling, most of it traditional, but 60 to 70 per cent stated that they were illiterate. The women were both unschooled and illiterate. The data are imprecise and deficient; nevertheless, the analyses are suggestive.

The demographic characteristics of the population of the farm operator households as they were reported by the enumerators are summarized in Table 3. The inconsistencies between age structures and the various measures of mortality and fertility are apparent. Birth rates seem to be lower, and proportions of youth less, in the Northern Plain

TABLE 2. AGRICULTURAL EMPLOYMENT AND EDUCATION, 1929–31
(*Per cent*)

	All regions	South	South-eastern Hills	Red Basin	Lower Yangtze to Hwai	Northern Plain	Northern Highlands
Men in Agriculture[a]	78.4	89.6	72.1	72.1	79.7	77.6	74.6
Full-time	48.8	52.7	42.2	52.2	56.8	48.0	32.5
Part-time	29.6	36.9	29.9	19.9	22.9	29.6	42.1
Some school[b]							
Men	45.9	41.9	69.0	48.5	50.5	43.8	37.1
Women	2.3	2.7	4.6	4.9	1.9	1.8	2.8
Illiterate[b]							
Men	69.3	63.8	60.5	61.3	67.2	72.1	76.2
Women	98.7	98.0	97.9	97.3	98.7	99.1	99.1

SOURCE: Population and vital statistics survey; unpublished data.
[a] Males age 7 or over reporting on occupations; no report from the Southwest rice area, incomplete in some other areas. [b] Age 7 and over reporting on education and literacy (incomplete).

TABLE 3. INDICATORS OF POPULATION DYNAMICS, IN FARM HOUSEHOLDS, 1929–31

Variables	All regions	South	Southeastern Hills	Southwestern Plateau	Red Basin	Lower Yangtze to Hwai	Northern Plain	Northern Highlands
Below age 15 (%)								
Men	36.0	38.0	36.2	36.1	37.3	37.3	35.0	33.9
Women	33.6	35.6	31.2	32.5	34.2	34.5	32.9	35.2
Age 65 and over (%)								
Men	2.7	2.0	2.8	1.5	2.1	1.9	3.4	4.1
Women	4.0	3.1	4.5	2.4	2.9	3.1	4.9	4.7
Males per 1,000 females								
0–4	1,102	1,145	1,185	1,110	1,209	1,083	1,082	1,108
All ages	1,085	1,123	1,184	1,028	1,114	1,095	1,068	1,185
Vital rates (per 1,000)								
Births	38.3	37.3	38.0	52.3	43.1	36.7	38.3	30.8
Deaths	27.1	33.8	25.7	26.3	39.0	27.4	24.8	19.0
Natural change	11.2	3.5	12.3	26.0	4.1	9.3	13.5	11.8
Single women (%)								
15–19	47.6	33.8	49.8	45.0	38.4	58.4	47.6	20.4
20–24	5.2	3.2	6.5	4.4	2.7	8.3	4.0	0.9
Fertility among married women 45 and over[a]								
Children per 100 women	527	553	579	630	488	549	499	570
Bearing 7 or more children (%)	30.4	29.5	38.6	48.3	24.2	10.1	26.0	9.8
Dead among children born to women 25–29 (%)[b]								
Sons	34.5	32.0	36.8	47.2	30.9	35.6	32.3	36.9
Daughters	36.1	26.4	38.0	49.0	33.3	37.8	34.3	37.8
Infant deaths per 100 live births	15.6	18.4	15.4	17.1	19.0	13.5	15.7	13.6

SOURCE: Population and vital statistics survey; unpublished data.
[a] Number of children ever born to currently married women.
[b] Per cent dead among children ever born to currently married women.

and Highlands. Death rates are high, even though the reported numbers of deaths are implausibly low in many of the study areas. The rate of natural increase, which is the difference between incompletely reported birth and death rates, cannot be accepted as accurate. The evidence of induced or assisted mortality among females is rather convincing. Although high proportions of women are married at ages 20 to 24 and almost all women eventually marry, proportions of single women are high at ages 15 to 19.

The direct relevance of these materials on population dynamics to the analysis of the family is not that the Chinese farm population was premodern. It is, rather, that the structure and dynamics of the populations of the climatic regions were complex and diverse, and theories presuming a simple peasant culture cannot apply here.

Families and Land

The numbers of persons per 1,000 households and families and the distributions of families by size are presented in Table 4. In these farm households, almost all persons were related in one way or another to the head. The average family included only 5.2 persons: the head and 4.2 others. The range in average family size was great, from 4.9 in the

TABLE 4. HOUSEHOLDS AND FAMILIES BY SIZE, 1929–31

Size	All regions	South	South-eastern hills	South-western Plateau	Red Basin	Lower Yangtze to Hwai	North-ern Plain	Northern Highlands
Persons (per 1,000)								
Households	5,296	5,830	4,680	5,067	5,513	4,935	5,530	5,676
Families	5,224	5,816	4,620	4,982	5,448	4,880	5,421	5,598
Families by size (%)	100.0	100.0	100.0	100.0	100.0	100.0	100.0	100.0
1	2.5	0.6	3.8	0.2	1.1	3.0	2.8	2.2
2	8.3	4.5	11.5	8.3	6.8	8.9	8.6	6.6
3–4	34.3	31.4	40.7	40.0	33.9	36.5	31.6	32.8
5–6	30.9	30.9	28.0	31.2	31.1	32.4	29.9	30.5
7–9	17.6	23.9	12.5	16.4	19.4	15.3	18.8	18.6
10–14	5.5	7.7	2.7	3.4	6.7	3.5	6.9	7.3
15 or more	1.0	1.1	0.8	0.5	1.0	0.4	1.4	2.1
Population by family size (%)	100.0	100.0	100.0	100.0	100.0	100.0	100.0	100.0
1–4	27.0	21.2	36.9	31.8	24.9	30.8	24.4	23.6
5–6	32.1	28.9	32.5	33.7	30.9	35.9	30.0	29.6
7–9	25.9	32.3	20.8	25.0	27.6	24.0	26.8	25.3
10 or more	15.0	17.6	9.8	9.5	16.4	9.3	18.8	21.5

SOURCE: Population and vital statistics survey; unpublished data.

TABLE 5. DISTRIBUTION OF FAMILIES BY NUMBER OF MEMBERS, 1929–31 (*Per cent*)

Fifths of land and size of family	All regions	South	Southeastern Hills	Southwestern Plateau	Red Basin	Lower Yangtze to Hwai	Northern Plain	Northern Highlands
First fifth	100.0	100.0	100.0	100.0	100.0	100.0	100.0	100.0
1–4	66.9	59.2	77.7	74.4	64.9	67.8	65.5	65.1
5–6	24.7	25.2	17.6	19.9	27.0	24.9	25.5	26.0
7–9	7.4	12.9	4.3	4.8	6.3	6.6	8.3	7.4
10–14	0.8	2.7	0.4	0.9	1.4	0.7	0.6	1.6
15 or more	0.0	—	—	—	0.4	0.0	0.0	—
Second fifth	100.0	100.0	100.0	100.0	100.0	100.0	100.0	100.0
1–4	55.1	44.2	64.9	56.7	53.2	57.4	54.2	51.2
5–6	31.1	31.3	26.5	33.9	29.2	31.2	31.1	35.0
7–9	11.9	20.3	7.9	8.5	13.7	10.5	12.3	11.4
10–14	1.8	4.3	0.7	0.9	3.9	0.8	2.2	2.1
15 or more	0.1	—	—	—	—	0.1	0.1	0.3
Third fifth	100.0	100.0	100.0	100.0	100.0	100.0	100.0	100.0
1–4	44.3	33.1	57.5	48.6	41.1	48.5	42.5	43.0
5–6	35.9	35.5	31.0	36.9	34.0	36.2	35.9	33.0
7–9	16.7	27.2	10.8	14.0	19.7	13.2	17.9	19.9
10–14	3.0	4.3	0.7	0.6	4.5	2.1	3.6	4.0
15 or more	0.1	—	—	—	0.6	—	0.1	—
Fourth fifth	100.0	100.0	100.0	100.0	100.0	100.0	100.0	100.0
1–4	31.9	29.2	38.8	34.5	29.9	36.5	27.5	31.6
5–6	37.8	33.4	39.1	36.8	36.6	40.4	36.7	35.8
7–9	23.6	26.2	19.0	24.2	25.8	19.9	26.4	24.1
10–14	6.0	10.4	2.9	4.0	7.0	3.1	8.4	7.2
15 or more	0.7	0.8	0.4	0.6	0.8	0.1	1.1	1.4
Fifth fifth	100.0	100.0	100.0	100.0	100.0	100.0	100.0	100.0
1–4	18.2	15.2	23.0	22.3	17.4	21.4	15.5	16.0
5–6	29.8	28.4	33.0	31.1	29.4	34.6	26.2	22.8
7–9	31.8	34.6	28.7	33.9	32.7	30.7	32.5	30.2
10–14	16.5	17.4	11.1	10.6	17.4	11.7	20.9	22.0
15 or more	3.6	4.2	4.3	2.0	3.0	1.6	4.9	9.0

SOURCE: All areas, Notestein 1937: 368–71; unpublished analyses.

lower Yangtze to 5.8 in the South. Single-person households were few (at the most slightly more than 3 per cent); large families were also relatively few, though they were more numerous than the single-person households. Only 6.5 per cent of all families included ten or more persons. The modal family consisted of three to four persons.

Regional variations occur mainly in the percentages of families by size. Higher proportions of larger families are found in the South, the Red Basin, and the Northern Plain and Highlands, and higher proportions of smaller families in the Southeastern Hills, the Southwestern Plateau, and the Lower Yangtze regions.

The processes of adjustment between population and land are difficult to measure even in modernized and statistically sophisticated societies, but it is possible to examine the extent of adjustment. Population per unit of land area is too crude a measure, for the proportions of the land that is cultivable and the quality of the cultivation that is possible differ widely among the regions. In his analysis of the data, Frank Notestein related size and structure of household to land and measured this in terms of fifths of cropland within each region (Notestein 1937: 363–71). (See Table 5.) In all families surveyed, the average size of family was less than four persons among those on the lowest fifth of the holdings, more than seven on the highest fifth. Families of four members or fewer were more than half those on small acreages, less than half those on medium holdings, one-third those on large holdings, one-fifth those on very large holdings. The reverse associations held for large families of more than ten members. Without exception, the larger the holdings, the less the relative role of small families and the greater the relative role of large families. For any given size of holding, the proportion of operators with smaller families was higher in the Southeastern Hills, the Southwestern Plateau, and the area of the Lower Yangtze to the Hwai. These relationships are suggestive of regional differences in the factors influencing farming practices and land utilization.

If the adaptation of family size and land involved expansion of the holdings as family size increased, then the proportions of owners who also rented land should increase as family size increased. This relationship existed in the Southeastern Hills, the Southwestern Plateau, and the Lower Yangtze regions. Elsewhere relationships were unclear. If land availability and the family codes permitted family division, tenants should include many nuclear families, and larger and cohesive families should remain in the owner or owner-tenant classes. These conditions obtained in the rice regions.

The associations of family size, crop land, and tenure suggest an

Table 6. Population Distribution by Relationship to Head, 1929–31

(*Per 1,000 households*)

Relationships and sex	All regions	South	Southeastern Hills	Southwestern Plateau	Red Basin	Lower Yangtze to Hwai	Northern Plain	Northern Highlands
Population[a]	5,734	6,026	5,235	5,465	5,910	5,383	6,021	5,902
Related persons	5,637	6,011	5,165	5,373	5,842	5,291	5,897	5,810
Line of male head	5,120	5,254	4,723	4,998	5,353	4,989	5,251	4,991
Collateral of male line	506	742	439	358	486	294	633	812
Other	10	15	4	17	4	8	12	8
Not related	97	15	70	92	68	92	124	91
Males								
Population	3,001	3,183	2,780	2,763	3,120	2,829	3,129	3,248
Related persons	2,912	3,169	2,719	2,676	3,064	2,746	3,013	3,157
Line of male head	2,628	2,742	2,470	2,476	2,775	2,576	2,668	2,682
Collateral of male line	279	420	247	194	288	166	339	470
Other	5	7	3	6	1	3	7	6
Not related	89	13	62	88	55	84	116	90
Females								
Population	2,732	2,843	2,455	2,702	2,790	2,554	2,892	2,654
Related persons	2,724	2,842	2,447	2,697	2,778	2,546	2,883	2,653
Line of male head	2,492	2,512	2,253	2,522	2,578	2,413	2,584	2,309
Collateral of male line	227	323	192	164	197	128	294	342
Other	5	8	1	11	3	5	5	2
Not related	8	1	9	5	12	8	8	1

Source: Population and vital statistics survey; unpublished data.
[a] Excluding single-person households and including only men reporting on relationship to head.

adaptability or a response of family size to resource needs that involved differences in migration patterns as well as differences in birth and death rates. The differences in family size in relation to land seemed more adaptive in the Southeastern Hills and the Southwestern Plateau, which were frontier areas being settled, and in the Lower Yangtze, which was an area of intensive agriculture influenced by urban demands. The traditional patterns were most evident in the South, the Red Basin, the Northern Plain, and the Northern Highlands, though the Red Basin could be considered intermediate between the adaptive and the traditional regions.

Paternal and Fraternal Relatives

Given the priorities of the male in Chinese culture, the absence of primogeniture, patrilocal (virilocal) residence, and the dominance of married roles for women, constructs of appropriate family structure could be developed quite simply. There would be flexibility in size and adaptability to change. Six corollary assumptions about structure and demographic processes can be tested empirically: first, the major component in families should be the direct male line of the head including the spouses of the males in direct line; second, the lesser component in families should be the brothers of the head (and their spouses and children), who would have been in the paternal line when they were the sons of the former head; third, the exodus of daughters at marriage and the influx of the wives of sons should maintain a rather balanced sex ratio in the direct male line, if no extraneous factors are involved; fourth, the retention of sons and brothers should increase the sex ratio, though their movements out for labor should reduce it; fifth, relatives other than those of the head and brothers should be few; sixth, lower fertility or higher mortality should reduce the numbers of persons in the lines of brothers available for inclusion and so increase the dominance of the direct patriline.

The numbers of related persons per 1,000 family heads were highest in the traditional regions of the South, the Red Basin, and the Northern Plain and Highlands. They were lower in the adaptive regions of the Southeastern Hills, the Southwestern Plateau, and the Lower Yangtze. (See Tables 6 and 7.) Almost 90 per cent of the related persons in families were in the direct line of the male head, including the spouses of the line. Relations of other male lines accounted for 8–14 per cent of the related persons in the traditional regions, 6–8 per cent in the adaptive regions.

Persons not related to the head were few in the households of the

TABLE 7. POPULATION IN HOUSEHOLDS AND PERSONS IN FAMILIES BY RELATIONSHIP TO HEAD, 1929–31

(Per cent)

Relationships and sex	All regions	South	Southeastern Hills	Southwestern Plateau	Red Basin	Lower Yangtze to Hwai	Northern Plain	Northern Highlands
Population[a]	100.0	100.0	100.0	100.0	100.0	100.0	100.0	100.0
Related persons	98.3	99.8	98.7	98.3	98.9	98.3	97.9	98.5
Line of male head	89.3	87.2	90.2	91.4	90.6	92.7	87.2	84.6
Collateral of male line	8.8	12.3	8.4	6.6	8.2	5.5	10.5	13.8
Other	0.2	0.2	0.1	0.3	0.1	0.1	0.2	0.1
Not related	1.7	0.2	1.3	1.7	1.1	1.7	2.1	1.5
Males								
Population	100.0	100.0	100.0	100.0	100.0	100.0	100.0	100.0
Related persons	97.0	99.6	97.8	96.8	98.2	97.0	96.3	97.2
Line of male head	87.6	86.2	88.8	89.6	89.0	91.1	85.2	82.6
Collateral of male line	9.3	13.2	8.9	7.0	9.2	5.9	10.8	14.5
Other	0.2	0.2	0.1	0.2	0.0	0.1	0.2	0.2
Not related	3.0	0.4	2.2	3.2	1.8	3.0	3.7	2.8
Females								
Population	100.0	100.0	100.0	100.0	100.0	100.0	100.0	100.0
Related persons	99.7	100.0	99.7	99.8	99.6	99.7	99.7	100.0
Line of male head	91.2	88.4	91.8	93.3	92.4	94.5	89.4	87.0
Collateral of male line	8.3	11.3	7.8	6.1	7.1	5.0	10.2	12.9
Other	0.2	0.3	0.1	0.4	0.1	0.2	0.2	0.1
Not related	0.3	0.0	0.3	0.2	0.4	0.3	0.3	0.0

SOURCE: Population and vital statistics survey; unpublished data.

[a] Excluding single-person households and including only men reporting on relationship to head.

TABLE 8. SEX RATIOS IN THE POPULATIONS IN FAMILIES AND IN
MALE LINES, 1929–31
(*Males per 1,000 females*)

Regions	Total population[a]	All related persons[a]	Line of male head	Other male line
All regions	1,098	1,069	1,054	1,229
South	1,120	1,115	1,092	1,302
Southeastern Hills	1,132	1,111	1,096	1,283
Southwestern Plateau	1,023	992	982	1,179
Red Basin	1,118	1,103	1,077	1,463
Lower Yangtze to Hwai	1,108	1,079	1,068	1,301
Northern Plain	1,082	1,045	1,032	1,151
Northern Highlands	1,224	1,190	1,161	1,371

SOURCE: Population and vital statistics survey; unpublished data.
[a] Including other relationships.

farm operators. Overall, less than one per cent of all households included a person not related to the head, and more than 98 per cent of all persons in households were related to the head. Though in theory the distinction between the household as a group of persons living together and the family as a co-living group of related persons is a major one, in the farm households studied a generation ago, differences between households and families were slight. It should be noted, however, that there were substantial variations among the regions. In all regions considered together, 1.7 per cent of all persons in households were not related to the head. This percentage extended from a low point of 0.2 in the South to 2.1 in the Northern Plain.

The nuclear families are relatively balanced in terms of sex and age. The collateral relatives of the line of the head consist primarily of brothers and the families of brothers, and the average numbers and the relationships of the male and female populations differed within regions and between regions. The number of males per 1,000 females in each relationship category, shown in Table 8, is an index of these regional disparities between the sexes. The sex ratios in the population of the line of the male head were somewhat greater than unity in all regions except the Southwestern Plateau; the migrations of men apparently had minimal influence on this component in the Chinese household. The high sex ratios of the population of the head's collateral relatives characterized all regions.

Wives

The roles of women were family roles: daughter, wife, mother, widow. The orientation of the daughter was to the father, that of the wife to the husband, that of the widow to the son or grandson who was head. But women also had roles with reference to women of other generations: the bride became the daughter-in-law and then the mother. Generations were, however, brief, for the mortality of women was high compared with that of men throughout infancy, childhood, youth, and the reproductive years. Daughters were few, for early marriage with childbearing soon after was common. The woman who married at 17 might have a daughter whose marriage at a similar age could make the mother a grandmother at age 36. This relationship would probably be outside the family of orientation, for the daughter would move to the house of the husband.

The changing roles of women in late middle and old age reflected the changing rates of mortality among men and women as well as certain basic aspects of Chinese society. Despite local practices and legends about young husbands, most of the wives were younger than their husbands, and the more vigorous women who survived the childbearing years lived on to be included within the family. The preponderance of grandmothers as contrasted with grandfathers was probably real, though the procedures of field surveys may be responsible for some of the discrepancy. Almost all heads of families were men who remained as head until death; the head's successor was usually a son. Hence fathers and grandfathers of heads were few. The widow of the head who lived with the son or the son's son became the mother or the grandmother of the head.

The prevalence of widows mirrored the high rates of mortality of men in the period and the greater longevity of women who survived childbearing in Chinese society. Accuracy about how many widowers there were who were grandparents is made difficult by the household rules of headship and the kin designations in relation to the head. The life cycles of men usually involved periods as sons of heads in childhood and youth and periods as heads in the middle and later years. In her life cycle the wife and widow of the paramount line of the head moved forward as mother-in-law, as mother of the head, or even as grandmother of the elder son of the elder son if she survived to truly old age.

The classic cycle of life for a woman was the life pattern of the girl who married the son of the head who was the successor designate. Some girls married the grandsons of the head, however, and so added junior status and their relationships to female ancestors of the husband in collateral lines to their problems of adjustment. Though speculation may be enticing, the data available for analysis are limited to the designations of females in families in terms of their relationship to the head.

TABLE 9. WIVES OF MEN IN LINE RELATIONS, 1929–31
(*Wives per 100 men*)

Relations	All regions	South	South-eastern Hills	South-western Plateau	Red Basin	Lower Yangtze to Hwai	North-ern Plain	North-ern High-lands
Related persons	43.3	43.7	49.6	45.9	41.8	41.9	43.9	41.5
Line of male head	44.4	45.1	50.2	47.7	43.1	42.8	44.9	43.3
Head	89.9	89.8	91.3	98.3	91.7	91.7	88.3	81.3
Sons of head	30.1	22.4	24.4	30.1	30.5	24.2	35.9	33.9
Sons of sons	7.2	7.7	8.4	2.6	3.9	5.2	9.0	8.6
Other male lines	32.0	33.8	43.6	20.1	27.7	26.9	34.9	31.4
Brothers	55.7	59.8	58.8	34.9	47.1	42.5	65.0	55.8
Brothers' sons	21.5	18.2	44.1	15.7	14.5	19.6	22.4	19.9

SOURCE: Lists of detailed relationships; population and vital statistics survey; unpublished data.

We know the numbers of wives of men in direct and collateral relations to the head of the family in generation sequences. The descendants of the head most likely to be found in the family were sons and sons of sons; the collateral relatives of greatest frequency were the brothers and sons of brothers. Heads were the oldest, followed in the direct line by the sons and sons of sons (Buck 1930). The brother was younger than the head but of the same generation; the brother's sons were likely to be younger than the head's sons.

The ratios of wives per 100 men in each of the relationship categories are presented in Table 9. The ratio of wives was 90 per 100 for heads, 30 for the sons of heads, 56 for the brothers, 22 for the sons of brothers. In general, the geographic distinctions were those between traditional and adaptive regions, with the Red Basin included in the adaptive group. The ratio of wives to heads was higher in the Southeastern Hills, the Southwestern Plateau, the Red Basin, and the Lower Yangtze; it was somewhat lower in the South and in the Northern Plain, and far lower in the Northern Highlands. In general, the ratios of wives to sons of the head, to sons of sons, and to brothers were higher in the traditional areas of large families. The prevalence of wives for sons' sons and brothers' sons was probably a function of age, for the average age of males in these categories would be higher in regions where residence in the parental home was customary. The variable prevalence of wives suggests age and sex structures less favorable to fertility in the coastal South and in North China than in the Southeastern and Southwestern regions, the Red Basin, and the Lower Yangtze.

The life cycles and changing roles of women involved geographic mobility. Some of these movements were included in reports on migra-

TABLE 10.   WOMEN MIGRANTS OF THE SURVEY YEAR BY RELATION TO HEAD
(*Migrants per 1,000 year-end resident population*)

Relation to head and migration	All regions	South	South-eastern Hills	South-western Plateau	Red Basin	Lower Yangtze to Hwai	Northern Plain	Northern Highlands
Daughters								
In	3.3	3.6	3.7	0.8	2.8	6.0	10.0	8.2
Out	27.6	22.2	39.6	25.9	28.2	20.2	33.8	27.4
Net	−24.3	−18.6	−35.9	−25.1	−25.4	−14.2	−23.8	−19.2
Sisters								
In	7.5	—	—	7.4	19.8	10.0	4.7	—
Out	78.0	118.5	146.3	22.2	99.0	62.2	98.3	—
Net	−70.5	−118.5	−146.3	−14.8	−79.2	−52.2	−93.6	—
Wives of:								
Heads								
In	14.3	9.6	7.2	21.1	8.1	19.7	12.1	8.3
Out	1.6	1.2	2.2	0.6	1.4	2.3	1.4	0.6
Net	12.7	8.4	5.0	20.5	6.7	17.4	10.7	7.7
Sons								
In	82.8	85.6	59.0	89.3	84.4	100.9	71.6	88.3
Out	5.6	—	19.7	4.9	—	9.9	3.1	13.0
Net	77.2	85.6	39.3	84.4	84.4	91.0	68.5	75.3
Brothers								
In	48.4	21.1	22.6	102.3	76.9	59.8	41.0	61.0
Out	6.4	—	22.6	—	—	11.2	6.0	3.4
Net	42.0	21.1	0.0	102.3	76.9	48.6	35.0	57.6

SOURCE: Lists of relationships for year-end populations and migrants of the survey year; population and vital statistics survey; unpublished tabulations.

tions to and from families in the survey year. (See Table 10.) The daughters and sisters of heads moved outward, presumably to marry and enter a new family. Wives of the heads, of the sons, and of the brothers moved into the families. The migrations of women were family processes rather than processes of economic adjustment.

The movements of wives are incomplete indicators of changing family size through marriage and only partial reflections of the life style of women. In the surveyed population of farm operators' families, in-migrants of the survey year included 26 concubines of fathers and two of sons. There were 50 fiancées of sons and 40 adopted daughters moving in, and nine adopted daughters moving out. These relationships may have been incompletely reported, however. The movements of women in directions contrary to the ones appropriate to their roles are a tantalizing aspect of the data in Table 10. Some of the daughters and sisters who moved in may have been returning to families of origin because of need; some relationships in the detailed data are suggestive of widowed women of the line returning with children. The out-movements of wives may have been associated with the out-movements of husbands. Few wives of sons or brothers were reported as out-migrants of the survey year. If these limited numbers are real (i.e., not products of failures to report departing wives of family members as members of the family), most migrations of sons and brothers occurred prior to or as an accompaniment to marriage.

Parents, Children, and the Nuclear Family

In the total population of families of farm operators, as Table 11 shows, more than 75 per cent were heads or the wives and children of heads. Nuclear relationships were more predominant in the Southeastern and Southwestern regions and the Lower Yangtze, where total family size was smaller. The major variations among the regions were those having to do with the non-nuclear rather than the nuclear relations. However, some of the variations in specific nuclear relations to the head suggest demographic differentiations. Numbers of wives per 1,000 heads were higher in the three adaptive regions plus the Red Basin, lower in the traditional regions of the South and the North. Sons were more numerous than daughters in all regions, but otherwise regional differentiations in numbers of children were not great and were unpatterned.

The families of the Chinese farm operators were classified as nuclear and non-nuclear families. (See Table 12.) More than 60 per cent of all families were nuclear, i.e., they included only fathers, mothers, and children. The proportion was less than 60 per cent in the South and in

TABLE 11. FAMILY MEMBERS IN NUCLEAR RELATIONS TO HEADS, 1929–31

Relations	All regions	South	South-eastern Hills	South-western Plateau	Red Basin	Lower Yangtze to Hwai	North-ern Plain	North-ern High-lands
Related Persons (%)								
Heads, wives and children	76.0	73.2	76.8	79.3	77.5	80.5	73.0	71.1
Persons (per 1,000 families)								
All members	5,224	5,816	4,650	4,982	5,448	4,880	5,421	5,598
Heads, wives, children	4,281	4,401	3,967	4,260	4,529	4,261	4,302	4,131
Head	1,000	1,000	1,000	1,000	1,000	1,000	1,000	1,000
Wife	899	898	913	983	917	917	883	813
Son	1,295	1,433	1,224	1,188	1,429	1,297	1,280	1,306
Daughter	1,087	1,070	830	1,089	1,183	1,048	1,139	1,012
Other members	943	1,415	683	722	919	619	1,119	1,467

SOURCE: Lists of relationships; population and vital statistics survey; unpublished tabulations.

TABLE 12. SIZE DISTRIBUTION OF NUCLEAR AND NON-NUCLEAR FAMILIES, 1929–31

Type and size	All regions	South	Southeastern Hills	Southwestern Plateau	Red Basin	Lower Yangtze to Hwai	Northern Plain	Northern Highlands
Persons (per 1,000 families)	5,224	5,816	4,620	4,982	5,448	4,880	5,421	5,598
Nuclear families (%)[a]	62.8	58.7	71.8	65.8	60.7	69.9	58.2	55.4
3–4 persons	90.3	91.0	89.4	90.2	92.6	91.9	89.1	87.7
5–6	61.8	64.5	68.8	57.7	58.6	67.5	58.7	54.1
7 or more	24.1	25.0	30.6	21.1	21.3	34.9	18.9	17.8
Size distribution, nuclear families (%)	100.0	100.0	100.0	100.0	100.0	100.0	100.0	100.0
2 persons[b]	13.7	7.8	17.5	12.6	11.7	13.3	15.3	12.2
3–4	49.3	48.7	50.7	54.8	51.8	48.1	48.4	52.0
5–6	30.4	33.9	26.8	27.4	30.0	31.3	30.2	29.8
7 or more	6.6	9.7	5.0	5.2	6.5	7.4	6.0	6.0
Size distribution, non-nuclear families (%)[c]	100.0	100.0	100.0	100.0	100.0	100.0	100.0	100.0
1–4 persons	9.5	6.9	17.6	11.6	6.5	11.0	8.8	9.4
5–6	33.7	26.9	34.0	38.8	33.5	38.1	31.4	32.8
7–9	38.5	45.2	35.0	38.0	40.3	37.2	38.9	35.8
10–14	15.5	18.5	10.2	10.1	17.2	12.4	17.5	17.1
15 or more	2.8	2.5	3.1	1.5	2.4	1.3	3.4	4.8

SOURCE: Tabulations by type of family by size for regions, unpublished. [b] Including a small number of families with one member present at survey but reported as nuclear. [c] A group designated as "large," defined as including non-nuclear members. [a] Excluding single-person households.

the Northern Plain and Highlands; it was 70 per cent in the Southeastern Hills and in the Lower Yangtze. The size distribution of nuclear families suggests the occurrence of high mortality and high fertility. Two-thirds of the nuclear families included two, three, or four members; the modal family had three or four members. Of the nuclear families 80 per cent had three to six members. The differences among the regions were variable.

The regional differences in family size and composition were greater in non-nuclear than nuclear families. Extended families were more prevalent, and the proportions of large families among extended families higher, in the coastal South, the Red Basin, and the Northern regions.

The Numbers of the Generations

Three-fourths of the members of the farm families were the heads, their wives, and their children. Three-fifths of all families were nuclear. Three-fourths of the relationships within families then, involved parents and children, and three-fifths of the families included no relationships other than two-generational ones.

The relationships tabulated in Table 13 pertain to the direct line of the head and his wife. More than four-fifths of the people in families were in the multi-generation line of the reference couple, the head and the wife. Roughly one in twenty was in a preceding generation, and one in ten was the child of a child. Regional differences were in the expected directions: there were smaller proportions in the direct lines in the coastal South and in the North, but differences were slight.

Computing frequencies of multi-generation families can be only hypothetical, for the generations of the parents and grandparents and those of the grandsons and great-grandsons may have been concentrated in those few families with extended membership. It is interesting to note, though, that the possible combinations of generations and the frequencies of such combinations differ markedly for males and for females. The surviving parents and grandparents of heads were mainly women; if the father of the present head were living he would probably have remained as head. Grandparents and parents of the head were 1.2 per cent of all men, but 10.7 per cent of all women. Sons of heads were almost 50 per cent of all men, daughters of the head only 34 per cent of all women.

Given complete dispersion of the grandparents and dispersion of the grandchildren subject only to the requirement that one grandchild be in a home with each grandparent, 1.2 per cent of the families could have included four generations of males. On comparable assumptions,

TABLE 13. MALES AND FEMALES IN THE LINE OF THE HEAD, BY RELATIONSHIP, 1929–31
(*Per cent*)

Sex and relation	All regions	South	Southeastern Hills	Southwestern Plateau	Red Basin	Lower Yangtze to Hwai	Northern Plain	Northern Highlands
All persons	100.0	100.0	100.0	100.0	100.0	100.0	100.0	100.0
Grandparents	0.0	0.2	0.2	0.1	0.2	0.2	0.3	0.2
Parents	5.2	6.7	5.6	6.0	5.3	4.8	5.0	5.5
Head and spouse	41.0	39.8	45.1	43.7	39.4	41.9	40.0	40.5
Children	42.9	45.7	41.4	42.2	44.8	44.3	41.6	41.9
Grandchildren	10.5	7.5	7.6	8.1	10.3	8.7	12.7	11.6
Sons' children	10.3	7.4	7.6	7.9	10.3	8.5	12.6	11.6
Daughters' children	0.2	0.1	—	0.2	0.0	0.2	0.1	0.0
Grandsons' children	0.2	0.1	0.0	0.0	0.0	0.2	0.4	0.2
Male	100.0	100.0	100.0	100.0	100.0	100.0	100.0	100.0
Grandparents (Grandfather)	0.0	0.0	0.0	0.0	0.0	0.0	0.0	0.0
Parents (Father)	1.2	2.3	1.2	2.2	1.7	1.1	0.9	1.9
Head	38.4	36.7	40.8	41.0	36.1	39.3	37.7	37.6
Children (Sons)	49.5	52.4	50.0	48.4	51.6	50.5	48.3	49.1
Grandchildren (Sons' sons)	10.5	8.5	8.0	8.2	10.4	8.9	12.7	11.2
Grandsons' sons	0.3	0.1	0.0	0.0	0.1	0.2	0.4	0.2
Female	100.0	100.0	100.0	100.0	100.0	100.0	100.0	100.0
Grandparents	0.5	0.6	0.5	0.2	0.3	0.3	0.6	0.4
Parents	10.2	12.5	11.7	10.3	10.0	9.3	10.4	10.9
Spouse	44.4	44.0	51.0	46.7	43.8	45.3	42.9	44.8
Children	34.4	36.8	29.7	34.9	35.7	36.4	33.0	31.4
Grandchildren	10.3	6.0	7.1	7.9	10.1	8.5	12.7	12.2
Grandsons' daughters	0.2	0.1	0.0	0.0	0.1	0.1	0.4	0.3
Total population in line of head	80.8	79.1	80.9	83.1	82.2	84.9	78.2	75.9
Male	86.8	85.6	88.1	88.2	88.6	90.0	84.7	81.9
Female	74.2	71.7	72.8	77.8	75.1	79.2	71.2	68.4

SOURCE: Lists of relationships, climatic regions, unpublished.

10.2 per cent of the families could have included four generations of females. The five-generation families can have been only a small proportion of the total. Grandparents and great-grandsons were too few to permit this except in a rare instance, whatever the capabilities of the family in retaining members. The realization of the ancient ideal of the multi-generation family might be achieved in some period remote from the years 1929–31 when the lower death rates of a modernizing economy and society would permit it.

Almost forty years ago the Land Utilization Survey of China obtained detailed population data for the households of farm operators in eight regions. Though interpretation is intricate, there were major and consistent regional differences in the relationship structures of the families of farm operators in the climatic regions of China. The variability lay more in the extended kin component than in the nuclear relationships. Social and economic factors were highly significant in family size and structure. It is tempting to speculate that the forces depressing fertility were greatest in the extended family. If so, the nuclear family, which is furthest from tradition and ideal, may be most conducive to population growth. This is not a conclusion, but a hypothesis relating to the population dynamics of the farm families.

Family Relations in Modern Chinese Fiction

AI-LI S. CHIN

The fiction of different periods of modern China affords varying insights into family relations. During the May Fourth period of the 1920's and 1930's (Chow 1960), the New Literature, belonging to a society in transition, revealed a deep interest in kinship, marriage, and the family. The same interest appears again, revitalized, in the stories of 1962–66 from the Communist mainland; but in the case of contemporary stories from Taiwan the topics are either ignored or treated with detachment. Paradoxically, some of the family virtues denounced in the fiction of the earlier period are now idealized in Communist fiction, but in the fiction of present-day Taiwan (where the old family ideology has official backing) family virtues are shown to lead to dissension and resentment. Conflict arising from the clash of old and new values abounds in the fiction of the May Fourth era; conflict emerges in the Communist stories of the 1960's as the product of dilemmas within ideology; but in Taiwan the prevailing mood in fiction is one of disengagement from family ties and of a disenchanted search for meaning in the encounters between liberated young men and women.

In this essay I first present the results of a classification and analysis of two sets of stories (from Taiwan and Communist China), and I attempt at the end, introducing material from the literature of the May Fourth Movement, to discuss the relationships between fiction and society in modern China.

To represent Taiwan I have chosen its foremost magazine, *Hsien-tai wen-hsüeh* (*Modern Literature Quarterly*) for the period from 1960 to mid-1966; for the mainland I have used the semi-official *Jen-min wen-hsüeh* (*People's Literature*) for the period from 1962 to mid-1966. I shall analyze these two sets of stories to see what they reveal about family roles in relation to the ideologies and structures of the two Chinese societies.

What is being compared? The two sets of stories not only arise from two different societies, but also stand in different relationships to the "social reality" they are supposed to illuminate. To make this clear, I shall try to sketch in some of the background of the two literatures and their societies in order to establish a basis, first, for assessing the meaning of the expressive patterns revealed, and, second, for relating these patterns to the ideology and family structure of the respective societies. For the second purpose I shall, in addition, draw on a previous study (Chin 1951) of stories from the 1920's and 1930's, the period when China first experienced a "family revolution."

Fiction has often been analyzed for the study of society, but the rationale of the method and the relation of the data so obtained to "social reality" are seldom made clear. The comparative or historical treatment of fiction in relation to society stands on still shakier ground. Although it has been recognized that the relationship between a literature and its society differs from case to case, there is no systematic framework for the study of the complex "tissue of connections" between literature and society. My statements about the circumstances that produced the Taiwan and Communist stories are based on a concept of the relation between literature and society that involves the following points.

The role of the writer of fiction. We have to try to understand the vantage point of the authors. Who are the authors, and how specialized is their role? What position do the writers occupy in the occupational structure? Is the role of the literary artist linked or merged with that of the educator, priest, or bureaucrat? How are the writers recruited, trained, and economically supported? Do the writers represent a particular generation?

The organization of publication, distribution, and remuneration. The effect on fiction of selection, editing, and other less obvious influences may be analyzed according to four main types of publisher: the author-publisher, the patron-publisher, the commercial publisher, and the state publisher.

Authority and literature. The extent to which official ideology is found in literature is governed by the mode and amount of state control. Does the same force govern literary forms and the choice of themes? What is the system of sanctions applied?

The structure of the reading public. How is this public composed? How far is it organized, and to what extent and in what manner can it make its preferences felt? Is the audience captive?

The four points are not equally relevant in all cases. In Taiwan, for example, who the writers are, what their status is as a group, and the literary influences to which they are subject are all important; their relations with authority and their channels of publication are less significant. On the mainland the situation is almost reversed: the thoroughness of political control over form and content is obvious, and the channels of publication are strictly policed; but the identity of the writers has less relevance for an understanding of content. The Taiwan stories tell us a good deal about the educated elite and their disenchantment with the social order, but nothing directly about the official ideology of their society. The Communist stories mirror faithfully official policy on family and kinship, but say very little about the reactions of the writers to the prevailing system of values. As for the stories of the 1920's and 1930's, when writers were in the vanguard of social progress, fiction expressed the repudiation of old family ideals and championed a new, minority, set of ideals. Writers and their readers jointly occupied a strategic position in their society.

However, it would be an oversimplification to characterize the literature of Taiwan as just one of disengagement, the Communist literature as simply one of ideology, and the May Fourth literature as merely one of social change. For all their rejection of family norms and failure to express ideals of any kind, the Taiwan stories must still be seen against the normative order being rejected by the characters (and their creators), for this is by no means a literature of escapism. The Communist stories may be closely controlled in terms of form and content, but beneath the ideological statements can be detected the portrayal of some patterns of response. That is to say, the writers, within limits, may include some "unintended" reality arising from reactions to "blue-print" relationships. In the stories of the transitional period of the 1920's and 1930's we find, amid the attacks on the old order and the advocacy of the new, indications of competing ideologies and differing patterns of response.

Taiwan: Source and Setting

Literature did not come into its own in Taiwan much before the 1960's. (See Tsi-an Hsia, "Taiwan," in Hsia 1961; and Chen 1963.) For the first five years after the Kuomintang move to Taiwan, the literary scene was dominated by established writers preoccupied with writing "epic" tales of the anti-Communist struggle. The repressive political atmosphere of those years did not, of course, encourage the free exploration of contemporary problems of Taiwan, and the ban on most of the literature of the May Fourth era removed an important stimulus.

By the second half of the 1950's the military and political tension had greatly relaxed, and a new college generation, come of age in the new environment, had begun to write about life as they lived it. Since then the writers have enjoyed a kind of freedom to express themselves within implicitly understood limits, being affected by government policy only in the sense that they have lived in a state of "national emergency." (See Hsia, "Taiwan," in Hsia 1961: 520f.) From the mid-1950's many periodicals and newspapers began to publish the new kind of realistic writing. Two of the literary magazines stand out in their dedication to serious writing. One is the now defunct *Wen-hsüeh tsa-chih* (*Literary Review*) founded in 1956 and edited by T. A. Hsia, then a professor at the National Taiwan University. By 1960 its place of eminence had been occupied by *Hsien-tai wen-hsüeh* (the magazine used in this study), which has been described in literary circles as "the most significant development" of recent years (Chen 1963: 83).

The writers this one magazine publishes cannot, of course, be taken as completely representative. There are at least two other important groups of writers of different orientations. One is the Young Writers' Association, sponsored by Chiang Ching-kuo but including authors of a wide range of views, some rather critical of the status quo. The other is the China Literary Association, which represents the more orthodox Kuomintang authors (Hsia 1961: 251f). However, since we are here concerned less with political ideology than with present-day responses to the reactivation of traditional norms and family values, we will confine our attention to *Hsien-tai wen-hsüeh*. The contributors to this magazine are for the most part young, many of them from the National Taiwan University. They come from both mainland and Taiwan families, and are nonpolitical in their writing. As members of the new educated elite, they are among the most sensitive to the tensions and problems of the younger generation.

Short stories in Taiwan enjoy a great vogue among the students, as they did on the mainland in the May Fourth era. In Taiwan the short story is more highly developed and is a medium of greater influence than the novel. Nevertheless, it has an important limitation as a source for our present purpose: much of the writing, in both style and content, is consciously modeled on European and American literature. With this limitation recognized, however, the stories in *Hsien-tai wen-hsüeh* will serve our purpose well enough. I have used a total of 49 stories from this magazine, this number being the total of the stories in the available issues since first publication that deal with kinship and family relationships and with marriage.

Taiwan: General Patterns and Topics in the Stories

The Taiwan stories may be characterized as a literature of disengagement, in which the heroes and heroines more often than not are alienated from society, are apt to reject rather than accept obligations, and are likely to display a high degree of normlessness in many interpersonal relations. It is ironical that a society subscribing to traditional values should produce such a literature, but perhaps the phenomenon is a reaction to the very reimposition of older virtues.

The general impression of disengagement is surprising because in real life the young intellectuals seem passive and obedient to standards of behavior defined by adults. Yet, on closer examination, the elite college generation, from which the writers come, can be shown to combine the verbal acceptance of adult norms governing the family with a readiness to rationalize away many deviations from them.* This pattern, in which the sincere acceptance of filial norms and the ready justification of deviance are combined, may lead the more sensitive among them—the writers—to perceive and express a mood of negation, of unresolved antagonism, and of despair about social relationships in general.

TABLE T-1. DISTRIBUTION OF FAMILY TYPES

Number of stories with no mention of family	21 (41 per cent)
Number of stories with families	28 (59 per cent)
Nuclear families (some stories have more than one)	32
Joint families	0
Married sons living with parents	0

The first striking feature of the stories is that the individual is shown as being isolated from his kin. There is no mention of the families of the heroes and heroines in 41 per cent of the stories. (These stories are about people in pursuit of boy-girl relationships or extramarital sex. "No-family" stories and "no-marriage-prospect" stories are excluded.) The remainder of the stories refer to families only of the nuclear type, four such families including an unmarried brother or sister. The three-generation family, known to be common in Taiwan, does not appear. The grandparent is totally absent; only one story refers to in-laws, and another involves an aunt and her niece holidaying together.

These figures demonstrate the preoccupation with the isolated individual. Otherwise, attention is focused almost exclusively on relationships within the nuclear family or leading to marriage. Perhaps the

* I base this statement on my fieldwork in Taiwan in 1962.

neglect of the joint family and what it implies for the network of lifelong filial and fraternal relationships is one way of responding to the problem of the persistence of tradition and the renewed emphasis on the old family ideal. The evasion of conflict issues can be a characteristically Chinese way of responding to such issues.

This analysis will concentrate on the husband-wife and parent-child relationships, the relationships leading to marriage, and those leading away from it (extramarital liaisons). The latter are prominent, forming 23 per cent of all the relationships listed in Table T-2. Against a background of Taiwan as a rather staid society, the literary importance given to sexual attachment may be taken partly as a product of the influence of foreign literature and partly as an indication of dissatisfaction with the prevailing norms for husband and wife and for young women contemplating marriage.

TABLE T-2. DISTRIBUTION OF RELATIONSHIPS NOTED IN 49 STORIES

Parent-child	48
Husband-wife	26
Boy-girl and the "intended"	25
Extra-marital liaisons	34
Grandparent-grandchild	0
Sibling	10
Other	4
Total	147

TABLE T-3. DISTRIBUTION OF PARENT-CHILD RELATIONSHIPS

Father-son	10
Mother-son	22
Father-daughter	7
Mother-daughter	9
Total	48

Within the family the mother-son theme is treated twice as often as the father-son. Traditionally and in modern times, the mother is closer than the father to the child. The Confucian ideal of the stern and remote father-figure makes contact with him a less rewarding and less varied emotional experience (except in the context of revolt against paternal authority, a theme nearly absent in these Taiwan stories).

Fathers and sons. The stories about fathers and sons are all highly charged; they express the theme of the mutual rejection of role obligations, whether defined in traditional or modern contexts. The portrayal of aggression, recrimination, shame, lack of understanding, and sheer heartlessness reveals an impoverishment of the traditional filial tie and a lack of any modern positive norms (such as mutual respect) to ease the loss. This pattern must be seen in the light of the traditional require-ment that the son undergo a lifelong subordination—a critical feature of the Confucian family system. When this tradition came under attack in the May Fourth period, the authority of the father came to symbolize the evils of the large family system, as stories of that time show. In present-day Taiwan fiction, the negative attitudes indicate not so much a pattern of revolt by the young (with a sense of righteousness) as an indirect expression of the resentment against the official reimposition of filialism in the face of the reality of waning parental authority.

In three of the Taiwan stories the father strikes his son. A stepfather habitually beats, scolds, and speaks sarcastically to his stepson (T60.3.4).* Another father slaps, beats, and threatens to strangle his young son who refuses to go to school; when the violence is restrained, father and son stare at each other in silent hatred (T61.9.2). In a third story a married son, having gambled away a sum of money donated by his fellow workers for his wife's operation, is rebuffed by his father when he seeks his help. The father's criticism is repaid in kind, the son blam-ing the father for his poor upbringing; the two men come to blows; the father is accidentally killed (T64.2.8). It is not always the father who is ashamed of his son; the son of a professor is ashamed of and hates his father for writing pedantic and stale research papers to get a govern-ment subsidy (T64.13.2). Another son avoids his father when the latter marries beneath his station; only at the death of the second wife does the son reappear—to attend the funeral (T64.22.1). In these examples there is little but bitterness between fathers and sons. The father is por-trayed as desiring the son's success, not his happiness. The son, on his side, fails to see the father as a person with feelings and individual needs. Shame also arises from the father's traditional concern with "face." One father scorns his second son for his poor performance at various schools, constantly praising his other sons as models. The father uses "face" with a friend to get the second son admitted to another school, and when the boy fails to appear for the examinations, the father is so ashamed that for days he will not show himself in public, mutter-ing that the boy "could not be of my seed" (T61.11.2).

Except in the last example, the reasons for the emotional outbursts are not exclusively or clearly traditional or modern. The context, that is to say, is not one of revolt against tradition so much as the expression of basic antagonism. The other stories illustrate the problems created by

---

* A story is cited by the year, cumulative issue number, and numerical order among short stories in the issue; it is marked "T" for Taiwan.

the passing of the old spirit of filialism and the new yearning for independence and individuality. The son of well-to-do parents is looking forward to his marriage with a beautiful girl of his own choosing. He feels that his parents merely assume that he is happy because they are happy—to them it is unthinkable that he might have different thoughts and feelings. In their approval of the match, the parents seem to the son to be "a little too eager," as if they had "set a net" for him. He is convinced that, were he to try to tell them about his hesitancy, they would only laugh in his face and ridicule him for being immature (T60.3.1). Another story tells of a similar gulf between a less articulate father and son, in which intellectualized self-questioning does not cloud the relationship. A boy of fifteen, on seeing a mural depicting the horrors of hell, enters a Buddhist monastery, where, after three days of searching, his father finds him; he is sitting motionless and refuses to show any sign of recognizing his father, despite the latter's tearful pleading (T64.2.4). In contrast with the dramatic negation of the father-son tie, we have the simple sorrow of a broken old man who is reduced to begging because his son is "no good . . . an ignorant, uneducated thing" (T61.6.4).

Mothers and sons. The mother-son relationship is both more prominent and more varied in its treatment; with it a little warmth is brought to the chill air. In the stories of the 1920's and 1930's, the mother is often portrayed with great sympathy, even though children may need to rebel against her in the cause of independence. But the mother of modern writing is treated differently: from the new, less clearly defined obligations between mother and son there emerges the pattern of the too dominant, too possessive mother, divested of her traditional duties and status, and coming up against the son's need to assert himself. The rebelliousness (tempered with sympathy) in the May Fourth writing is replaced in the Taiwan stories by resentment, evasion, and quiet disobedience.

In the mother-son relationships in the Taiwan stories we do find the traditional type of mother who echoes the father's harsh treatment of the son without daring to take a firm step herself (T61.11.2). Another mother tries to soften the father's anger: after helplessly watching the father beat the son for his refusal to go to school, she sends her older son to find out from the teacher what may be troubling the delinquent boy (T61.9.2). The type of mother who sacrifices herself for her son may be traditional or modern: the widowed singer in an opera troupe refuses an offer of marriage because the man objects to her keeping her infant son (T61.10.2). Similarly timeless is the simple warmhearted mother: a desperately poor washerwoman with seven children buys a few cakes and carefully distributes them among her delighted offspring (T61.10.3).

The modern mother-son situations are more complex. In one case the woman resents her role as mother: a hard pressed mother of three, finding her husband grown insensitive to her, blames her children for her "drooping breasts," grumbling at the youngest child who has just wet the bed, "Do you want my life too?" (T60.2.5). Another modern pattern is the mother encountering the son's annoyance or evasive acquiescence: the college graduate agrees, on his mother's insistence, to drink a hot-weather remedy, but quietly slips away to experiment with wine and women (T62.13.2). But evasion is not always so easy: another college educated son rejects with hatred his mother's plea to let her come and do his chores for him; now for the second time widowed she has nowhere else to go (T60.3.4). Or a son's rejection of his mother may be complicated by her neurotic hold on him: one such mother, disabled by crippling anxieties about her son, wants to keep him near her all the time; he secretly pays repeated visits to a young divorcee to satisfy erotic fantasies in advance of his age (T60.2.1). Other mothers are shown to be overly possessive and jealous of their sons' girl friends, some allowing their sons to maintain erotic attachments to themselves well into adolescence.

Fathers and daughters. The father-daughter relationship is less charged emotionally. After all, in the traditional system the father could afford to treat his daughter with greater indulgence because of the impermanence of her membership in the family. But the modern daughter shares the same family environment with her brother, and we may expect her to suffer the same tensions, although at a lower emotional pitch.

Some of the strains between father and daughter in the stories arise from unfortunate events rather than from rejection of roles. For example, a girl is sold into prostitution by her poverty-stricken parents (T64.19.4); a widowed farmer sorrows because, striving for better and better matches for his daughter out of his love for her, he loses her to the first boy who lays a caressing hand on her shoulder (T60.4.5).

But there is also disobedience, ranging from occasional disregard to persistent defiance. A high-school student goes out jitterbugging against her father's wishes (T62.13.2). A professor's daughter, knowing of his disapproval of her appearance, clothing, manner, and male company, carries on with her ways: "What can father do about it?" In a more thoughtful moment she asks herself "This is my way of revolt, but what exactly am I rebelling against?" (T60.3.4). The only instance of direct confrontation with paternal authority concerns the marriage of a Tai-

wan-born girl and a mainlander. The father pronounces a dire prohibi-
tion on the marriage; defied, he declares his daughter unfilial, and she
retorts, "It is useless to say anything more—I will follow this man and
no one else" (T61.10.3). This story is reminiscent of the 1920's and
1930's when youthful rebelliousness was most evident in life as well as
in literature.

Mothers and daughters. The relationship between mother and daughter is similar to the father-son and mother-son relationships no doubt
because of the greater degree of equality in the treatment of sons and
daughters. However, the intense antagonism in the father-son relationship and the emotional complications of the mother-son relationship are
lacking here. Instead, the independent-minded daughter of the present
day can oppose the insecure modern mother, so that we find the same
kind of aimless negativism in a daughter toward both her mother and
father. A girl who is poor at her college studies is provided with tutors
by her mother; she will not take things seriously, why, she herself does
not know, though she knows she is causing her mother much pain
(T64.22.6). Ready to set out abroad to study, a girl receives a cable from
her divorced father in Japan urging her to pay him a brief visit en route;
the mother hysterically forbids her daughter to do so, terrified at the
idea that her ex-husband may "take my angel away from me." In tears
the mother clings to her daughter, begging her not to make the visit "for
my sake." The daughter wonders, "Is this a mother's love?" (T61.7.3).

Boys, girls, and love. The boy-girl relationship, which in Communist
fiction is defined ideally as full of restrained anticipation and in the May
Fourth literature as expressing the exhilaration of a new-found sympathy between independent personalities, is in the Taiwan stories charged
with suspicion, the fear of being deceived, used, or ridiculed. Intimacy
—one is given to understand—may turn out to be a trap; nor should one
trust one's own feelings. The contrast with the Communist stories is
striking. In them the ideal portrayal of the boy-meets-girl situation con-
veys faith that understanding awaits the ripening of friendship even
when, as in some cases, the friendship is prearranged. From the Taiwan
stories we may speculate that the young intellectuals are in real life
disenchanted with the state of marriage and interpersonal relations.

My first example—a story with heavy symbolism—hints at the ephem-
eral, almost unattainable, quality of understanding in love between two
people. A young man and his girl are walking by the calm sea. He finds
in this silent, mysterious girl someone who understands him perfectly,
but somehow something is missing: she is "almost too pure." He starts
going out with another girl, just temporarily (he tells himself) to make

the first take notice. When he decides to tell her that he needs her, he returns to the beach to find that she has gone and is never to be found again (T61.10.6).

More explicit situations are used to convey the message that a display of affection is not to be trusted. A girl known for her aloofness is finally invited to the movies by a boy. She accepts eagerly, and the two classmates engage in warm and animated conversation. But seeing another boy, also a classmate, watching her and her companion outside the theater, she concludes that the invitation was the result of a dare, and she abandons her escort at the ticket window (T61.10.1). A college girl who cannot live without the company of boys finds herself alone with a shy boy, whom she proceeds to tease by a show of affection. By the time he loses his equilibrium she abandons him for someone "more exciting" (T60.3.4). Another girl tries to seduce a shy boy in an empty classroom when her own boyfriend fails to show up for a rendezvous. The boy later feels remorseful and writes to the girl to apologize, admitting his loneliness. The girl shows the letter around, and his classmates go about mocking him: "I am lonely!" (T61.11.2).

One's own feelings are not reliable either. A quiet girl, typed as a model student uninterested in boys, desperately wants to be popular. At a mountain outing she is walking along a narrow path with a boy she has admired at a distance. In a daze of confused excitement she backs to the edge of the precipice, and the boy grasps her arms. Taken by surprise, she responds warmly and clings to the boy for a fraction of a second. She feels him disengaging himself, a hint of a smirk on his face. She is certain he will spread the story around. Ironically, she will be rid of her unwanted reputation, but in exchange for a more painful one (T60.2.2).

Husbands and wives. If romance is so devoid of tenderness and empathy, marriage and the new family in fiction have not much to build on. In these Taiwan stories we find the husband-wife relationship described negatively, although examples of marital devotion are not absent. The two main themes are fear of domination and lack of sympathy and understanding. Perhaps both themes express the gap between the traditional conjugal relationship of inequality and the Western type of marriage maintained by the thin thread of romantic love. When love proves illusory, there is left only the mutual resentment of dominance between two people whose duties are not clearly defined. Whereas in the May Fourth stories the old hierarchical family was under attack, now husband and wife are their own enemies, struggling against mutual insensitivity.

In the few cases of marital devotion—for there *are* happy endings —tragedy nevertheless arises from external circumstances. A pedicab driver works feverishly at the edge of a typhoon, and comes home late to count his earnings before his sick wife, saying "We may have enough money to take you to the doctor tomorrow" (T61.11.1). The invalid wife of a professor, shunned by relatives and friends because she was once a servant girl, nevertheless lives happily in a fine house; she is made content by her husband's devotion (T64.22.1). A poor gambler is hiding from the police, being suspected of patricide. The harassed wife, knowing nothing of his crime, defends his name to the police, saying that he drinks and gambles but would not break the law. When later he comes to her and confesses that he has fatally wounded his father, she helps him to escape, offering him her meager wedding jewelry (T64.21.8).

The following stories illustrate ambivalence toward submission. A happily married young woman, seeing her former lover, recalls their days together at college when each was constantly aware of the unexpressed mood and thoughts of the other, each being unwilling to accept the sacrifice the other silently and gladly offered. To have married this man would have brought too much suffering and tension. But the brief encounter also jolts her into realizing that her two years of married life have cost her her selfhood. Her husband has made every decision for her, even answered her letters, and unquestioningly has accepted her sacrifice. And she has felt happy and peaceful in this surrender, choosing the peace of submission to the bitter-sweet tension of intimacy. She even convinces herself that there really was no choice (T61.6.2). When a Taiwan-born wife learns of her husband's other wife and children on the mainland, now refugees in Hong Kong, she sets out to win her husband's "respect for her." She takes up washing to make an independent living, and gradually achieves complete control over him by persuading him to quit his job and live on her earnings. Now she has him all to herself, a kept man (T61.10.3). A man who does not play cards is yet grateful for his wife's card parties because they give him the chance to sit unobtrusively near her, hoping she will be too absorbed to drive him away. But at one party he has let the coffee burn and is enduring a public scolding. His presence is now a nuisance. "Why can't you go out somewhere like other men?" his wife shouts. The assembled ladies, impressed by the wife's daring, say "You are indeed a remarkable wife to treat your husband like that! We think the poor thing is rather amusing" (T61.8.2).

By far the commonest feature of the conjugal relationship is lack of empathy, an emphasis made more striking by reason of the freedom exercised in the choice of marriage partners. Two-thirds of the fifteen marriages in this group are shown to be corroded by a feeling of alienation between two people who have chosen to spend their lives together. In one case a mellowness finally sets in after a lifelong estrangement that began when the wife discovered the husband in a compromising situation with the maid. It takes her son's unhappiness in love to bring her belatedly to forgive her husband, now dead (T62.12.1). In other stories there is no such mitigation.

In several stories the beloved, when married, turns out to be a stranger. A girl comes shyly to a teacher of English for her lessons and, during the courtship that follows, displays a tender love for animals and other people's children; now, married, she refuses to have children and will not even let her husband keep a bird. Her interest in English has long since vanished (T64.22.1). Even a marriage that appears perfect to others may leave the husband with unspeakable ennui, as in the story of a chance reunion of three classmates. The teacher-writer who considers his wife "one of the successes of his life," nevertheless feels life is so "empty" that it leaves him with nothing to write about (T64.22.5). To epitomize all the stories of marital estrangement we refer to the story of the woman who "doesn't know how she got married." The husband who comes to her bed seems to her a total stranger, leaving as silently as he approaches. She only knows that he demands his daily food, a clean shirt, and polished shoes, and that he pounds the table when the meals do not please him (T60.2.5).

Sexual relations outside marriage. There are more extramarital liaisons in the stories than marriages. These liaisons include one or two involuntary ones (as when a girl is forced into prostitution), but most are the results of acts of "will." Some are merely passing incidents, but perhaps these, even more than the longer-lasting attachments, express the anomie of the characters. Casual or episodic sex, it appears, is the last test for the person who finds normal role relationships meaningless; when he comes face to face with the opportunity, he merely succumbs to sex, often with a stranger who happens along, instead of actively searching for it or finding in it the assertion of individuality. Sex does not even serve as a symbol of rebellion: when the hero or heroine enters into such a relationship, he or she typically finds it empty.

Some of the liaisons are of the maid-in-the-garden, the male-boarder, and the youthful-passion-in-the-woods varieties. These violations of the norm do not in a direct sense threaten the marriage institution itself. There are also variants of the modern "emancipated sex" themes: heavy petting in the dark corner of a teahouse, homosexual attachments, and the premature eroticism of the very young adolescent. But who are the violators of the norms and what are the attendant emotions? One story starts with the wife afraid of losing her husband because of her inability to bear him a son. In an attempt to hold on to him, she proposes that he go out with her younger sister. The expected happens. There is now in the menage a little boy who calls the unmarried mother "auntie." The father of the child, who once promised "to take care of everything," is now silent before both women (T60.4.2). A college girl moves out of her sister's house because she dislikes her new brother-in-law, but to please her sister she returns for a long vacation. Meeting her brother-in-law in the garden, she is captivated by the gentleness in his eyes. Daily exchanges of stolen glances culminate in his suggesting that they go away together to a famous resort—"we two ... and your sister" (T60.4.4). Another story about a brother-in-law has him widowed to marry his wife's sister (T60.1.4). Then there is the man who seduces his best friend's happily married wife while the husband is away on a long trip (T60.3.2). It appears that people who should be trustworthy, by reason of kinship or friendship, are the very ones to violate the norms.

The note of distrust in these stories is matched by the note of despair —not exhilaration, bold defiance of convention, or a sense of liberation. A married woman, exploited by her husband, leaves him in a daze of silent anger. After walking in the streets and, for the first time in her life, drinking in a bar, she wanders into the woods, where she submits to an unknown man. The story ends with her walking into the river to cleanse herself, the water slowly rising above her head (T60.2.5). The college graduate of well-to-do parents is about to marry a beautiful girl. They seem perfectly matched and have everything to make them happy—a house, a car, and the prospect of a trip abroad. She has been intimate with him, and he says he does not know whether he loves her or not: "This kind of thing is enjoyable if it is not done too often!" (T60.3.1). This theme is baldly put in a story called a "fable." A young man stares out of the window of a bare room, a woman lying half awake on the bed. After two months of this—same room, same view, and even same weather—the young man says to himself, "They all say this is hap- piness. *But how loathsome, how ugly it was!* Is there nothing happier?" (The italicized words are in English in the original.) That afternoon the man kills himself (T60.5.3).

Interpretation of the Taiwan stories

In these stories from Taiwan we have found patterns of response to ideology and norms of marriage and family rather than idealized or descriptive versions of family roles. We may interpret what we see in this fiction to be the work of a group of writers expressing the sentiments of a generation who in real life are faced with the task of reconciling the officially endorsed return to tradition with life in a modernizing society, and who live in the context of a suspended family revolution. The tendency is to avoid a frontal attack on family problems, rather than to deal directly with them by protest against the old and advocacy of the new, as in the May Fourth literature. In addition, the almost total neglect of the older generation in these Taiwan stories tells us something of the latter's relevance to the psychic world of the young.

We must now attempt to sketch the reality, insofar as we can observe it, which serves as the springboard for this fictional view. In the 1960's, those who in their youth had participated in, or at least had witnessed, the early wave of the family revolution in China are themselves parents or grandparents. This generation has, to all appearances, failed to carry forward the struggle for the values of self-assertion and self-determination; it has sat by while an orthodoxy of traditionalism has been imposed on this tenuously integrated island society. This orthodoxy includes the reappearance of the *yen* father—the remote and unapproachable figure of authority. Whatever forces lie behind this turn of events, here sits a transplanted generation divested of its power to enforce parental authority or other traditionalized values. The young are now less dependent than they were on their family for the opportunity to rise educationally and occupationally. The children of both mainland- and Taiwan-born parents have to make their way mainly by ability and by depending on government or foreign-supported channels for studying abroad. The semi-*yen* father is an empty, helpless figure. The son cannot see him as a substantial enough authority to rebel against, or as a staunch enough image to emulate. The result (as the data here as well as research in Taiwan would indicate) is that the younger generation show a tolerance of the father and a tendency to accommodate parental wishes and expectations in face-to-face situations, but in other circumstances they tend, without soul-searching, to discount or ignore the importance of meaningful parental sentiments or deep-seated needs.

We can perhaps see why in the Taiwan stories the primary focus is not on family obligations but on the lone individual, apparently unencumbered by a sense of family duty, wary of too much emotional dependence on parents, and unwilling openly to fight for independence. Contrast this situation with that in the May Fourth literature, where youth was seen as righteously struggling to free itself from what was viewed as a formidable authority figure in an oppressive family system. That battle is in fact far from won, but in the Taiwan stories the individual chooses to disengage himself from family and society, and sees himself, without cushioning relationships, pitted helplessly against other, equally isolated, individuals.

The mother has in present-day society won a degree of emancipation from the traditional family but has not fully consolidated her gains by participating actively in the wider society. In real life the son finds her less the oppressed figure of a generation ago than a figure to be set aside. In the stories she is sometimes seen as trying to exercise an emotional hold on her son, who finds this emotional dependence an unwelcome burden. Yet the kind of hostility in the stories between father and son is not found between mother and son, for the mother symbolizes not traditional values but a modern aberration. Here once more fiction gives us a pattern of response that represents a selected and extreme form of reaction, one that is nevertheless highly suggestive of tensions in society.

Although in a somewhat aimless way, the daughters in contemporary Taiwan carry forward the spirit of defiance of the earlier generation of youth in revolt. In fiction the daughter too finds paternal authority less formidable than its traditional counterpart. She shares with her brother the annoyance at the emotional hold of the mother. In these responses the daughter in part expresses the newly won sense of equality with males and in part shows that a daughter rebelling against the father is after all engaged in a less serious struggle.

The loss of clearly structured roles in real life provides material for the fictional portrayal of husband-wife and boy-girl relationships. The extramarital encounter is robbed of the meaning of rebellious gesture or fleeting pleasure. What is supposed to be the romantic interlude before marriage is, for the characters in the stories, fraught with suspicion and fear of deception and public ridicule. Now, in contrast to the stirring portrayals in the earlier fiction, boy and girl find a void between them. They play a game in which each hopes to win by not showing his hand. Carried over into marriage, these uncertainties are translated into fear of being dominated and a view of the partner as a stranger. One cannot be open with one's husband or wife, or even with oneself: those close to us may betray us. These sentiments in fiction indicate an intensified response to a family system in suspense between ideologies. During the earlier period the new ideology produced a sense of comradeship between the sexes. Now, with the passing of the grand gesture of rebellion, the present group of elite youth appears to be floundering. That there are submerged tensions in the present-day Taiwan family left unresolved by the imposition of traditionalism is revealed by the pervasive search for satisfying ways of relating to others and by the accompanying mood of despair.

Yet we must by no means overlook the threads of continuity between the early and latest phases in the modernization of the family. Then and now, family bonds are weakened; intensity of interpersonal attachments, which never characterized traditional relationships, does not seem to accompany the emergence of new roles either in the early years of modernization or at present. Chinese society has had no institutionalized permissive outlets for personal indulgence or emotional excess in or outside the family—as, for example, can be found in Japan. Thus, faced with freedom between the sexes, modern youth in Taiwan experiences not a sense of personal fulfillment but a pressing need to search for meaningful bonds.

I venture a final conjecture on the spirit of negation found in the Taiwan stories. While Western avant-garde literature may be characterized by the theme of the alienation of man from himself and from his very existence as an individual, the elite youth in Taiwan is, through its writings, expressing something different: the individual's detachment from structurally important role relations. We may call the latter a literature of disengagement, the former a literature of alienation. If the modern Chinese is to find his meaningful self, more likely he will do so through social relationships rather than in terms of the individual self or "significant other." Alienation from self comes after the discovery of a strong core of the self, which in the West has been building up from antiquity through the development of the Protestant ethic to the present.

Communist China: Sources and Setting

In the years 1962–66 Communist China appeared to take a new direction in family policy. Regaining its balance after the economic disasters of the Great Leap Forward and the early commune experiments, the government stressed agriculture, the moral education of the young, and the veneration of the *lao-pai-hsing*, the masses. All these major policies point to a consolidation of the family and a greater respect for the older generation, phenomena richly revealed in literature.

In comparison with the stories published before 1962, those appearing in the three or four years after that date unmistakably mark the solidarity of the nuclear family, the renewal of wider kinship ties, and a respect for elders in general and for the father in particular. For the first time since China started to modernize, the father as a literary image is again held up as a model for the son. We can even find the

Confucian ideal image of the *yen* (stern) father modified to fit the Communist mold.

We should expect these new emphases to produce difficulties with regard to marriage choice and relations with the mother-in-law; and that is what we do find in the stories, in which the preoccupation with the "semi-arranged" marriage and the mother-in-law–daughter-in-law relationship suggests that writers are attempting to understand or portray the interaction of several roles.

The political element remains in these stories, but it recedes before the newer family issues. Nevertheless, all matters remain subject to the criterion of ideological correctness; hence the consistent application of the latest principles conflicts with the individual's duty to the society. For this reason the stories show many ambiguities in their approach to the topic of the *ta-fang* (socially competent) young girl, for example, or the matter of parental influence on choice of marriage partners.

The *Jen-min wen-hsüeh*, the widely circulated publication of the All China Association of Literary Workers, gives us the most orthodox view of kinship ideology. All but two or three of the issues of this magazine (which began in October 1949) are available and have been perused. The stories are contributed by a great number of authors, who seldom write more than one story each. No study has been made of family relations in the post-1962 literature, although some Western accounts are available for the earlier years (Borowitz 1954; *China Quarterly* 1963; Hsia 1962; Hsia 1963), written primarily as literary criticism. By concentrating on the stories of the 1960's we are able to ensure greater comparability with the Taiwan data and sufficient homogeneity of the Communist material to allow us to detect significant patterns. I have studied every available story in the chosen period, a total of 47 in 35 issues, that is relevant to this inquiry.

Control over literary production is exercised both through general policy directives and by specific post-publication criticism, sometimes in the same magazine in issues immediately following. The critics are fellow writers, literary critics, and sometimes important party members. Thus by following all the criticism of a given story, it is possible, though tedious, to get at the nuances of the interpretation of policy.

The short story, because of its simplicity and speed of production, is a more sensitive medium than the novel for the translation of fluctuating policies into fiction. The general thematic emphasis of the stories follows changes in national policy over the last decade and a half, and I draw attention to some of these major shifts in the following discussion.

We should note, to begin with, that in Communist China's literary history there has never been a concerted attack on the legal family or marriage as an institution. The "free love" theme and the "glass of water" theory of sex have never gained a foothold in literature or in real life, contrary to the situation in Soviet Russia in the 1920's. A puritanical tone is maintained in the fiction of Communist China. Even in the early years, when divorce was encouraged and the oppressed wife and daughter-in-law urged to "speak bitterness," the integrity of the nuclear family was assumed or upheld. Members of a family in fiction often begin on different sides of the political fence (especially during the land reform and collectivization drives), but for the most part the stories lead to the "thought conversion" of the backward member—unless an entire family is beyond redemption. It is a rare story that breaks up the immediate family because one member turns out to be "an enemy of the people."

In the first three or four years of the Communist literature the popular themes are land reform and the exploits of the Liberation Army. Parents out of stupidity oppose land reform, refuse to join a cooperative, or choose the wrong kind of son-in-law or daughter-in-law, whereas the son or daughter falls in love with a progressive and joins in the vanguard of revolutionary change. Sometimes the old peasant, having suffered oppression, is given revolutionary stature. In the case of industrial workers, a frequent theme in these early stories is the ideological gap between husband and wife—with the backward member finally being reformed.

During the three-week period immediately before the Hundred Flowers Movement of 1957, great diversification appears in the stories, but the period was not long enough for changes in family relationships to be portrayed. Thus in late 1956 we find a few unabashed love stories, with ideology in a supporting role. During the Great Leap Forward and the height of the commune movement in 1958–59, stories glorify production duties in preference to home duties. C. T. Hsia describes this trend (Hsia 1963), and my own previous study of the stories of another magazine for the year 1960 (Chen 1964) suggests it. Differences in dedication to work and revolutionary enthusiasm may introduce tensions in the family, but most difficulties are overcome in the course of the story.

Earlier Communist short stories, though they did not describe the family as destroyed, did show the solidarity between the generations and between husband and wife as strained. During the period of the Great Leap Forward and the commune experiments, the individual was shown sacrificing family unity in order to answer the socialist call, subordinating a narrower to a greater loyalty. There were stories glorifying the temporary separation of family members, but the marriage bond was portrayed as enduring. Now we may begin the detailed examination of the stories from 1962 to mid-1966.

Communist China: Some General Patterns in the Stories

The heightened interest in kinship in the stories of the period 1962–66 is quite noticeable. Three preliminary observations may be made. First, kinship terminology appears more frequently after 1962 than before: village people in the stories often address one another by some kinship term, even when they are not related, and between husbands and wives one sees again the old teknonyms such as *t'a-tieh, t'a-ma* ("his father, his mother") or "father of (child's name)"; even the party secretary may refer to himself as "your uncle," when talking to an unrelated girl (C62.12.4; C64.8.5).* Second, there are positive statements about the solidarity of kin: one character quotes the old saying "relatives are like flesh and bone; they stick together" (C63.3.1); a father talking to his daughter about her difficulty in gaining admission to a dance academy says, "We leaned on your aunt and uncle as revolutionary cadres. Do not lose face for your elders" (C62.7.3). Third, a considerable number of relatives appear in the stories: of the 232 relationships coded, 9 are grandparent-grandchild, 26 are in-laws, and 3 are between other kinds of kin; these figures are much greater than in the Taiwan sample.

TABLE C-1. DISTRIBUTION OF RELATIONSHIPS IN 47 STORIES[a]
(*Not necessarily residing together*)

Parent-child	62
Husband-wife	28
Grandparent-grandchild	9
Siblings	11
Boy-girl	77
"Intended"	16
In-laws	26
Other	3
	232

[a] The 232 relationships are spread fairly evenly throughout the 47 stories, averaging about 5 relationships per story.

Three-generation families are also fairly common. Among the families described in the 47 stories, 11 show parents (or a surviving parent) living with one married son and his children, though the joint family (i.e.,

_____

* Stories are cited by year, issue number, and order, and are marked "C" for Communist China.

with more than one married son) is not found. The grandparent has of course been valued in Chinese Communist society for his services as nursemaid, but his glorification as the progressive member of the family can be taken as one aspect of a new pattern of respect for age.

TABLE C-2. DISTRIBUTION OF FAMILY TYPES (BY RESIDENCE) IN 47 STORIES[a]

	Frequency
No family	4
Nuclear family	35
Parents with one married son	11
Joint family	0

[a] Some stories describe more than one family unit.

Whereas ideological issues form the major theme of the earlier stories, the political orientations of most characters in the new stories are either less sharply opposed or more ambiguous. In many cases, differences in political views are minor and may even be irrelevant to the development of the story. This change does not simply reflect the settling down of the revolution, for the call for revolutionary fervor has by no means subsided; the change reflects a shift in emphasis during this period to wider forms of interpersonal relationships.

TABLE C-3. ENUMERATION OF MARRIAGE THEMES IN 47 STORIES

Stories in which marriage or the "match" is the central theme	11
Stories in which marriage or the "match" is the subsidiary theme	3
Stories in which marriage arrangement or interference by parents or relatives is involved	7
"Matches" in which girl shows greater initiative than boy[a]	6
"Matches" in which boy shows greater initiative than girl[a]	0

[a] In many matches it is unstated or unclear who takes greater initiative.

It is obvious that there is a considerable interest in the circumstances surrounding the match, since in 11 of the stories this is the central theme. What is even more interesting is the number of cases (7) of matches in which there is a parental arrangement or an attempted parental interference. These moves, though not always successful, are by no means unsympathetically portrayed, nor are they shown to be unwelcome to the young people themselves.

TABLE C-4. DISTRIBUTION OF PARENT-CHILD RELATIONSHIPS IN 47 STORIES

Father-son	11
Father-daughter	14
Mother-son	23
Mother-daughter	14
Total parent-child relationships	62

Fathers and sons. The consistent father-son solidarity described in recent Communist stories is quite striking. Most of the fathers are now progressive, aligned with their sons and daughters; the father no longer represents the backward or stubborn peasant unwilling to take the socialist road. His skill and devotion to work, worthy of his children's respect, are emphasized. Surprisingly, we find the partial return of the *yen* (stern, laconic) father as hero. The stress on family unity in these stories is not just a strengthening of the nuclear family with relatively independent members; it is a partial return to the old pattern of paternal authority and the solidarity of the father-son tie, with an implicit subordination, though qualified, of the younger generation.

In the eleven father-son relationships of the stories, only one father is ideologically on the wrong side: he is a merchant. His son is also bourgeois-minded, dreaming of fame and comfort as a writer, but the son's steady girl is a true progressive. The story tells of the father tempting the son into profiteering deals and hastening the break with the girl (C64.1.1). A second father, a middle-class peasant, is steered toward anti-progressive behavior by a domineering second wife, the widow of a former landlord. She stirs up so much trouble in the family that the father is forced to drive out his beloved son by his first marriage, giving him only a poor hilly portion of the family land. Again at the instigation of his wife, the man tries to get credit from the commune, without having earned enough work points, on the borrowed "face" of the son as Party Branch Secretary and Deputy Team Leader (C62.12.9).

The other ten fathers are strong progressive men, worthy of emulation by their sons, for legitimate authority in a Communist society must be built upon ideological correctness. It would be difficult to document this point briefly, but the skill and ability of the fathers can be simply illustrated. A son who fails the entrance examination for college reluctantly joins his father as a forester. While the boy looks for his father in the forest reserve, he meets some workers who praise his father's skill and dedication. The boy is filled with pride and respect for his father, and he resolves to stay and work by his side and to persuade his mother and cousin to join them (C63.1.3). Respect and admiration can be mutual. An apprentice driver has his license suspended for discourteous driving, by his father, the head of the motor transport pool. But the son finally wins the respect of his father, when in a later incident the man discovers that his injured son in the hospital is not the negligent person he used to be but a new hero who has saved his truck and the lives of some comrades as well (C63.3.2).

We have already noted the reappearance of the *yen* father. Some of the changes noted in this paper seem to be in the nature of patterns of adjustment, but the *yen* father emerges more deliberately than that—to be part of a normative pattern. Here are some examples. A farmer who comes home to find his wife angry at the children because of the pressure of her self-imposed high standards of care, lays down the rules for a simplified family routine, allocating household duties to each member of the family (C63.12.2). A boy eagerly awaits his father's homecoming to tell him his school news, but when he hears the footsteps of two people, he is disappointed because he knows that when his father brings home a guest to talk about work, he never allows interruptions: "Father is a *yen* person anyway" (C62.8.4). In a three-generation family, the patriarchal head (the true progressive) storms into the house and tears up a red banner with traditional New Year inscriptions on it. His cowed wife, who had asked a neighbor to write the banner, orders her grown-up son to fetch brush and ink for his father. The son obeys but starts to explain some misunderstanding. When he sees his father's face he "does not dare continue to cross words" with his father. Without a word, but wearing a stern expression, the father takes up the brush and writes a fiery revolutionary slogan, revealing himself to be the most progressive—and feared—member of the family (C64.8.5).

Fathers and daughters. The father's treatment of the daughter also includes strictness, in accordance with the *yen* image, but it involves even more an element of affection, a pattern harking back to traditional times when the father disciplined the daughter less strictly than he did the son. Yet when in the stories the father's authority is concerned with marriage choice, we see a more complex response pattern. The former Communist line simply condemned arranged marriages; now the values of authority and independence have to meet, as they did in an earlier phase of China's modernization. When such a conflict appears in the present stories, the younger generation shows a minimum of open defiance or indignation; self-determination is not invoked as a right. Instead, some ideological answer resolves the question. Perhaps we may take this as more than a mere literary device; perhaps in real life some ideological crutch can be found to lean on when a child wants to disobey even politically progressive parents.

Here is an example of the strictness of the new ideal father. A girl has worked for a year as an apprentice in a factory, and has done well. People at the factory all praise her; she is successful because "her father disciplines her with strictness" (*kuan-t'a kuan-te chin*) (C66.3.1).

The father-daughter relationship in the stories is characterized above

all by affection, simply portrayed in the case of the man who tells the
news of his election as Production Team Leader to his lame eldest
daughter before he tells anyone else (C63.7/8.1). A daughter confides
in her father about her choice of a husband (C64.3.3). A father com-
forts his little daughter when she is slapped by her mother, humoring
the child with a joke and soft words (C63.12.2). Another father's sentiments are revealed when, having advised his wife not to insist on their
daughter coming home for a vacation, he calls out her name in his sleep
(C64.6.2). Affection can also lead to a kind of camaraderie between
father and daughter, as in the following tale. A girl returns to her village to help with the farmwork and, disappointed at not being met,
starts to walk home carrying her luggage. As she passes a group of farmers she sees her father among them with the cart that was to have carried
her things. The girl accuses her father of failing to meet her at the station, and he retorts, "You are over twenty years of age and possessed
of feet and legs!" Then he adds approvingly, "Such a spirited girl with
big hands and big feet makes a good farmer." The girl then teases him
about book-learning at his advanced age, snatching away his notebook.
Yet this daughter is fundamentally respectful of her father, saying "One
could learn much revolutionary spirit from him" (C64.8.2).

As we have said, in some stories ambiguities arise in the accounts of
the choice of marriage partners. One daughter gets the approval of her
father (C63.2.5), and another loses out because she dare not oppose
her father's incorrect thinking—his insistence on a high brideprice
(C63.2.5). In a more subtle story a carpenter with a history of having
"eaten bitterness" from the rich arranges a match for his daughter with a
hard-working laborer in town. The girl goes from her village to town to
meet and go out with the boy. When later her father asks her opinion,
she hangs her head in demure silence. Unaccustomed to making decisions, she searches her heart for an answer: "Maybe I would do the right
thing if I followed father's advice." But many days later, on the eve of
her wedding trip, she rejects the father's advice, not on the principle of
self-determination, but on the grounds that she is too young to marry
and agricultural work needs her more (C62.12.4).

Another marriage dilemma is "solved" by a literary device. An able
farm girl is much admired by the boys. Her parents, worried about her
reputation and its effect on her marriage prospects, pick up the gossip
that she has chosen a *tui-hsiang*, "an opposite party," and has been ex-
changing messages with him. The mother identifies the *tui-hsiang* as a
cart-driver, a local bumpkin, and she and her husband decide to order
their daughter to have done with the boy in no uncertain terms. Know-

ing that her parents have taken the message-carrier for the boyfriend but not wanting to contradict them, the girl puts on a show of tears and starts to write a letter to break off relations. But every time she echoes her parents' words "Quit him!" she writes down "Let us marry!" All ends well when the parents discover that the true *tui-hsiang* is a young farmer of irreproachable reputation. The mother even meddles a bit on her daughter's behalf by maneuvering a visit to the prospective in-laws' house and "settling the match with the boy's mother" in the absence of the young couple (C63.4.2).

Mothers and sons. In the earlier phase of Communist fiction the mother was portrayed as the socialist producer who put her family duties in second place. In the more recent stories this role, less prominent, is joined by two other kinds of maternal behavior. The mother has the right and duty to take part in the choice of her daughter-in-law. She plays an important part in her son's household. The appearance of so family-oriented a mother is understandable if indeed there is now an emphasis on filial solidarity, since for the integration of the family a dominant father requires a more home-oriented wife less bent on pursuing independent goals.

Although the theme is now less common, we should look first at the way the newer stories carry forward the older Communist image of the mother who sacrifices her duties to her children in favor of her obligations to the socialist society. A progressive factory worker takes her infant on three different buses to her new place of work. She stays late at the factory to learn new techniques and leaves the child in the nursery for long hours (C64.6.2). A woman tractor driver sends her two small children to their maternal grandparents in order to devote all her time to her work (C64.4.3). A mother can *also* be devoted to her family, though the balance may be delicate: as one story shows, too much concern with family welfare, even when motivated by the desire to preserve the health and productivity of busy workers, should be corrected (C63.12.2).

The reappearance of the mother playing a role in the choice of marriage partners is not always met by acceptance. After insisting that all members of her family put on new shirts in honor of the visit of the future daughter-in-law, a mother orders the shy groom to entertain the guest and then to accompany her part of the way home. Although the central interest of the story is the colorful description of the girl's visit, a minor theme is introduced at the very end when the mother wants an early marriage but the young people decide upon a later date (C62.2.4). Sometimes a mother restrains her wish to interfere in her son's marriage plans, as in the case of a widow who, undoubtedly because of her disadvantaged position, agrees to her future daughter-in-law's conditions "for fear of spoiling her son's chances" (C63.6.2). One mother regrets that her son's cultural level is not high enough to attract the right girls and that he is too busy as Secretary of his Party Branch; she appeals to her brother to make a match for his nephew (C63.4.2). Another mother keeps probing until she worms the secret out of her son that he has already chosen a girl, whereupon she at once sends her husband to look the girl over (C64.2.4). These and other attempts at maternal intervention do not appear to be resented by the son; on the whole, the efforts seem to support his own aims.

There are enough instances of the desirability of a mother living with her married son to make this seem a new positive goal. In two stories, sons want their mothers to live with them in their new places of work (C63.1.3; C63.1.4). The mutual need of mother and son is expressed in a story about a teacher who spends his evenings tutoring his mother. She, out of concern for his health, indicates that she has understood the lessons, but the son pleads with her to pursue all unanswered questions in order that he may improve his efficiency as a teacher (C62.8.4). The new sense of the mother's role is epitomized in the highly traditional words of a village woman: "Wait until you bring in five daughters-in-law. Then you will really enjoy the happiness and good fortune of a mother-in-law!" (C62.8.2).

Mothers and daughters. The stories of the mother-daughter relationship do not show so clear a pattern. Perhaps the stories, instead of simply being statements of ideals, reveal more the tensions resulting from the fast emancipation of women during the Communist period. At any rate, we find examples of solidarity and friction, competition or rejection, as well as mutual support.

The ideal mother image of the earlier writings remains—she sacrifices her daughter to her work (C63.9.2)—but the mother is just as likely to be solicitous of her daughter's welfare: she makes shoes for her grown daughter, urges food upon her, and thinks of her with "heartache" (C63.12.2; C64.8.2; C64.6.2). A mother can be harsh (C63.12.2), but she is drawn with sympathy, for she is shown to be eager to provide what she thinks are proper services for her family. But a more reprehensible mother is also described: she is a greedy village woman who advises her daughter against honesty. This mother tries to get her daughter to join her in making a profit from the sale of production-team apricots; but the daughter abandons her in this enterprise, and in the end the mother is exposed in a team meeting (C63.11.4).

Mother-daughter competition shows up in the story of the struggle between two progressive women. The mother, a pig-keeper, refuses her daughter's help, saying that the daughter's time is more valuable to the production team. The mother's real motive, however, is to have the credit all to herself so that she may earn the model-farmer award, since the daughter had received a first prize in the family-contest-and-criticism meeting after she had reported helping her mother with the chores before going off to her own team assignment (C64.6.4).

The ambivalence of the relationship causes the daughter more often than the son to reject the mother's intervention in the choice of a marriage partner. One mother still lives in a bygone world recalling her tears on the eve of her own wedding at the misery of becoming a daughter-in-law; she fails to understand that her daughter weeps over her indecision about whether to marry the good city worker of her father's choice or to remain at home contributing to agricultural production (C62.12.4). In another story, a mother is rebuffed when she tries to get some information out of her daughter about her *tui-hsiang*; the girl will tell only his age and will talk only about his membership in the Youth League. "Mother, how about not asking these questions?" When the mother wants to invite the young man to the house, the girl flatly refuses, and the mother is reduced to calling on him instead (C63.2.5).

In other stories something of the rebellious spirit of the May Fourth era is apparent. A daughter overhears her mother and her maternal aunt plotting a match for her. Despite the girl's objections, the two women invite the boy to a nine-course dinner to impress him; the girl refuses to come out of her room to eat with them and later slips out of the house to cut wood. The boy follows her and meets with an insult about his opportunistic family. The girl all the while has been cultivating a relationship with a childhood friend now in the army (C63.3.1). This sort of open defiance is infrequent. Nevertheless, although the dominant theme in the stories is family consolidation, the newly liberated young girl is described as difficult to keep in a subordinate position.

Boys, girls, and tui-hsiang. Although romantic love is not a prominent theme, the boy-meets-girl situation is a popular subject in the stories. Usually the accounts describe the delicate friendship of two shy young people who meet (the origins of their acquaintance often shrouded in mystery), reach some understanding, and pass the long waiting period before marriage. The shift in interest away from "love" to "getting to know each other" fits in so well with the general family pattern that we seem to have before us in the stories a blueprint for a return to a conservative family policy. But we cannot know whether the accounts mirror real life, or whether they are mere policy statements that may have been interpreted by the writers.

The understanding reached by the young couple is not marked by public ceremony. We may loosely translate *tui-hsiang* as "intended," but it can mean either a special friend of the opposite sex or somebody one is pledged to marry. Thus a young person can go to *kao tui-hsiang* to meet someone chosen as a possible marriage partner by a parent or intermediary, but such a meeting does not bind the young people to any obligation.

The values of the society are clearly represented in the stories. In both boys and girls the desirable qualities are technical skill and willingness to work, good character, and good temperament. Appearance is seldom elaborated beyond a simple description of regular features, sturdy build, and perhaps ruggedness in the boy and competent demeanor in the girl. Shyness and modesty are valued in both boys and girls, but in girls there is the contradictory virtue of being *ta-fang*, socially unreserved and competent. The nation needs the outgoing girl, and yet the new emphasis on the mutually interdependent family of three generations requires the ideal of the self-effacing girl.

A story entitled "Introduction" gives the flavor of the new Communist version of the "semi-arranged" match. Set in the traditionally sophisticated city of Soochow, it concerns a young technical worker (*chi-shu-yuan*) and a waitress in a famous tea-shop. The young man, careless about his clothes, shy and tongue-tied, goes to meet his "intended" with his mother and *erh-shen* (his father's brother's wife). He takes one look at the girl and is ready to leave; he is satisfied but impatient to escape the embarrassment. The aunt points out how rude it would be to leave so quickly, for in the old days such an insult could have led to the girl's suicide. The aunt then goes on to praise the girl's virtue: her good character, good nature, skill at sewing are rare qualities in a modern girl. The mother fears that the girl may look down on the proposed match, but the aunt reassures her that the girl's family has been solid working class for three generations; besides, the boy is a technician, and young ladies nowadays look at the man and not his family background. The aunt then coaches the boy: "The most important thing is your mouth—to talk love depends on your mouth. First impressions are especially important. She wants to understand (*liao-chieh*) you; you want to understand her. So you must talk—about your temperament, your family background ... but not about machines. If she does not understand machines, she would think that you were looking down on her. . . . Then inquire about her sisters and ask if they like the movies. Use that as an excuse and make a date to take them all to the movies. That way you solve the problem of the next meeting. . . . Young ladies are not lions or tigers—they will not bite you." When the little family group comes face-to-face with the girl they greet one another as if the meeting were accidental, and they decide to sit together for a cup of tea. The aunt quickly leads the mother away so that the young people may be left together. Minutes of silence follow, the aunt peeking around the corner in an agony of suspense. The girl starts to play with a flower; it is blown out of her hand, and the boy remarks that if they had a vacuum machine they would be able to catch it. Then the conversation turns to machines, a subject of interest to the girl, contrary to the aunt's prediction. The girl even wants the boy to come and look at a broken *wan-t'an* machine in the tea-shop, and when the boy suggests looking at it the next day, the girl asks, "Why not right now?" The two walk happily away, the mother being restrained from joining them by the alert aunt (C62.9.4).

Dating several people is censured: a girl who is said to have changed *tui-hsiang* three times is looked down upon by her friends (C62.12.4); if a boy has a *tui-hsiang* he feels he should not return the smile of another girl who is interested in him; to do so would be "immoral" and "base" (C62.9.1). But there is an odd kind of innocence in this puritanical code: a man may accept personal services from a girl when there is no marriage pledge between them. A young accountant, who has not yet committed himself, allows a girl admirer to collect his muddy clothes, in full view of their friends, and to wash and deliver them the next day (C62.11.5). Is this merely socialist service to a fellow citizen?

Ambivalence toward the forward girl comes out in the stories. One story (C64.2.1) tells of a boy who, awaiting his city sweetheart's decision, finds a village girl looking for a chance to show her admiration. She stops at his vegetable farm to bring him some choice apricots. Holding out her hands with the fruit concealed in them, she makes him guess what she has hidden. When he puts out his hand to receive the gifts, she jokingly slaps it and rebukes him for not thanking her first (C62.9.1). This is flirting, Communist style. When a girl visits her future husband's house, she goes forward to meet the shy farmer boy, who hesitates to greet her. At the time of parting, the boy has to be told to escort her part of the way, but the girl is ready with a letter explaining her plans for a late marriage. The two sit down by the path to discuss the subject, the boy hesitantly, the girl straightforwardly. Touched by her thoughtfulness, the boy weeps after they part. The girl notices and comes back to comfort him, "holding his right hand in both of hers." At the beginning of this story, the girl, arriving at the boy's house, is met by a group of staring villagers, some commenting on her flowered jacket and long trousers, others on her long black braids. Two older women wonder at the sight of this "modern" girl. One says, "The young ladies nowadays, really!" The other responds: "Yes, they are so *ta-fang,* unlike girls of former days." "Yes," the first woman comes back, "girls never used to be seen by their future husbands' families, let alone come unaccompanied to visit them!" The present-day young woman finds herself in a delicate situation: she is glorified for being capable and progressive, and yet in the appropriate context she must be demure.

Husbands and wives. The new pattern for the relationship between husbands and wives is less ambivalent. On the whole, spouses are portrayed as equal partners, one of them helping (not harshly criticizing) the other in minor ideological deviations. There is joking and good-natured teasing between them, as if marital differences are to be handled with a light touch.

Humor is applied in situations ranging from petty annoyances to fairly serious cases of "incorrect thinking." On the lighter side is the wife who calls her husband "old coffin" and jokingly scolds him because he likes to sing old opera tunes as soon as he gets up. The husband replies, "After so many years of marriage, aren't you yet used to it?" (C64.3.3). The wife of a Party Branch Secretary, who does not visit her for two weeks after she gives birth to their first son, awaits his arrival with a mixture of anger and eager anticipation. She jokingly pretends not to let him in, saying that their son will not call him father. Soon all is forgiven; he is exhausted, and she mends his jacket as he falls asleep at the table (C64.2.4). Husband and wife can vie with each other in being progressive, and can soften their prodding with humor: a Team Leader tactfully leaves his wife a volume of Chairman Mao's works, open at an appropriate page, when he thinks she is growing discouraged in her efforts to learn how to drive a mule-cart, but the wife laughs, "You are firing the cannon after the enemy has gone—I have my own copy!" (C66.3.6).

Soft persuasion and the gentle touch are brought in to settle important differences in political thinking: another Team Leader criticizes his formerly progressive wife for having slipped into family-centered selfishness; in the midst of his lecture the wife asks, "And who wakes you up in the morning?", thus forcing the husband to admit his own weakness and to promise to "reform" (C63.12.2).

Other aspects of the conjugal relationship show nothing remarkable or new. Married life is painted variously, showing now the husband, now the wife, in a more favorable ideological light. We conclude that respect for the older generation is a more important ideological theme than the solidarity of the family.

In-laws. There is a great deal of interest in relationships with in-laws shown in the stories. In several of them, parents bring together the two prospectively affinal families to confirm the match (C63.2.5; C63.4.2; C64.3.3). Even greater attention is given to the selection of children-in-law, the prospective daughter-in-law being discussed far more often than the prospective son-in-law (13 daughters-in-law against 3 sons-in-law). The reason for this disproportionate interest is clear: it is the structural consequence of the conflict between patriliny and the values surrounding the modern girl.

The new ideal is, of course, for the bride to live harmoniously with her parents-in-law. Parents are frequently congratulated on their fortune in having a good son- or daughter-in-law, but the voice of skepticism is also heard, especially from the mouths of village women. One mother remarks, "Daughters-in-law nowadays have deaf ears"; and a neighbor warns a bride, "Beware of being oppressed in your in-law family . . . but no," she corrects herself, "daughters-in-law nowadays are put on a pedestal, beyond oppression" (C63.6.1; C62.14.2).

The ideal characteristics of a girl are those that qualify her as daughter-in-law rather than as wife or mother. In fact, these seemingly old-fashioned virtues are frequently expressed by parents-in-law. A mother has her eye on the girl next door as a bride for her son because she is "good-natured, accustomed to hard work, and *tung-shih* (has social tact)" (C63.4.2).

Few stories describe the daughter-in-law's position after marriage; conflicting expectations in the society make this situation a difficult one to handle. The ideal of the old-fashioned daughter-in-law who holds her tongue in the presence of her elders is mentioned in one story (C64.8.5). And the technique of evasion, so common in the Taiwan stories, is found here too: one mother-in-law, having promised before her son's marriage to allow the new bride to continue her outside activities, is displeased at her daughter-in-law's election as Leader of the Women's Production Brigade; when she advises the younger woman to be an inactive leader, the latter "just smiles" and fails to comply (C63.6.2).

This and another story say a great deal about the potential for conflict in the mother- and daughter-in-law relationship. A woman and her daughter-in-law vie with each other in picking tea until the son orders his wife deliberately to let the mother win the contest. The story ends according to good ideological principles: the girl refuses to "lose," because she must win the village women over to the new technique she is using (C63.1.2). It is not clear in the story, however, that the daughter-in-law has public opinion on her side.

Interpretation of the Communist Stories

We have seen a shift in kinship values from the pre-1962 to the 1962–66 period; presumably other modifications will result from the Cultural Revolution begun in 1966. Nevertheless, the basic Communist dilemma must remain: should family ideals stress authority and dedication to the new society, or should they emphasize rebellion and the assertion of independence? The first emphasis having been chosen in the early 1960's, we find in the fiction a straightforward representation of the policy. The literary criticism of the period confirms the emphasis. But in fact the stories go beyond what was planned when they bring up family matters that are consequences of the official policy.

The significance of the new family ideology for the wider society should be noted, for the parallel between the father-image in the family and the national father-figure is clear. If the family father is strong, competent, ideologically correct, and therefore worthy of respect and emulation, he may be said to possess the respected qualities of the state as father-figure. To honor the progressive elements in the older generation is to preserve the authority of the old revolutionary generation, that of the Long March and the resistance to the Japanese. The family patterns we have discussed are largely those of the rural population, a distortion due partly to the emphasis on agriculture during the period and partly to the fact that stories with urban themes tend to escape our net because they concern the job situation, not the family. We may note, in passing, that a trend parallel to one we have described in the rural stories is found in the urban ones: the respect for age and authority is revealed in the new model of the master-apprentice relationship, in which the experienced *shih-fu* is like a father to the *t'u-ti*.

The stories as a whole show a relatively uniform pattern of father-son relations that is worth noting. The father is occupationally capable and politically progressive, and the son never fails to show the appropriate respect and admiration. In contrast, there is ambivalence in the relations between women of different generations. The mother-daughter relationship is sometimes upset by the daughter's reluctance to accept the mother's intervention in the matter of her marriage. The position of the new daughter-in-law constantly creates potential for conflict: the emphasis on the authority of elders and the basic doctrine of individual responsibility for national goals are results of rival ideologies. That conflict does not show itself as obviously in the relations between fathers and sons does not mean that they have no problems; it suggests that the male generational axis is too central an ideological base to allow the exploration of ambiguities, for this is the relation around which others are built. In contrast, the dilemma of the liberated woman—is she to be independent or demure?—seems to emerge in the stories as a response to ideology, not as a statement of it. A similar response to ideology is the hint that the renewed emphasis on family solidarity may lead to nepotism and family favoritism.

Peer-group relations—sibling ties and friendship—are not at all stressed in the stories. Although the spirit of camaraderie is emphasized throughout Communist writings, the regime at the same time has frowned on strong friendship ties because of their potential threat to national and party loyalty. Because it becomes necessary, therefore, to distinguish between comradeship and intimate friendship, it may be that avoiding the issue of strong sibling ties and friendships is one way out of a dilemma.

The continuity between the themes of the stories and the older tradition must be noted. The Chineseness of these stories is beyond question: the characters are Chinese in their expressions and behavior, in their sense of propriety and "face," and sometimes in their characteristically Chinese way of meeting authority with accommodation. But to judge the full significance of this continuity is premature at this point.

Three Kinds of Fiction in Modern China: Conclusion

Three groups of fictional stories have been discussed in this paper: stories of contemporary Taiwan, of contemporary Communist China, and of the May Fourth era. They need now to be put side by side.

The Communist stories, in the main, attempt to translate official ideology into fiction, and in so doing they reveal patterns of response that arise as consequences of policy. The literature of the May Fourth Movement attacked the prevailing ideology by challenging existing norms; it described reactions to both the rejected old relationships and the innovations. The Taiwan stories represent yet another response of writers to their society: these authors tend to ignore both official ideology and current role definitions, expressing their rejection of both in favor of negation and disengagement.

The May Fourth literature denounced the values of father-son solidarity and respect for age and replaced them with the values of individual development and personal independence. The traditional ideals were making a qualified reappearance in the Communist stories of 1962–

66, but were absent in the Taiwan stories even though these ideals are part of the ideology of the Nationalists. The May Fourth stories reject or only conditionally accept the traditional filial roles. These roles are ignored in the Taiwan stories, but are given approval by the Communist writers. Perhaps because of the critical importance of the filial role, the problematical aspects of the father-son relationship are not explored in the Communist stories, whereas the stories of the 1920's and 1930's abound with situations of conflict between the generations, situations that may be seen as a result of competing ideologies during the early family revolution. In a more limited fashion, the Communist themes of "arranged" marriage and the mother-in-law problem are portrayals of the dilemmas arising from different requirements. In the Taiwan stories, on the other hand, there is no direct confrontation with the revival of traditional ideology, and hence almost no exploration of direct role conflict and resolution.

In the literature of the May Fourth period love is introduced as the basis of marriage; this theme involves fairly rational considerations of the criteria for choosing a mate and of love as an individual person's right. Romantic love loses some of the romance as it is fitted into the life of a generation intent on remaking society. In the Communist stories private emotions in the boy-girl and husband-wife relationships are played down. In the Taiwan stories it is only the intensity of antagonistic feelings between father and son that stands out, not the kind of emotional intensity resulting in positive satisfaction or personal indulgence. Furthermore, there remains in personal encounters a vulnerability to shame and ridicule, a control mechanism that was functional in the traditional society but is now an anachronism. The Chinese self was accustomed to finding meaning in terms of well-defined sets of relationships rather than in terms of the individual; this may be why the characters in all three groups of fiction do not find in romantic love or eroticism any meaning of personal assertion or self-indulgence.

The theme of the revolt of youth, central in the May Fourth stories, takes on an elusive and indirect mien in the Taiwan stories, which as a body represent a token of "rebellion" by a particular young elite against society. By avoiding the issue of generational conflict (except in terms of personal antagonism) and by portraying the disengagement from rights and obligations within the family and the emotional detachment from significant interpersonal relations, the Taiwan stories constitute a psychological response to a social environment. This response, though different, is as significant as the responses to ideology and social structure found in the May Fourth and the Communist stories.

Land and Lineage in Traditional China

JACK M. POTTER

Collective property in the form of ancestral estates was extremely important for the creation, maintenance, and internal structuring of the Chinese lineage. In this paper, I will discuss a number of aspects of the relation between land and lineage in Traditional China (between the twelfth and the twentieth centuries), using material collected in the New Territories of Hong Kong as my primary exemplary data. Going beyond specific cases, I will hypothesize about factors affecting the distribution of strong lineage organization in various parts of China.

Land Tenure and Lineage Segmentation

An important relationship between land and lineage in China was the effect that differential ownership of ancestral property had on the internal segmentation of the lineage, a topic first discussed by Maurice Freedman in *Lineage Organization in Southeastern China*. Freedman hypothesized that differential ownership of common property was responsible for the asymmetrical segmentation of the Chinese lineage. In a more recent work, he notes that his "guess" seems to have been richly confirmed by his experience in the Hong Kong New Territories and by my analysis of the Ping Shan Tang lineage (Freedman 1966: 37ff).

My fieldwork in the New Territories* was aimed specifically at testing whether Freedman's analysis of the internal structure of the Southeastern Chinese lineage was useful and accurate. The Ping Shan data confirmed his analysis in all important respects and supported his hypotheses about the importance of ancestral property in determining the nature of the internal segmentation of Chinese lineages. (See Potter 1968: 22–26 and Ch. 4.)

* My fieldwork in Hong Kong from 1961 to 1963 was supported by the Ford Foundation Foreign Area Training Fellowship Program.

The members of the Tang lineage of Ping Shan live in a cluster of eight villages located near a common central ancestral hall devoted to the founding ancestor of the group. The Tang lineage is a good example of the large, powerful, wealthy, and highly differentiated lineages discussed by Freedman (1958). It represents in many respects the epitome of lineage development in China and is certainly one of the most highly developed lineages that have been studied. Although the Ping Shan lineage has been weakened and has lost many of its functions since it was incorporated into the Colony of Hong Kong in 1898, it is still very much a going concern, and from currrent information it is possible to reconstruct the essentials of its structure and operation in traditional times. The lineage, which dates from the twelfth century, has grown to include about 3,000 persons; over the centuries it has undergone an elaborate process of internal segmentation, so that now there are eight major branches of the lineage. Although the eight villages and the eight lineage branches do not actually coincide, I use village names here for economy of presentation. (To sort out branches and villages would only complicate the discussion without adding to the points I wish to make.)

The process of asymmetrical segmentation has operated from the very first and is now present at all levels of the lineage. Over the centuries the various maximal branches of the lineage have achieved differential success. Three of the branches produced members who have pursued successful careers as scholars, officials, and merchants, many of whom left sizable ancestral estates in trust for their descendants. At present these ancestral estates are the focal points for the internal structure of the lineage, with lineage subsegments being defined in relation to ancestral estates and/or ancestral halls in exactly the way Freedman predicted. (These wealthy and differentiated lineage segments are good examples of lineage structure Type Z, as described and formulated by Freedman.)

The other five branches were made up, in traditional days, of poor peasant farmers and were much less differentiated than the three wealthier branches. (The smaller villages are an almost perfect example of Freedman's Type A lineage. See Freedman 1958: 131ff.) Each poorer branch had only a single ancestral hall for the entire group below the Central Ancestral hall level, and it was a very crude building that was more important as a village meeting place than as a center for ancestor worship.

The differences in structure among the various branches of the lineage are definitely associated with differential ownership of ancestral property. Hang Mei, the major focus of my study, owned about 455 acres of land, 93 per cent of which was held in ancestral estates collectively owned by subbranches of the group. Two other fairly wealthy branches of the lineage, Hang Tau and Fui Sha Wai, owned 86 acres of land each, whereas the other five branches owned only 22, 10, 8, 5, and 2 acres. Although I have no breakdown on the percentages of common land owned by branches other than Hang Mei, it is clear that the five weaker branches had little or no common ancestral property (Potter 1968: 96ff).

The relation between differential property ownership and the internal segmentation of the lineage is evident at a lower level of segmentation within Hang Mei, which is both the wealthiest and the most highly differentiated branch of the Ping Shan Tang lineage. Within the Hang Mei branch there were thirty different ancestral estates that varied from one acre to as much as 178 acres of land (Potter 1968: 98). Four of these ancestral estates were of major importance, and three were physically symbolized in major ancestral halls. The important features of the internal groupings of the Hang Mei branch can be seen in the following figure, much simplified and telescoped for convenience of presentation. In the diagram the Hang Mei branch is shown as Yat T'ai Hall, after the name of the ancestral hall-estate on which it depends. Yat T'ai Hall is the ancestral hall that serves as the ritual symbol and

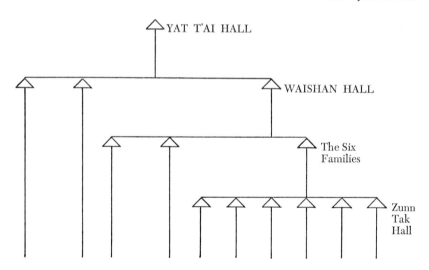

THE STRUCTURE OF THE HANG MEI LINEAGE°

° This diagram is taken from Potter (1966:25) and is reproduced with permission of the University of California Press.

focus of the Hang Mei branch of the lineage, and almost all the Tangs
of Hang Mei are descended from the man in whose honor this hall was
built. Membership in Yat T'ai Hall and the accompanying ownership of
shares in the ancestral property attached to this hall separate Hang Mei
from the other major branches of the lineage with whom the Hang Mei
sublineage shares membership in the central ancestral hall of Ping Shan.

Within the Hang Mei sublineage the three highest level branches are
descended from the three sons of the Yat T'ai Hall ancestor. The process
of asymmetrical segmentation continues to operate at this level. Of the
three Yat T'ai Hall branches the Wai Shan branch is by far the dominant
one in terms of numbers, wealth, and prestige, and it is much more differentiated. Whereas the Wai Shan branch contains 72 families, the
other two branches of Yat T'ai Hall together contain only 33 families.
The Wai Shan branch is further differentiated in a complex fashion by
the presence of several important ancestral estates and ancestral halls,
whereas the other two branches have relatively simple structures. The
only ancestral estates in the other two branches are at the highest level
of segmentation, and these are small and of little consequence. In terms
of prestige, the Wai Shan branch is made up of several subbranches
famous in the New Territories; the other two branches are composed
mainly of tenant farmers and laborers.

Continuing down the Hang Mei genealogical charter, we see that the
Wai Shan Hall branch is further divided into three subsegments descending from the three sons of the Wai Shan ancestor. Of these, the Six
Families is by far the dominant group within Wai Shan Hall. Of the 72
families that belong to Wai Shan Hall, 50 belong to the Six Families
branch and 22 to the other two branches. Again, the Six Families group
is both wealthy in ancestral property and internally highly differentiated, containing several branch ancestral halls. The other two Wai Shan
Hall branches are relatively undifferentiated internally; moreover, they
have little collective property and have no branch ancestral halls.

Finally, the principle of asymmetrical segmentation continues to operate at the lowest levels within the Six Families group. Three of the six
branches that compose this group are ritually separated from the other
branches by branch ancestral halls, and each has its own ancestral estate.
Of the six branches, one branch, Zunn Tak Hall, is the wealthiest and
has more power and prestige than the other five branches. Although at
the Six Families level the branches are only a few generations deep, it
is evident that further differentiation is in process within each of the
groups.

The Ping Shan data show, just as Freedman had predicted, that the internal structure of the Tang lineage is determined by the differential ownership of collective property in the form of ancestral estates. Their 27-generation genealogy presents a great number of potential genealogical points at which the differentiation of social groups within the lineage could occur. But the crucial points of lineage segmentation, at which important subsegments of the lineage are formed, coincide precisely with the genealogical location of sizable ancestral property. Sublineage A separates itself from sublineage B because sublineage A has rights to the ancestral property and the branch ancestral hall left in the name of the ancestor of group A. Sublineage B is in turn separated from other groups in the village because its members are a corporate group that holds ancestral property B in common. Ancestral estates are so important that lineage members usually refer to a subgroup by the name of its ancestral estate. For example, the villagers call the Six Families group "Chap Ng Tsoh," the name of the ancestral estate that is the economic foundation of the group.

The lineage branches and subbranches are, of course, not mutually exclusive units. Almost all lineage members belong to several corporate kin groups and have shares in several associated ancestral estates. At the lowest level of lineage segmentation a person shares with his brothers in the ancestral property left by his father. If he is a member of a highly differentiated and elaborately segmented group like Zunn Tak Hall, he has a share in the property of this estate at the grandfather level, and he also has a share in Chap Ng Tsoh, the ancestral estate of the Six Families branch of the lineage. Since the Six Families are, in turn, one of the three branches of Wai Shan Hall, this person—ego—will also have a share in the ancestral property of the Wai Shan ancestor and be a member of the group formed in relation to Wai Shan Hall. Still further up the Hang Mei genealogical charter, since Wai Shan Hall is one of the three groups that make up Yat T'ai Hall, ego will also have a share in this estate and be a member of this hall. Since the Hang Mei sublineage is one branch of the Ping Shan Tang lineage, which includes all of the eight villages, ego is a member of the Ping Shan lineage and has rights in the Central Ancestral Hall and its estate. Moving further still, we find that ego is also a member of the Tang clan of the New Territories, which includes several major lineages similar to the Ping Shan branch such as the Kam Tin and the Ha Tsuen.

The asymmetrical structure of the lineage insures that power is not equally distributed among the segments as it would be in a more homogeneous society. In Ping Shan the Six Families group, with their very rich ancestral estate, have predominant power, wealth, and prestige.

This is because their wealth and numbers enable them to dominate proceedings within the Wai Shan Hall group, and since Wai Shan Hall is by far the most powerful segment of Yat T'ai Hall, the Six Families are also able to dominate the Hang Mei branch of the lineage and therefore the lineage itself. It is no accident that the most important leaders of Ping Shan have come from the Six Families branch of Hang Mei. If the Ping Shan example is at all representative, the distribution of political power within Chinese lineages may be said to have been determined largely by the distribution of ancestral property. This must also have been true in traditional society, for landed wealth in the form of ancestral estates enabled wealthy branches to educate sons for the examinations, making it probable that wealthy branches would have more prestige and political connections than poorer branches. Again, if Ping Shan is a reliable example, it appears that the wealthier branches on the whole had more members than the poorer branches, adding strength of numbers to their preponderant wealth and prestige.

Even the ancestor cult of the Ping Shan lineage is greatly influenced by the differential distribution of ancestral land. The internal divisions within the lineage, defined in relation to important ancestral estates, are reinforced by the cult. In Ping Shan, worship at ancestral halls and tombs occurs mainly in the fall of the year. Then, during a period of about one month, members of the lineage spend day after day marching out into the countryside to worship at the ancestral tombs. Usually starting with the most remote ancestor and moving down the genealogical ladder, they ritually define all important features of the lineage structure. On a fixed day, all the Tangs in the New Territories come together to worship the first ancestor who settled there. On subsequent days, all the men in Ping Shan worship the founder of the Ping Shan lineage, thus ritually separating themselves from the other maximal Tang lineages of the New Territories. Then all men of the Hang Mei branch go as a group to worship their common ancestor; in effect they are ritually recognizing their separation from the other major branches of Ping Shan. On subsequent days, the three branches of Yat T'ai Hall separate to worship their own ancestors' tombs; then the three branches of Wai Shan Hall do likewise. Finally the separate families of the Six Families group divide to worship their respective ancestors.

The ancestral rites are important occasions because they symbolize the social structure and define membership at the different levels of lineage segmentation. Most members of the Hang Mei branch of the lineage, for example, usually do not read the genealogical charter set down in the clan register and are only vaguely aware of the intricate pattern of segmentation within the lineage, particularly at the highest levels. During the complex ceremonial cycle the various groupings within the lineage divide to worship at separate ancestral graves, becoming progressively smaller as they move down the genealogical ladder. This enables all members to see just how closely they are related to every other member of their lineage. One old gentleman of the Tang lineage, when asked how the men of the lineage remember their genealogical charter, said (without prompting) that it would be difficult if it were not for the yearly ancestral sacrifices when people can see clearly just how closely they are related to everyone else and how the different groups are related at all levels. The men of most groups marching off into the countryside to worship an ancestral grave have only the vaguest notion about who the ancestor is or what his exact position is in the genealogy. Usually all they know is the name of the grave itself. So in effect when they carry out collective ancestral rites at the grave, they are actually worshiping little more than a symbol of the group itself![*]

The ritual structure of the lineage is directly related to the distribution of ancestral property. Collective worship takes place in most cases only at graves that have land attached to them to pay for the expenses of worshiping and the distribution of sacrificial pork. Graves of remote ancestors attached to little or no ancestral property are seldom visited. On those rare occasions the descendants pay for their own ceremonial expenses and worship at the grave singly as families, not collectively. Graves not connected with ancestral estates are ignored after a few generations and are not even ritually recognized as important reference points for the internal segmentation of the lineage. Ritual structure, in this instance, closely follows the social structure of the lineage, and both are closely related to the economic structure.

Ancestral Estates and Lineage Solidarity

Implicit in the discussion so far is the view that collectively owned land in the form of ancestral estates is a *sine qua non* for the development of strong lineage organizations in China. There were, of course, lineages in China that owned little or no collective property, but these were lineages in name only, whose functions were limited to perfunctory ritual and whose solidarity was at best diffuse. Collective property basically financed the building of ancestral halls and supported ancestor worship; most important, however, was the role of ancestral estates in attracting lineage members for economic reasons and in maintaining lin-

[*] The relevance of Durkheim's ideas to this situation is clear.

eage solidarity. As in almost all other discussions of the Chinese lineage, I must start with a quotation from Freedman:

When the landlord was often the agnatic group of which the tenant was a member, and when being a member of such a group meant having a prior right to tenancy, the poorer people had every reason to stay in the community rather than go to try their luck elsewhere. In other words, the surplus economy of the region, mediated by the institution of collective ownership, created a fund of property which tended to keep the lineage members at home. When corporate land was either rented out to members of the corporation or circulated for use among them, the privilege proved a centripetal force. (Freedman 1958: 127.)

It is true that poor farmers who belonged to weaker branches of a large landowning lineage were sometimes able to rent land from their lineage or one of its subbranches with secure tenure and sometimes at a price much lower than they would pay elsewhere (Fei and Chang 1945: 77ff); thus they were given a strong incentive to remain members in good standing of their lineage. However, this economic benefit for poorer members of a lineage should not be overemphasized: arrangements for renting land to lineage members varied greatly from lineage to lineage. In the Tang lineage of Ping Shan most tenant farmers of the lineage rented land from branches of which they were not members, and usually they were charged the same rate as outsiders (Potter 1968: 81). This is not peculiar to Ping Shan, for many lineages specified in their rules that ancestral property should be rented to outsiders (Liu 1959: 111). The reason for this was that business relations and kinship obligations tended not to mix very well and often ended in ill feeling between lineage members. Fei and Chang (1945: 78) mention a case in Yunnan in which the lineage manager had great difficulty collecting proper rent from tenants who were members of his own lineage, and I suspect that this was not an isolated example. But in spite of these exceptions, it does seem that ancestral property did give economic advantages (if only in terms of secure tenure) to some poorer members of a lineage.

Another important attraction of ancestral estates for lineage members, and one that perhaps has not been fully recognized, is the personal income for lineage members that sometimes was provided by division of surplus funds. In the Ping Shan Tang lineage the collectively owned ancestral land is so extensive that many branches of the lineage receive a sizable personal income even after the ritual expenses have been paid. Members of the wealthier branches often receive sufficient income to support their families without having to work for a living. Members of lineage groups that are so wealthy have such a strong economic interest in remaining with their group that only few would permanently leave their lineage.

Over the centuries, maintaining a strong lineage organization was made easier once this degree of wealth had been achieved. Members of really wealthy lineages were furnished with such a secure economic base that they could devote all their attention to studying for the Imperial Examinations or engaging in commercial enterprises to further increase the wealth, power, and prestige of their group. In most parts of China family wealth and position seldom lasted for more than a few generations; families tended to decline rapidly as a result of the rule of partible inheritance. But this principle did not operate, or operated much more slowly, for members of wealthy lineages. Unlike family property, which rapidly disintegrated in a few generations, ancestral estates were more permanent; this gave members of such groups a much greater opportunity for social mobility than was enjoyed by members of weaker kinship groups. Large ancestral estates, then, exerted a powerful attraction for even the wealthier members of a lineage because the secure economic base of the ancestral estate allowed them to compete for social honors and, if unsuccessful, return in their old age to live as "termites of the ancestral hall." Wealthier lineages or lineage branches were probably more stable than poorer lineage groups because they offered economic benefits to all members, both rich and poor. Collective property was then crucial for the maintenance of a strong lineage organization.

There were, of course, other factors such as mutual aid and protection, prestige, and sentiment that served to maintain solidarity among Chinese kinsmen. These factors were important, but the economic attractions of collectively owned ancestral property were necessary and primary factors in maintaining a strong lineage organization. Although it is difficult to prove this argument, there are synchronic and diachronic arguments that serve to support it. For example, the correlation in the Hong Kong New Territories between the presence of common landholdings and strong lineage organization is significant. Moreover, my study of the changes that have taken place in the Tang lineage of Ping Shan in recent years strongly suggests that the common property of the ancestral estates was the only factor preventing the disintegration of the group in the modern social and economic context. Over the half century since the incorporation of the Tang lineage into the Colony of Hong Kong, the lineage has lost its main legal, political, and prestige functions and has probably become sentimentally less important than in traditional days. The lineage is, however, still in existence as a going concern largely because the immense holdings of ancestral land still motivate members to retain membership in the group (Potter 1968: 167). Without the economic attraction of the ancestral lands, the Tang lineage would soon cease to be socially important. This research indicates that common property was the most important single element maintaining the traditional lineage organization. Conversely, the fate of lineage organization in Communist China suggests that the confiscation of lineage property during the land reform was probably crucial in the destruction of lineage organization there.

The Distribution of Strong Lineages in Traditional China

Almost every scholar who has written about the Chinese lineage has made the observation that strong lineages were more prevalent in South and Central China than in the North (Hsiao 1960: 326; Hu 1948: 11; Lang 1946: 178; Freedman 1958: 1), and the evidence we have on the distribution of lineages appears to support this opinion (Hsiao 1960: 327; Gamble 1954: 53ff; Gamble 1963: 14ff; Hu 1948: 14ff; M. Yang 1945: 134). Nevertheless, our evidence on the distribution of strong lineages in China is meager, and, as Freedman (1966: 159) says, we must accept this conclusion with caution. One reason for caution is that much of the empirical evidence advanced to support this conclusion is phrased in terms of the presence or absence of single-surname villages; it is reasoned that lineage organization will be strong in a village inhabited entirely by one surname group. But this is a shaky premise, for it is quite possible that a single-surname village may lack property, power, and organization, and at the same time form a lineage in name only. I know of many cases in the New Territories where tenant villages of the powerful Ping Shan Tang lineage were inhabited by a single-surname group, all the members of which were descended from a common ancestor yet lacked ancestral halls and common property. Furthermore (and I know this from hearsay only), several villages in the Yuen Long area of the New Territories were inhabited by members of more than one surname group and yet one or more groups still exhibited an extremely strong lineage organization. If this is at all representative of other parts of China, it should caution us against always correlating single-surname villages with strong lineage organization.

Another reason for caution is that even in parts of China, such as Kwangtung Province, where large and powerful lineages exist, the number of such lineages is only a small percentage of the total number of lineages in any given area. For example, in the several hundred villages in the Hong Kong New Territories, only a few lineages were really prominent. Strong and well-developed lineages were, then, rare even in Kwangtung Province (of which, up to 1898, the New Territories was part).

We have so little information about lineages in North China that it is simply not possible to say anything conclusive about the distribution of strong lineages there, although the literature does describe several North China lineages that appear to be fairly well developed. The lineages in Ten Mile Inn, as described by the Crooks (1959: 12f), were apparently strong and well organized. Gamble (1963: 14) also mentions a village in Hopei Province that formed a lineage of several hundred members owning all the village property in common. Hsiao (1960: 324) mentions in passing a case in Chihli where 24 villages were inhabited by one surname group. Gamble (1963: 229) describes a village that contained a prosperous lineage descended from an immigrant from Kiangsu Province. In an earlier work, although Gamble does not stress the presence of strong lineages in Ting Hsien, some examples he gives of lineage activity indicate lineages with wealth and organization (Gamble 1954: 392ff).

These random examples from North China (and unfortunately we do not know how random they are) at least suggest that strong lineages were by no means absent in that area. Given the present state of knowledge concerning the distribution of large, powerful, wealthy, and differentiated lineages in China, I will proceed on the assumption that some strong lineages were found throughout China but that there were more strong lineages in the central and southern parts of the country. This differential distribution of lineage organization in China can be explained only by the joint effect of several variables—cultural, social, political, ecological, and economic—a task of explanation that I do not attempt here. Why the Chinese were more motivated than other traditional peasant groups to use lineages as important features of their social structure is a question that also requires a complex explanation. It is sufficient here to say that the cultural values of the Chinese underlay the formation of lineages, and I, with Freedman (1966: 8), will proceed on the assumption that the Chinese had the desire to form as strong and prestigious a lineage village as they were capable of forming. Given this motivation, it was no more possible for every group to organize a strong lineage than it was for every person to establish and maintain a patrilineal extended joint family over several generations. Culturally defined ends are pursued in an environment whose means and conditions profoundly affect their realization. Only if certain conditions were present was it likely that a strong lineage organization could be created and maintained. What were these conditions?

Perhaps the most obvious and often mentioned set of factors affecting the distribution of strong lineages in China is ecological and economic. Since the distribution of rice agriculture in China corresponds to the area in which the strongest lineages are found, it seems reasonable to assume that this association was not mere chance. Freedman (1966: 159f) has suggested such a correlation; Hu (1948: 15) states that strong lineages were present in the agriculturally richer sections of the country; and Hsiao (1960: 329) has written that in the poorer regions of China strong lineages were not found because poverty made it impossible to gather the surplus necessary to support a lineage organization.

Going a step beyond these opinions, I will tentatively hypothesize about the relation between agriculture, land tenure, and lineage organization. I suggest that one of the reasons strong lineages are less prevalent in North China is that the ecological factors of soil, rainfall, and climate allow an agricultural system less productive than that of the south. Wheat, millet, and kaoliang, the major crops of China north of the Hwai River, give on the average a much smaller yield per unit area than southern rice crops. Basing his statements on information supplied by O. E. Baker, Cressey cites average yields of 124 catties per mow for wheat, 144 catties per mow for millet, and 271 catties per mow for rice agriculture (1934: 100). Rice agriculture, then, yields on a single-crop basis as much as wheat and millet combined. As one moves south in China the growing season becomes progressively longer, and two-crop rice agriculture becomes more common. It is clear that the south is agriculturally richer than the north in terms of total production. What is not so commonly realized is that per capita income was not balanced by a greater density of population in the central and southern rice regions (Buck 1937: 45). On the average, the Chinese in the central and southern parts of the country were wealthier than in the north because their production per capita was one-fifth greater. This difference in agricultural productivity was of great significance for large-scale lineage organization; the agriculturally richer central and southern rice regions had enough surplus on the average to finance lineage organizations more easily than poorer regions of China.

It was much easier for a lineage to get started in the south than it was in the north. Although the old adages "land breeds no land" and "one can't get rich in agriculture alone" generally held for all of China, they were probably less true in the south than they were in the north. In South China, and especially in the two-crop rice region, it was possible for a small group to save enough from rice agriculture to purchase a small estate, add to it over several generations, and gradually accumulate the economic base necessary for a modest ancestral estate. This situation must have been even more typical before the southern part of the country was completely settled and the population density had increased. Freedman suggests that some lineages could establish a landed economic base by jointly carrying out reclamation projects (1966: 159–61); such opportunities were more frequent in the south than in the north, where irrigation was much less common. In the southernmost part of China there was a constant ebb and flow of small ancestral trusts within the successful branches of already established lineages and in small undifferentiated lineages (Freedman 1966: 35). These represented initial (and mostly rather feeble and short-lived) attempts to establish a property base on which to develop a stronger lineage. Of the thirty ancestral land estates in the village of Hang Mei in the New Territories, 50 per cent were from one to fifteen acres in size (Potter 1968: 97). These represented budding attempts at establishing important lineage subsegments. Only a small percentage of these attempts resulted in the establishment of strong lineages or strong subbranches within larger lineages, but the potential was always there. These efforts were probably much more frequently successful in the south than in the north. Freedman suggests that "we cannot understand the differential development of minor segments within the lineage unless we take account of the perpetual ebb and flow of small trusts" (Freedman 1966: 35). These small trusts are particularly significant because they illustrate a phenomenon that explains in part the differential distribution of strong lineage organization in China. The roots of lineage organization were continually sending up shoots in the agriculturally more productive environment of South China, while lineage shoots were rapidly stunted in the less favorable agricultural milieu of the north.

Not only were lineages more likely to appear in the south, they were also more likely to grow into powerful, wealthy, and enduring organizations. It took time to create a strong and wide-ranging lineage in China, and it was difficult to maintain lineage strength over long periods. As Liu (1959: 98) notes, "in looking over the history of many clans, one finds that they have not lasted very long. Either their line of descent has become disrupted, or their descendants have dispersed far away from the native place. In the latter case, nine out of ten clans no longer enjoy prosperity." To maintain itself and grow in numbers and wealth a lineage had to increase its base of common property and preserve its residential compactness. In the north, for example, less productive agriculture was not the only factor that weakened a lineage's strength and lessened its chances for survival. Uncertain rainfall and frequent droughts coupled with annual floods and famines resulted in a constant movement and shifting of population to escape these natural disasters. If we also consider the population movements resulting from invasions and wars in the North China Plain over the centuries, it is easy to understand just how difficult it would be for a lineage to maintain its common property base and residence over long periods of time. From numerous examples of these large population movements, Gamble (1954: 3f) describes a relevant case:

The T'ang and Sha rivers that flow from west to east across the hsien have often been the scenes of bloody battles as the armies of the succeeding dynasties have fought up and down the coastal plain. In 1401 Yen Wang and his army swept through Ting Hsien on the way to Nanking. He besieged, assaulted, and captured the walled hsien city and so depopulated the area that it is said that at the time "the roof swallows nested in the trees." The area was repopulated later by bringing in large numbers of famine sufferers from Shansi. Many of the present Ting Hsien families trace their lineage back to ancestors who came from Shansi at that time.

Such disasters were apparently much more frequent in North China than in South China, where more favorable agricultural conditions prevailed and the civil unrest caused by competing armies near the northern centers of power was less frequent.

The factors we have discussed, although important, by no means give a complete explanation of the differential distribution of strong lineage organization in China. Since large landholdings in the form of ancestral estates were necessary to maintain a strong lineage organization, the presence or absence of the capital necessary to purchase land and create the economic base for a strong lineage must be explained. Although it was occasionally possible in rich agricultural regions to create a lineage estate through agricultural savings alone, most lineages were established by one or a few wealthy ancestors who bequeathed a large ancestral estate, and, of course, it was much easier to establish a lineage this way. In traditional Chinese society, land was the most common investment for accumulated wealth because it was fairly secure, permanent, and gave high social prestige. Since in traditional times wealth came mainly from an official or business career, it follows that the more wealthy and affluent men a given area could produce, the stronger the lineages would be.

Wealth gained from official careers was an important source of funds for founding lineages in all parts of the empire. Although the distribution of successful examination graduates was not even, every part of China had some successful candidates who might enter official careers. The considerable wealth that could be obtained this way was often used to buy land and establish lineages, and thus a certain number of fairly strong lineages would be found in all parts of the country. I suspect that most strong lineages in the north and in other poorer sections of the country were founded in this way by wealthy officials.

Commerce was the other method of obtaining wealth sufficient to establish ancestral estates that could serve as economic bases for building a powerful lineage. However, opportunities to gain sizable fortunes from commerce were not equal for people living in different sections of the empire. From Sung times on, Central and South China were not only the richest agricultural regions of China, but were also the most commercially developed. This can be explained partly by the presence of an agricultural surplus that stimulated trade and partly by the presence of foreign trade. Wealthy merchants were also found in North China, but wealth gained from commerce was more prevalent in the central and southern regions. Much of this commercial capital was invested in land, and some of it was left as ancestral land vested in lineages. Since merchant capital was an important addition to capital gained from official careers, again we would expect to find a greater number of powerful lineages in the central and southern regions of the empire, and especially in the more commercially developed areas. We see, then, that although lineage organization has usually been considered a "primitive" form of social organization, in China it was in the more "modern" and more economically developed regions that lineage organization was most developed.

Another variable that affected the distribution and strength of Chinese lineage organization was the degree of governmental control in a given rural area. Governmental control was strongest near the capital; it was especially weak in rural areas such as Fukien, Kwangtung, and other border regions where minority languages were spoken. In such weakly controlled areas, conditions often approached a state of near anarchy, and strong lineage organization was one method of mutual protection and self-help. The lineage here would take on important legal, political, and military functions, whereas in areas more closely controlled by the central government these functions would be deemphasized by the lineage. Hu (1948: 98) notes that the imperial government only tolerated a lineage organization strong enough to maintain effective control over its members. When lineages grew too large and powerful, the government saw this as a direct threat to its power and authority and exerted every effort to limit lineage strength (Hsiao 1960: 353). Given the more or less natural tendency for lineages to assume as much power as possible, it seems that there would be a definite correlation between weak governmental control and strong lineages.

This supposition has temporal as well as geographical implications. It is highly probable that the strength of the Chinese lineage was greatly influenced by the dynastic cycle. During periods of dynastic decline, lineages increased their strength and influence on the local level. Once imperial control was reestablished, the power of the local lineages diminished in proportion to the distance they were from the seats of imperial authority.

Another important and related variable affecting the distribution of lineages in China was the value of strong lineage organization in settling frontier areas (Freedman 1966: 162f). It was no accident that strong lineage organization was characteristic of South and Southeastern China, both frontier areas settled late in Chinese history. In the great southward migration Chinese agriculturalists moved into areas inhabited by non-Han minority peoples, establishing themselves mainly by force as enclaves within hostile populations. They had to protect their property and lives, sometimes for centuries, against these hostile peoples with little aid from the Chinese government (Wiens 1954). Under frontier conditions, strongly organized and highly integrated lineages were almost essential for continued survival, and the land won by these pioneering lineages often provided the economic base for strong organization that lasted down through the centuries. This pattern describes the history of the powerful Tang lineages of the Hong Kong New Territories, which settled that area as early as the twelfth century. At that time they occupied the best valley land, a property base that together with tight organization assured their domination of this area for almost a thousand years (Potter 1968: 22ff). Other things being equal, it is probable that lineages in frontier areas tended to be stronger than lineages in more anciently settled areas of the country.

This hypothesized connection between frontier settlement and strong lineage organization seems to hold for Kwangtung and other areas of Southeastern China. There is some indication that in Yunnan Province, another area of late settlement in Chinese history, lineage organization was stronger than in Central China at least (Fei and Chang 1945: 11), although Hsu disputes this (1948: 129n). The lineage situation in Szechuan is another example of how lineage organization thrived in frontier conditions: after bandits had massacred a large part of the population in the seventeenth century, settlers came, formed many clans, and occupied large areas (as many as several thousand mow) where they established single-lineage settlements (Hsiao 1960: 324). This evidence, though meager, suggests that, in Sahlins' terms (1961: 323), under frontier conditions the Chinese lineage could serve as an effective "organization of predatory expansion," as "a social means of intrusion and competition in an already occupied ecological niche."

The hypothesized factors favorable to the development of a strong lineage—a rich agricultural environment, frontier conditions, the absence of strong governmental control, and commercial development—all were present in the New Territories of Hong Kong, where the Ping Shan Tang lineage flourished. One of the strongest lineages described in the literature, the Ping Shan Tang lineage is located on a rich and productive rice plain in the two-crop rice region of southernmost China. The sizable ancestral estates owned by the lineage and its subsegments were partly obtained during the first settlement of the area. Because it is in one of the richest agricultural regions of China, the income from its extensive ancestral estates has been high, furnishing funds to build ancestral halls, keep the fields in good repair, pay taxes, supply charity for needy members, and still have enough surplus to furnish a substantial personal income for members of the wealthier branches of the lineage. The Tang lineage is a good example of how a strong lineage can arise under frontier conditions and be maintained under favorable environmental conditions.

Furthermore, the Tang lineage developed in a region long on the fringes of the empire, where imperial control was notoriously weak and the countryside often approached a condition of near anarchy. In this situation the Tang lineage took on important political and military functions, protecting its property and honor against the inroads of other lineages in the vicinity, and using its economic power, influence, and strength of numbers to exploit weaker tenant lineages over whom the Tangs for centuries had exercised almost despotic control. That the Tang lineage has been strongly organized is directly related, I believe, to its distance from the seat of imperial control. Finally, the Tangs were located in one of the most commercially developed areas of China, only thirty miles from Hong Kong and ninety miles from Canton, one of the oldest centers of foreign trade in China. Although reliable information on the history of the lineage is lacking, it is probable that part of the success of the Tangs was due to the merchants produced by the group, who have added to the ancestral estates by wealth gained through commerce.

The evidence represented by the Ping Shan data would support a hypothesis that the strongest lineages would tend to be found in the agriculturally most productive two-crop rice regions of China, in frontier regions far from central government control, and especially in areas where industry and commerce were highly developed. The weakest lineages would tend to be located in North China's poorest agricultural areas, in long-settled areas where effective governmental control was present, and in regions characterized by subsistence agriculture and little commercial development. Moreover, in all areas lineage organization would tend to be weaker under strong dynasties and stronger in interregnal periods or under weak dynasties.

The four variables affecting the distribution of lineage organization in Traditional China—basic environmental features affecting agricultural productivity, the degree of commercial development, the degree of effective governmental control on the local level, and the presence or absence of frontier conditions—can form a set of interrelated hypotheses that, if validated by further research, would allow us to predict when and where strong lineage organization tended to appear in Traditional China.

The Chinese Genealogy as a Research Source

JOHANNA M. MESKILL

The Chinese genealogy (*chia-p'u, tsu-p'u, tsung-p'u*, etc.) has only recently begun to receive the attention it deserves. The very nature of the
document, its confidential character as an internal record of a kinship
group, kept it out of the hands of outsiders until the 1930's and the time
of the war, when hundreds of genealogies first became available (Makino 1936: 261, 273; Hu 1948: 51). Many are now in the public domain
and are accessible to scholars in public or university libraries. Many
more, of course, remain in private hands, and some, at least in Taiwan
and the New Territories of Hong Kong, are occasionally made available
to researchers.

In the past, limited access to genealogies was matched by limited interest. As pioneers in the study of preliterate societies, anthropologists
at first stressed field observation and oral evidence even when they studied literate societies such as China; early field reports by anthropologists
and sociologists on individual Chinese communities and kinship structure gave only passing attention to genealogical materials (Fei 1939:
84; Yang 1948: 135, 137–38; Hsu 1948: 122). Only in the last few years
have some of the younger scholars in the field begun to pay more attention to genealogies. Meanwhile the use of the genealogy as a docu-
mentary source, outside the context of fieldwork, had been pioneered
by the Japanese sociologist Makino Tatsumi (Fairbank and Banno 1955:
242–43) and, in the United States, by Wolfram Eberhard and Hui-chen
Wang Liu (Eberhard 1954–56 and 1962; Liu 1959). Similarly, historians have made little use of genealogies. What could become their most
worthwhile field of inquiry, the history of individual families and kinship groups, has barely begun, though Denis Twitchett has pioneered
here with his history of the Fan clan, and Eberhard has tried to reconstruct the histories of two South Chinese clans (Twitchett 1959; Eberhard 1962).

My study of the Wu-feng Lins, perhaps the most prominent lineage of mid-Taiwan in the late nineteenth and early twentieth centuries, combines the resources of the genealogy, of fieldwork, of the voluminous historical record, and of the various administrative surveys and statistical inquiries undertaken by the Japanese government-general at the turn of the century. This should be the first study that will permit us to gauge the methodological value of the genealogy as a historical source in comparison with a variety of other materials.

For the purposes of this paper, I draw on my acquaintance with various Taiwanese genealogies and a small sample of genealogies in the Columbia Library, in addition to an indirect knowledge of a large set of printed genealogies that has been analyzed for us in a recent splendid bibliographical study by Taga Akigoro (Taga 1960a). Taga provides an inventory of nearly 3,000 genealogies, of which about 500 are in the libraries of mainland China, close to 1,000 in the United States, and over 1,200 in Japanese libraries.

Limitations of the Sample of Available Genealogies

Taga has studied some of the characteristics of the genealogies in Japanese libraries. His conclusions, and Liu's in regard to the smaller group she studied in the Columbia Library, suggest certain limitations in our sample of the publicly available printed genealogies.

First, the geographic distribution of the printed genealogies in the public domain is uneven, a heavy majority of them coming from the lower Yangtze valley and especially its urban centers; Kiangsu and Chekiang, for instance, make up over three-fifths of the 1,228 genealogies examined by Taga and an even higher proportion of the 151 genealogies whose places of origin Liu has identified (Taga 1960a: 63; Liu 1959: Appendix Table 1). In Liu's sample, Anhwei and Hupeh are the places of origin of the next largest groups of genealogies. Taga's sample, moreover, clusters heavily in certain very wealthy centers, especially in those cities that have had a long tradition of orthodox Chu Hsi Confucianism. We know even less of the distribution of the much larger group of printed or manuscript genealogies still in private hands, but they seem to be numerous in Southeast China, to judge from those available in Taiwan and Hong Kong's New Territories. It would be unrealistic to hope that genealogies in private hands can ever be collected or inventoried; this especially applies to genealogies that may survive today on the mainland, where such documents are distinctly out of favor with the authorities (Freedman 1966: 179–80).

What does the geographic distribution of the known printed genealogies mean? Since the genealogies come predominantly from the wealthiest section of China, one that in recent centuries moreover has produced the largest share of scholar-officials, but one where lineage organization was only moderately well developed,* we may have to revise our ideas about what it took to produce printed genealogies. It may be that, far from having to be well organized to produce a genealogy, a lineage need barely exist. In the case of many first editions of genealogies, at any rate, the editing and printing of a genealogy created the organized kinship group, rather than vice versa. That is, making a formal genealogy may have been the first step on the road that led an agnatic group to incorporate property and thus to create itself a lineage. Even updated editions of older genealogies, except for those printed at frequent intervals, do not necessarily presuppose that a highly organized lineage maintained itself in the interval between editions. In many instances, all it seems to have taken to produce a first or later edition of a genealogy was a few wealthy individuals who could defray the printing and other expenses. That "charter and grouping may interact" (Freedman 1966: 28, in a somewhat different context) is clear from the following episode from a Shantung village:

Recently, three leading families of the [Yang] clan having risen economically and socially, the clan decided to have a copy of the clan book brought from their kinsmen in a neighboring village [which was used to help make the new genealogy]. This action stirred up a great deal of clan consciousness among the younger members and as a consequence quite a few of them advocated the strengthening of the interrelationship among the clan's families. (Yang 1948: 135; see also Liu 1959: 98.)

A similar thing happened in the case of the Wu-feng Lin genealogy. After a period of several decades when lineage organization had languished, the work on the genealogy marked a revival of formal kinship organization under the aegis of two or three prominent members. These same men were the leading spirits in the erection of a clan temple and the formation of a clan association in nearby Taichung at about the same time.

Another limitation of the sample of genealogies may be put as a question: if the printed genealogies are proof mainly of the wealth of some editors, rather than the degree of prior organization of the kinship group, are we to assume that only wealthy persons and their immediate kin are covered in the genealogies? Not necessarily. Printed genealogies, since they most often relate to the kind of lineage Freedman has designated Model Z—a large, highly segmented lineage with considerable

* Liu (1959: 13) speculates that lineage sentiments may have been strong enough in Southeast China as late as the thirties to prevent massive sales of genealogies from that region.

social differentiation in its membership (Freedman 1958: 132)—will usually include agnates at varying levels of the socioeconomic scale, but the wealthy and prominent have a better chance to be included and fully covered than the poor and insignificant. Clan rules in fact had to warn against this unequal treatment of kinsmen (a fourteenth-century rule to that effect is quoted by Eberhard 1954–56: 212), but the bias was probably inevitable. The heavier representation of the prominent and rich on the editorial boards accounts for it, and so does the greater wealth of the data; since the richer and more prominent segments of a lineage usually held more corporate property, they also presumably kept more careful records of their membership than did the poorer less literate segments. These circumstances, and the purpose of the gene-alogy, which will be discussed further on, probably weighted the record inevitably in favor of the prominent and wealthy.

Keeping these geographic and socioeconomic limitations in mind, we see that certain standard demographic questions should not be asked of the genealogy. For example, I suspect that data in genealogies bearing on age at marriage or life expectancy reflect upper-class conditions rather than those prevailing among a cross-section of the population.

Data on the segmentation of kinship groups are also affected by this upper-class bias of the genealogies. Since there is a tendency to "shed" or "slough off" humbler segments from the genealogical record, we can never know whether a configuration such as that illustrated below re-flects a biological fact (the extinction of one branch) or a social reality —the "sloughing off" of the poor relations by their mightier cousins. This example is adapted from the Wu-feng Lin genealogy (Lin 1935).

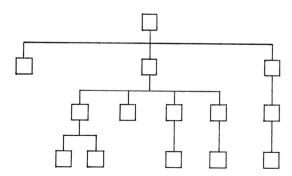

A final limitation of our sample has to do with its chronological spread. Taga's Japanese set is weighted heavily in favor of the nine-teenth and twentieth centuries; in fact, up to 1937, genealogy making hardly seemed to slow down. Out of a total of 1,197 datable genealogies, only fourteen originated prior to the Ch'ing. Since the accidents of preservation favor the newer genealogy, something like this distribution was to be expected. But how much we have lost is suggested by another of Taga's tabulations, in which he estimates the rate of genealogy production by the dates of all the prefaces of earlier editions that appear in his 1,228 extant genealogies (Taga 1960a: 58 and table facing page 60). I have combined the two sets of figures in a table as follows:

ESTIMATED PRODUCTION AND PRESERVATION OF GENEALOGIES BY PERIOD

Period	Dated genealogies in Japan		Dated prefaces in genealogies	
	Number	*Per cent*	*Number*	*Per cent*
Republic	312	26.0	212	5.7
Ch'ing	871	72.8	2,365	64.3
Ming	13	1.1	765	20.8
Yüan	1	0.1	60	1.6
S. Sung			216	5.9
N. Sung			61	1.7
Total	1,197	100.0	3,679	100.0

Again, we can only speculate about what these data mean in terms of the conditions conducive to genealogy making. It may be that families in the wealthy lower Yangtze provinces, and perhaps especially families with comprador wealth, found in the genealogies a convenient status symbol as late as the second and third decades of this century. Not only can we visualize a good deal of genealogy making being carried on without well-organized kinship groups backing the enterprise; we have also come to realize (Fried 1966) that urbanization and modernization need not corrode clan bonds and attendant sentiments (as expressed in the genealogies). This may well explain the otherwise puzzlingly high level of genealogy making at a time when kinship bonds had been thought to be weakening in the face of modernization, especially in coastal China.

The chronological limitations of our sample, then, preclude a full view of the genealogy in all its stages; yet one must be aware of what the Chinese genealogy has stood for in its different phases of historical development before one can hope to use it with discrimination.

The Changing Function of the Genealogy Through Time

When we speak of the Chinese genealogy today, we generally mean the type of document that developed in the Sung Dynasty and after. But that genre itself probably owed something to its pre-Sung predecessors. In its origins, the Chinese genealogy was linked to the aristocratic structure of Chinese society in its early period (Hu 1948: 11–12; Taga 1960b: 116–17, and *passim*). The earliest prototype of the genealogy, the descent lines of the royal and ducal houses of the pre-imperial period, can be found in the earliest Chinese histories, including that of Ssu-ma Ch'ien. Between Han and T'ang and particularly during the Six Dynasties, when great families (*shih* and *tsu*) continued to dominate politics and society, their genealogical records (*p'u-tieh*) were a recognized historical genre, with its own section in the Literature Treatise of the dynastic histories (Makino 1936: 261). With both civil service appointments and marriage strategies based on considerations of descent, the government maintained a genealogical bureau (*p'u-chü*) to check on the genealogical labors of the great houses (P'an 1933: 109).

We may assume that many of these pre-Sung genealogies survived the general decline of the aristocratic houses that had rendered them politically insignificant by the tenth century, and that these records influenced the reformers of the Northern Sung, who revived the genre under new auspices. In many fundamental respects, however, the "modern" genealogy dating from the Sung breaks with its predecessors. It is, for one, an exclusively private document. (In the seventeenth century, Ku Yen-wu recommended the reestablishment of a government bureau to control the number of spurious genealogies that were being manufactured to serve as charters for surname associations that he judged politically dangerous. See Hu 1948: 50.) More important, its revival is closely linked with the neo-Confucian cult of the family institution, the intended training ground for Confucian character building.

Pioneered by reformers of the Northern Sung, especially Su Hsün (1009–66, the father of Su Tung-p'o) and Ou-yang Hsiu (1007–72), the "new" genealogy at the outset belonged to the religio-moral sphere of neo-Confucian concerns. Some Sung thinkers thought it to be a narrowing of the genealogy's function. The great Sung historian Cheng Ch'iao (1104–62) in his treatise on clan and family, for instance, contrasted the earlier genealogy with its double function of assisting the government in selecting officials and the great houses in arranging marriages, and the new genealogy that had been reduced to the mere function of "revering and uniting the lineage" (P'an 1933: 119).

The religio-moral aspect of the new genre is reflected in a long debate over the principles that were supposed to govern inclusion of forebears in the genealogy. Su Hsün began his line of descent with his great-great-grandfather, not because he was ignorant of earlier ancestors, but for reasons of propriety. As long as rites to earlier ancestors were not per-

mitted, their inclusion in the genealogy seems to have appeared im-
proper too. (Makino reports on a debate extending from Sung to Ch'ing
on the propriety of worshiping one's first ancestor. Treatment of that
personage in the genealogy seems to have followed the cultic practice,
and as the rule forbidding commoners to worship the first ancestor was
in practice disregarded, he tended also to be accepted into the genealogy. See Makino 1949: 177–78.) Similarly, both Su and Ou-yang, at
the same time commenting on the difficulty of establishing data on collateral (*p'ang*) relatives, believed that in any case not all collaterals
should be included in the genealogy, so that a confusion of the near and
far would not violate human feelings (Makino 1936: 278–79).

Though the new genealogy may have appeared to some as a deliberately sparse document, the conceptions of the Sung reformers actually
caused the genealogy's contents to proliferate far beyond the simple
listing of descent lines (*hsi-p'u* or *shih-piao*), which had constituted the
genealogy in the pre-Sung period and remained its core later. In the
course of time, and apparently especially from the Ming on,[*] full-
fledged genealogies regularly contained, in addition to descent lines and
"vital statistics" (*shih-lu*, sections listing birth and death dates, burial
place, spouse's name, offices if any), large additional sections with prose
biographies of eminent clansmen, and a vast apparatus of honorific materials—poems and calligraphy by eminent men in honor of lineage members, for instance. (The Wu-feng Lin genealogy goes so far as to display
the calligraphy of Confucius and the Duke of Chou, in passages honoring Lin ancestors.) In addition, there might be functional records such
as clan rules and material bearing on clan ritual and the administration
of clan property. Suffice it to say here that genealogies vary tremen-
dously in the relative amount of space they allot to these different parts.
If there is any pattern to this variety, a sampling of Taiwanese genealogies suggests that genealogies kept by lineages (groups with corporate
property who might wish to control access to it) stressed the lines of
descent; the genealogies of some of the modern clan associations or surname groups that do not own property and cannot demonstrate common
descent of necessity stress the honorific material.

The revival of the genre at the hands of the neo-Confucian reformers
had certain important consequences for the genealogy. Shaped by the
more extreme sense of Confucian familism that only began in the Sung
(Twitchett 1959: 101), the contents and editorial principles of the modern genealogy mirror the moral standards of the great tradition. Con-

---

[*] Liu (1959: 65) and Makino (1936: 278) agree that the proliferation of the contents of the genealogy increased markedly in the Ming.

fucian standards of propriety, which may themselves have become more rigorous at about this time, directly influenced genealogy making. As in the histories that had pioneered this device of moral censure, admission to the genealogy was open only to morally worthy kinsmen. Persons who had violated family morality (sons becoming monks, widows re-marrying, kinsmen engaging in political rebellion, etc.) were omitted from the record if their behavior could not be disguised by euphemism. (The Wu-feng Lin genealogy is a good example. A famous Taiwanese rebel of the Ch'ien-lung period, Lin Shuang-wen, was most likely a close relative, but has been edited out of the genealogy; in fact, I know of no Taiwanese Lin genealogy that claims him. Less drastic censure is visited on a nineteenth-century black sheep of the family, the only man of his lineage segment and generation who is not accorded a biography. Yet the formality of this censure-by-omission is clear enough, since the major elements of his story are told in the biographies of his closest relatives.) Conversely, special attention, mainly in the form of a separate biogra-phy, was lavished on the moral paragon. One clan rule not only reflects awareness of these editorial principles, but suggests that genealogies very properly employ even stricter moral standards than histories. Whereas both genres serve as "mirrors," it is argued, the history proper-ly includes the good and the bad to trace order and disorder in society; the genealogy, by contrast, is concerned only with the integrity (*cheng*) of the clan, and hence properly excludes all the bad (Taga 1960a: 11, quoting a clan rule).

While religio-moral propriety may have been the chief concern of the Sung pioneers and certainly continued to affect editorial standards in genealogies later, genealogies came in time to be viewed as so many points in the game of social one-up-manship. The more fluid social con-ditions of the Sung and post-Sung world must have made it natural for families newly arrived at the pinnacle to borrow some of the aura of the great old houses by creating their own genealogies and, in the manner of the universal parvenu, if possible attaching themselves genealogically to one of the eminent houses of the pre-Sung. Families still struggling for higher status tended to boost their prestige by borrowing that of their betters through various forms of genealogical "interloping."

In Southeast China, where the lineage was the focus for much of the informal political structure in the countryside, genealogies more often had an overtly political purpose. They served as foundation charters for the large combinations of scattered lineages or for the common surname associations that emerged as the basis for joint action (vendettas in im-perial China, preelection alliances in contemporary Taiwan, etc.) and that often appeared uncomfortably powerful to the state. (See Freedman 1966: 29–31, and *passim*. For contemporary political uses of the clan in Taiwanese elections, see Fried 1966.)

When genealogies were made to support such social or political claims, their historical value as evidence inevitably suffered in the process. Descent lines were extended vertically into prehistorical times to garner prestige, or the genealogy was inflated laterally to connect hitherto unrelated kinship groups, even though many clan rules warned against such abuses of the genealogy (Hu 1948: 48).

To make allowances for these historical inaccuracies, some students have suggested that we distinguish an early (pre-Sung or pre-Yüan) and presumably unreliable portion of most genealogies from a later, more trustworthy part. Others have urged special caution in regard to lateral connections of branches, on the assumption that the straight lines of descent for most localized lineages deserve more confidence. (Suggestions for such distinctions are made in Hu 1948: 45, 51; Freedman 1957: 71, n. 2; Freedman 1958: 70; Freedman 1966: 42.) Actually, as we shall see later, the matter of authenticity may be more complicated than this; fortunately, the written Chinese genealogy often carries within it the internal evidence for such tampering as may have occurred.

It is clear, then, that the written Chinese genealogy shares some of the features of the oral genealogy: it speaks to some extent of the present in a language purporting to deal with the past. Current moral aspirations are presented in the language of past paragons of virtue; status achieved or hoped for is discussed in terms of venerable ancestry; among minority groups, the current wish to "pass" into the greater Han society is voiced in terms of demonstrated Han descent. (On the phenomenon of non-Han families establishing Han credentials via genealogical interloping, see Hsu 1948: 46 and Eberhard 1962: 200–201.) How do these characteristics of the genealogy affect its ability to answer some of the questions that social scientists and historians are likely to put?

Some Basic Questions

On the primary question of the nature of the group that the genealogy represents, many genealogies are stubbornly silent. Let me raise but one question—the key distinction between lineage and clan. In Freedman's terms, the distinction hinges on the presence or absence of "common property and the ritual obligations and privileges entailed in that property" (Freedman 1966: 21). Most of the genealogies that I have studied from Taiwan do not record the existence of corporate property even in cases where such property exists. The existence of corporate property at some time in the lineage's history may be inferred from lineage rules that bear on its stewardship; but even here the genealogy will tell us nothing about the long-term fortunes of the lineage property, the rhythm of accumulation and dispersal that seems to have prevailed in most lineages over time. Another distinction, whether a lineage is localized or dispersed, is not usually evident from the genealogy either, since place of residence is not part of the data provided in the "vital statistics."

For the historian, the meatiest part of the genealogy will be the "lines of descent" and "vital statistics," sections that are presented in slightly different tabular form in the Su and Ou-yang styles of the genealogy. Supplementary information may be found in the more extensive biographies that appear in some genealogies, honoring men of marked distinction. With these data available, the historian can usually dig further in other historical records, such as local gazetteers. Gazetteer biographies are not, however, always an independent check on genealogy biographies. The Taiwanese historian Lien Heng, who helped compose the Wu-feng Lin biographies in the genealogy, incorporated identical biographies in his *General History of Taiwan*, from which editors of later gazetteers have recopied them. Similar situations presumably prevailed in other counties of China where the editorial boards for county gazetteers would be recruited from gentry families who were also active in genealogy making.

For the demographer, the genealogy may hold more frustration than fulfillment. Many standard demographic questions cannot be answered from genealogies. Family size, for instance, cannot be discovered, since genealogies usually record only males who have survived a certain childhood age; daughters were usually omitted altogether. (For customary practices in Taiwan, see Sheng 1963.) Although no one has seriously thought to derive estimates of infant mortality from the genealogies, an attempt has been made to chart adult mortality rates (Yuan 1931), an enterprise of dubious validity, I believe, because of the bias in the genealogies in favor of upper-class persons.

To come to more specifically anthropological questions, much can be said about marriage on the basis of some genealogies, but certain limitations must also be kept in mind. For one, genealogies seem to vary widely in the degree to which data on spouses are recorded. Eberhard's Wu genealogy, for example, lists 4,331 males but records only 397 spouses. And this may not be an extreme case: there are other genealogies that do not list wives at all. In the Wu-feng Lin genealogy, there are vital statistics (birth and death dates) for virtually all the wives, as well as their family and personal names, and often their burial places. Secondary wives (*fu-pi*) are recorded as well as main wives, and sons are usually carefully attributed to the mother if the father had several wives, though these attributions are sometimes spurious. (For example, if a son's true mother, because of some moral lapse, had to be omitted from the record, he is, for the sake of convenience, attributed to another woman.) Whether concubinage is always as openly admitted as in the Lin genealogy, I do not know. Some genealogies, I have been told, use different typographic devices (different inks, for example) to distinguish ranks of wives. It is also plain that a concubine's status in the genealogy, as presumably in many other respects (whether she will be listed or not, how fully documented, etc.) depends on whether or not she produced a son.

Widowhood and remarriage are treated within the limits of the moral conventions and the family's search for an impeccable image. Among the Lins, for example, there is no record of remarriage (nor did I learn of such cases orally), but several chaste widows are expressly mentioned in the biographies of husbands who died young. There may be considerable regional differences in this matter; Eberhard's study of the Jung clan recorded more remarriages of widows than cases of "chaste widows"—those widowed before the age of thirty who did not remarry. (In Eberhard's Jung genealogy, there is also a small number of divorces listed. See Eberhard 1962.)

The subject of marriage strategies cannot be pursued very fruitfully in the genealogies. Since the great majority of genealogies record only a wife's surname and personal name and nothing about her family background, we can never know whether two ladies with the same surname who appear as a man's mother and wife, represent in fact an example of the much-discussed matrilateral cross-cousin marriage. Some anthropologists (e.g., Hsu 1948: 80–81; Eberhard 1962: 122–26) have tried to deduce preferred marriage patterns from this crude measure of spouse's family names, a highly questionable procedure in my view, especially in those regions of China in which a very few surnames make up a very large proportion of the population and where on simple statistical grounds reappearance of one and the same surname for spouses may be expected.

Another related limitation of the genealogies is the omission in most cases of daughters, and, of course, of any data on the families they marry into. The matter of a kin group's matrilateral and affinal relations thus remains beyond most genealogies. If these relations are indeed as important as has recently been claimed (Gallin 1960), the standard genealogy is too faithful a mirror of the official agnatically oriented kinship system to make a record of the matter.

A second set of data, of interest to the social scientist as well as the historian studying a particular family that is omitted in most genealogies, bears on the geographic and social background of the spouses. Only occasionally can we pick up a helpful clue in the biographies of the genealogies (he married the daughter of a *hsiu-ts'ai*, or scholar, from X). In my researches on the Lin family the genealogy disappointed me most in this respect. From the impersonality and anonymity of the genealogical entries it would have been impossible to discern the rather interesting pattern of marriages and shifting marriage strategies that the family underwent as it climbed the social ladder of late Ch'ing Taiwan: from their early and obscure days when they tended to marry peasant girls from nearby villages, to a second stage when they could aspire to the daughters of businessmen and lower gentry from nearby towns, to a final stage when an occasional marriage with a mainland girl (always the most prestigious match for a Taiwanese) was contracted. Here, of course, neither the vital statistics nor the fairly stereotyped biographies were of help.

Adoption, too, cannot be studied thoroughly by using the genealogies. Clan rules, it is true, chart something of the changing attitudes toward the practice (Liu 1959: 72–77), but whether the practice itself is accurately mirrored in the genealogies is a question. Adoption for ritual purposes, to continue the male line, and from within the kin group (*szu-tzu* or *kuo-fang tzu*) is frequently recorded within the Lin genealogy. Other forms of adoption, at times from outside the surname group (*ming-ling-tzu*) are often disguised, and may have occurred more often than the genealogies indicate. In the case of the Wu-feng Lin genealogy, disguises were used occasionally, but not consistently: *ming-ling-tzu* adoptions by fathers who were powerful members of the lineage could not be admitted; they were admissible in the case of the less exalted members.

Segmentation of the kinship group, another key question for the anthropologist, is only fitfully illuminated by the genealogies. At the highest level, segmentation of the lineage into what are usually called *fang* (and the terminology is surprisingly consistent) is generally recorded; the *fang* are usually thought of as having been established by the sons of the first ancestor who settled in the family's current place of residence, so that division into *fang* usually occurs in the second generation of the most recent generation sequence, often ten or twenty generations prior to the last recorded generation. Where vital statistics are given by individual, individuals are arranged by *fang*, and within each *fang* by generation. Below this level, segmentation is usually not explicit in the genealogy; again, the failure to record corporate property ("trusts") held at such lower levels deprives us of the most clearcut indicator of segmentation at these levels. Rather, generation members appear in their proper places regardless of individual chronological age or socioeconomic status, as if the genealogy meant to deny the differentiation that usually develops among segments in the larger lineages.

We can, of course, fall back on a certain amount of internal evidence to discern segmentation, though the functional significance of the segments that appear cannot usually be determined on the basis of the genealogy. We come across a certain number of generation members who share an element of the personal name; others of the same generation do not. Presumably there is some particular cohesion among these members, perhaps at the branch (*chih*) or compound (*hu*) level. Even more revealing may be the quality or consistency of the vital statistics provided in the genealogy. If consistently fuller data are given for a segment that nests in the larger *fang* than is given for individuals surrounding the segment in the "family tree," we may be dealing with an organized branch that has in fact some device for keeping better track of the members' life data. We may suspect a joint ancestral shrine at the segment level or perhaps even joint property incorporated at that level; usually, however, only an examination *in situ* can confirm such a conjecture. (In Taiwan, the Japanese land and population registers from the turn of the century give extensive information on joint residential arrangements and jointly held property that can be profitably correlated with material in the genealogy.) If three brothers, but none of their collaterals, have secondary wives, we may suspect that a wealthy segment is beginning to differentiate itself from the rest of the lineage.

A mass of hypothetical segments, proliferating for as many as twenty generations below the *fang* level, does not complicate the scholar's task as much as we might think. What might, in the absence of specific sub-segmentation in the genealogy, look like an unwieldy and amorphous record becomes more structured because of the already mentioned "sloughing off" of branches that for one reason or another have failed to maintain ritual and other contact with the segments that *are* recorded and that presumably have done the recording. The very pattern of omissions or lapses of descent lines may therefore help us understand the reason for segmentation.

In some cases, the biographies can supplement the "descent lines" and provide information on the functional significance of segments. These data, however, are usually unsystematic and will consist of incidental episodes that document military cooperation of segments in one instance, joint worship in another, or perhaps a falling out over the management of joint property in a third case. If we are lucky enough to get hold of a genealogy that has been published in different editions for different branches, this of course will give us additional information about the important lines segmenting the unit.

Types of Genealogy

We can pursue the subject of segmentation and put it in a broader context, that of the varying size, depth, and complexity of kinship groups. The printed genealogies, in their diversity, make clear that there are wide variations among the groups they represent; we can use these differences to construct a typology of genealogies and of the agnatic groupings they stand for, moving from the simple to the complex.

We have first the simple group represented in the Northern Sung genealogy of Su Hsün (Su 1698: ch. 14), an early genealogy that has come down to us in the collected works of its author. While Su's postface mentions ancestors as far back as the pre-Han period, the descent lines begin with his great-great-grandfather (*kao-tsu*) and descend to his (yet unborn) son's generation. In other words, the group included is almost identical with Su Hsün's mourning grades. Ritual reasons, as we have seen, rather than ignorance, determined his principles of inclusion and exclusion. The group included is not formally structured, there being no subdivisions at the *fang* level or lower. Internal evidence, such as the pattern of the common element in the personal name, throws some light on what were the most significant subsegments. Depth (six generations) and size (a maximum of twenty-four persons in a single generation) are held low. We may well assume that this simple chronologically shallow record may represent the form of genealogy often kept by individual households in handwritten form. The vital statistics are also sparse, there being entries only on the direct forebears of Su Hsün (the taboo on their personal names is, incidentally, observed), and these include only such matters as whether office was held or not, the wife's family name, and the subject's month and day of death. The omission of the year of death makes clear that we are dealing here with a document from the sphere of neo-Confucian ritual, rather than with a historcal record proper.

As the practice of genealogy making caught on in the Southern Sung and Ming, and as reluctance to stop the record with one's *kao-tsu* waned, we get a genealogy with a fixed apex and a longer descent line, roughly fifteen to twenty generations in depth and including in the last or last-but-one generation anywhere from fifty to two hundred males. In genealogies of this size, division into *fang*, established at or near the second generation, usually prevails to make the organization more manageable, though I believe a closer look at these genealogies will confirm my suspicion that not all *fang* are equally well documented. From the data we cannot tell to what extent the lineage is localized, or whether branches that have "died out" represent those who migrated away.

The third type in order of complexity is represented by the Wu-feng Lin genealogy, and I would like to discuss it in greater detail. This genealogy was produced in the mid-1930's by an editorial committee recruited from three eminent lineages in the Taichung area: the Wu-feng Lins, the Shu-tzu-chiao Lins, and the Ta-li Lins. The committee produced three different genealogies, one for each of the lineages, and a number of variant subeditions of the Wu-feng Lin genealogy, to accommodate the special interests of some prominent segments of the Wu-feng lineage, the branches in T'ai-p'ing and in T'u-ch'eng. These variant editions had descent lines and vital statistics identical with the main Wu-feng edition, but they varied in the biographies and photographic material included.

These editorial labors seem to have created, perhaps for the first time, a common genealogical framework for three important lineages in mid-Taiwan. We do not know in what terms they had conceived their genealogical relationship earlier, but we do know that political and economic ties between the lineages had existed since the nineteenth century. The Wu-feng Lins had been mid-Taiwan's "first family" since the 1860's, gradually transforming themselves from the region's premier "local bully" to public-spirited "local gentry" by the end of Ch'ing rule in 1895. In their days as bullies they had occasionally been crossed by the more law-abiding Shu-tzu-chiao Lins, but as the Wu-feng Lins themselves became more staid, political cooperation replaced rivalry. The Ta-li Lins, economically several notches below Wu-feng, had been business agents for the Wu-feng Lins in the market town of Ta-li since the turn of the century. Pressures having to do with Japanese occupation policy may account for the joining of the three lineages. Accompanied as the union was by the founding of an endowed temple in Taichung, the merger created a clan whose "clanship has once more been condensed into lineage bonds." (Freedman 1966: 21 sets forth the basic terms as now understood.)

The three lineages, which have a genealogical depth in Taiwan of between four and six generations, had to go back to their mainland forebears to establish their common origins. In this effort, they were able to make use of several mainland (largely Fukien) Lin genealogies with which they proceeded to demonstrate (authentic or spurious?) affilia-

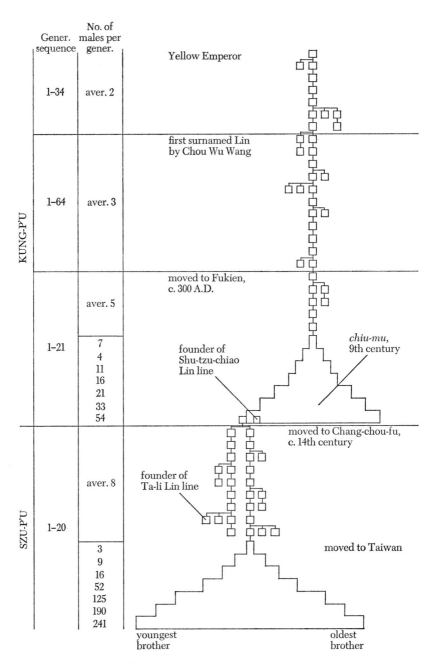

Gener. sequence	No. of males per gener.		
		Yellow Emperor	
1–34	aver. 2		
		first surnamed Lin by Chou Wu Wang	
1–64	aver. 3		
	aver. 5	moved to Fukien, c. 300 A.D.	
1–21	7 4 11 16 21 33 54	founder of Shu-tzu-chiao Lin line	*chiu-mu*, 9th century
	aver. 8	moved to Chang-chou-fu, c. 14th century	
		founder of Ta-li Lin line	
1–20	3 9 16 52 125 190 241		moved to Taiwan
		youngest brother	oldest brother

KUNG-PU

SZU-PU

WU-FENG LIN SIMPLIFIED DESCENT LINE

tion. Among the earlier genealogical materials that were available, the Taiwanese editors distinguish between a chronologically earlier portion, called the "common *p'u*" (*kung-p'u*), and a later, so-called "private *p'u*" (*szu-p'u*). The *kung-p'u* may be a fairly widely accepted version of an early Lin descent line, prepared perhaps in the early Ming. It lists 117 generations, arranged in overlapping sequences of 33, 63, and 21 generations. The time span covered by these sequences extends from the Yellow Emperor (the first ancestor) to the fourteenth century A.D. The first sequence comes down to the time of King Wu of Chou, who bestowed the family name Lin on an ancestor, a man of the thirty-fourth generation, who thereupon became the starting point for a new sequence. The third sequence begins *c.* A.D. 300 when the family first entered Fukien. The descent line is depicted in the chart.

To connect the three mid-Taiwan lineages, it was necessary to go back to the *kung-p'u* in one case and to the *szu-p'u* in another. I might add that these "joints" are not very convincing, though more care might surely have been taken to disguise the matter, had this been the wish. (The Wu-feng and Shu-tzu-chiao lines come together in a portion of the *kung-p'u* that is very questionable. In this portion, part of the first "pyramid," many elisions must have occurred, since the genealogy spans six centuries in seven generations. The Wu-feng and Ta-li lines come together in more recent times, in the *szu-p'u*, perhaps early in the Ch'ing period. Below the Ta-li ancestor who appears in both the Ta-li and Wu-feng genealogy, the Ta-li genealogy records blanks for the next three generations, with neither vital statistics nor even personal names known.) It is perhaps an argument for the authenticity of the record that the twentieth-century pecking order (which most certainly was Wu-feng, Shu-tzu-chiao, Ta-li) is not perfectly mirrored in the genealogy, where the order of seniority is Shu-tzu-chiao, Wu-feng, Ta-li. In the absence of all records used by the editorial committee thirty years ago, a further check into their editorial standards and policies was impossible.

Though the chronological depth of this genealogy is considerable, the size and complexity are kept to a minimum, first by the device of preparing separate editions for the three related lineages, and secondly and chiefly because collaterals have been recorded only sparingly, as the chart with its long thin descent lines and only two broad-based pyramids demonstrates. The first pyramid has a depth of seven generations and reaches its base with 54 males in the seventh generation; the second, more substantial pyramid (of the Wu-feng lineage, in this case) also encompasses seven generations, reaching a base width of 241 males. Formal segmentation terms are used sparingly throughout, and appear in neither of the two pyramids. Patterns of shared name elements can be seen in the genealogy, but the more significant segmentation of the lineage (which covers a wide range of people in terms of political and economic status) only emerges from the biographies and from personal acquaintance with the lineage members themselves, from their oral testimony, and from an inspection of the residences of individuals and segments, to mention only one socioeconomic criterion.

The genealogy in addition does not tell us whether this lineage is in any strict sense localized. The biographies fill this gap in part, giving us an occasional clue that branches other than those at T'ai-p'ing and T'u-ch'eng (for whom separate editions of the genealogy were prepared) were scattered over villages near Wu-feng. Whether unnamed branches have moved further afield, or even migrated back to the mainland, is not discernible from the genealogy.

More research in other Lin genealogies is required before the accuracy of individual portions of this record can be judged. Since none of the sources used by the compilers was available, only an indirect examination of the Wu-feng descent line's authenticity is possible. From conversations with persons who have studied other Lin genealogies, I conclude that the "first pyramid" may be authentic and may be based on a genealogy of the pre-Sung or early Sung period. Its pièce de résistance is the *chiu-mu* (nine governors), nine territorial officials of the T'ang, brothers who held office simultaneously and who may have been famous enough to have had their genealogy prepared shortly after their time. At the same time, the Lins of my study are not descended from the *chiu-mu*, and their direct forebears in T'ang times have only a most tenuous and questionable connection with the group called the *chiu-mu*.

Further along in time, the more detailed information, or vital statistics, only makes its appearance for that section of the genealogy that is called the private *p'u*, i.e., the last generation sequence, which is different for each of the three editions. The fairly consistent and full set of data may indicate the authenticity of that part of the record, or at least its earlier section pertaining to a mainland lineage. The records on the three shallow Taiwan lineages are no doubt also authentic, but the manner in which these Taiwan descent lines are attached to the continental main stem also gives the historian pause. The Lin genealogies, then, show a pattern in which apparently authentic portions of the record are punctuated by questionable connections and "splicing" in fairly late historical times.

A somewhat more complex group is represented by the Wu clan, studied by Eberhard and identified here only on the basis of his description and analysis. In many respects similar to the Lin group, the Wu clan is more complexly structured. (There are more clearly designated *fang* and subsegments in given localities.) Its size is far larger, too: 4,331 males as against 1,192 in the Wu-feng descent line. The title of their genealogy (*tsung-p'u*, not *tsu-p'u*) also indicates that we are dealing here with a different kinship group, a "clan" rather than a "higher-order lineage."

Much like the Lin genealogy, this one at first traces a thin single line, with only an occasional collateral, from prehistoric to historic times, specifically to the Five Dynasties period. Lateral expansion in the form of several pyramids occurs from the late tenth century on, as a number of *fang* develop to reach maximum base widths around the year 1400. The pyramids represent the success and proliferation of a number of families who rose to eminence at the Sung court and who, after its demise, established themselves in Kwangtung, Kwangsi, and Fukien. It is from around 1400, too, that we find the greatest number of prefaces in the twentieth-century genealogy, and hence presumably of earlier genealogies now lost. From these prefaces it is quite clear that by 1400 the major *fang* had been satisfactorily spliced and tied together by the genealogists. The "splices" are not always convincing (Eberhard himself is skeptical at times), but we may assume that we are dealing here with the establishment of a surname association that must in some way have been related to the individual lineages' needs and troubles in the turbulent time of migration southward and Mongol overthrow. For all the pyramids, the descent lines thin out shortly after 1400, evidence, I should think, of lagging genealogical labors and not necessarily of a decline of the lineages. The lines become so tenuous in places that even the placing of individuals in specific generations is in doubt. Only in the last century or two do we once more find pyramids building up, proof at least of the renewed genealogical labors of certain lineages or sublineages that in some cases had attained considerable wealth (one such example is a Cantonese Cohong merchant family that is included). Working with inadequate genealogical records, the twentieth-century editor was forced to rely on a great deal of guesswork and interpolation to connect the hundreds of Wu lineages he knew of in Kwangtung and Kwangsi with the attested lineages of the early Ming genealogies. Eberhard (1962: 55) describes his method for us:

[The author] certainly knew that the clan had more than the few hundred living members which he mentions at the time of his writing; his general information seems to indicate that by 1933 far more than a million people in

Kwangtung and Kwangsi had the clan-name Wu and claimed to belong to the clan he studied. Most of these people were simple farmers, as the names of the places in which they live indicate. Here, the author has limited himself to find all villages in which Wu live and to establish the name of the first settler. In most cases, then, he succeeded in identifying the founder with one of the main branches [established by Ming times in the numerous genealogies of that period] and with a definite generation.

This, if not the earlier material on the "splicing" undertaken by early Ming, makes clear that we are dealing here with one of those vast surname groups that seem typical of South China.

Freedman, who has analyzed this "giant genealogy" with its vast "panorama of fission" (1966: 26–28) finds the rationale for such a document not in "sociology" but in "history": he implies that we are not dealing with a charter for a group about to embark on joint action; rather, we get a retrospective document, inspired by "filial piety, hunger for prestige, and scholarly appetite for writing history." At the same time, because of the questionable authenticity of major portions and "splices" in this massive genealogy, the historian will not take its data on social or geographic mobility at face value, in particular because much that bears on these subjects comes from the more suspect or puzzling portions of the record. Ex post facto alignments of widely scattered lineage segments by the twentieth-century editor cannot simply be taken as evidence of actual migrations centuries ago. Similarly, the meagerness of the thin descent lines in many houses over several centuries (especially 1400–1800) should caution us against making sweeping generalizations about mobility patterns over such vast periods of time when only occasional data on occupational status are given.

An even more comprehensive genealogy is represented by the typical twentieth-century clan genealogy available in Taiwan through commercial channels or clan temples today. I can best speak of the all-Taiwan Lin genealogy I picked up through a firm in Taichung that is in the business of making genealogies (Lin-shih 1963). The number of persons to be included—many, I understand, pay for the privilege of having their photograph included—had grown to such tremendous proportions that any attempt to construct a consistent genealogical framework for them was abandoned. The editors simply borrowed what we already know from the Wu-feng genealogy—the prestigious but often dubious *kung-p'u*, which stopped in the fourteenth century. They made no attempt to connect the myriad Taiwan Lins with their forebears of the Ming. In other words, the heart of the pre-Sung and post-Sung genealogy, the descent lines, has been removed. As if to make up for this gap, the genealogy abounds in honorific and decorative materials. A portrait series of Lin ancestors, once rejected by the Wu-feng editors as too anachronistic, is here reproduced in full. Photographs not only of members, but of clan association meetings and clan temples as far away as Manila and the United States abound. Nor is the opportunity to include eminent *t'ung-hsing* neglected; for example, the goddess Matsu, née Lin, a Boddhisatva and legendary rescuer of Taiwan fishermen in distress, comes to grace the record, on the same level as the mythological first founders.

This, the fifth and last type is, of course, much less ambitious as a historical or quasi-historical record; it no longer does what the genealogy had always done, i.e., establish links between individuals and groups in accordance with accepted principles of descent. Although almost worthless as "history," this document nevertheless has considerable sociological significance; it is on the basis of such genealogies, understood as charters of surname associations, that contemporary Taiwanese form alignments for political and other purposes.

Conclusion

The Chinese genealogy is the product of a particular ideological environment. It reflects to a larger extent than the social reality of Chinese kinship the standards and aspirations of the Confucian tradition during its last centuries. Although genealogies cannot wholly obscure the ways the real world of families and lineages departs from the Confucian canon, they tend to record primarily what agrees with accepted standards and is relevant to them. In the process, genealogies make the reality look more uniform and conventional than it ever was. Despite these limitations, the social scientist and the social historian can benefit from the study of genealogies. Used with caution and imagination, the Chinese genealogy can answer a good many questions. For the historian, the data it contains on specific persons may be of the greatest value; for the social scientist, questions of the general structure of kinship groups and their social function may be paramount. In any case, the record will speak the more clearly the less we have to rely on it alone, and the more we can supplement it with information gained in the field. For the time being, this restricts the most effective research in genealogies to Overseas Chinese communities and to Taiwan and Hong Kong (including the New Territories). In all these areas, we can supplement information from genealogical records with our own observations in the field (interviews, examination of ancestral tablets, graves, etc.) and with the statistical and administrative surveys undertaken by the colonial powers (Britain in Hong Kong and Malaysia, or Japan in Taiwan). When the genealogical labors of Chinese editors can be combined with the investigative resources of the modern state and the inquiries of contemporary social science, the value, and the limitations, of the genealogy will become fully clear.

It has been thought that the Chinese genealogy, which is usually a written document, is more immune to alterations or "fudging" (to serve social or political purposes) than are the oral genealogies of preliterate peoples (Freedman 1957: 71, n. 2). This may be true in a very general sense, but I believe the inhibitions against later genealogical manipulation are somewhat weakened by the fact that few kin groups seem to preserve the old editions of genealogies when newer editions have superseded them. In fact, the most tempting and most frequent kind of manipulation of genealogical materials in the light of recent demands, the creation of fictitious relationships to express recent political and social alignments, was not inhibited by the written nature of the record. The written form becomes a boon to the researcher mainly in that it makes more difficult the disguise of such manipulations. The written genealogy, more than the oral, therefore contains the traces of its own historical evolution—illuminating both the development of the document and the history of the grouping to which it refers.

While the study of individual kinship groups and their histories is one fruitful area for future research in genealogies, our general understanding of kinship groups and their historical evolution might be advanced by other approaches to the genre. Taga has already suggested that genealogies can be divided into different types, *chia-p'u*, *tsu-p'u*, *tsung-p'u*, etc., according to the kind of kinship group to which they relate. A more extensive inventory of available genealogies might be undertaken, using the categories of historical depth, size, and complexity that I have suggested, so that we can see roughly what proportion of kinship groups in any given time or place falls into one or another of these broad categories. To get a better idea of the kinds of kinship group that produced genealogies, such an analysis should also try to discover what proportion of the genealogies are later editions in a fairly straight line of descent and at frequent intervals from earlier editions, how many are creations purely new, and what proportion can be considered seminovel in that they connect chronologically shallow kinship groups, through a process of often farfetched "splicing," with older and better documented groups. Such a further, even cursory, analysis of available genealogies can serve several purposes. It can help us clarify further the problem of an adequate vocabulary and typology for the whole range of agnatic kinship groups that we find in Chinese society. It can help us learn in what times and places particular forms of agnatic groupings have been found. Now that Freedman has raised a fundamental question by suggesting that the Southeast Chinese pattern, so far from being the primordial order, was rather the result of specific historical processes, the study of genealogies may help us chart the history of particular types of agnatic grouping during earlier centuries of Chinese history. Does the formation of strong lineages coincide in some way with the process of colonization on the agricultural frontier of China, as Freedman has suggested? Is there some correlation between periods or regions of political and social stress and the formation of lineage or clan combinations for purposes of self-defense and protection? Are these corporations of agnates in some way part of the whole trend toward the vigorous growth of voluntary associations (including guilds and *hui-kuan*) in the late traditional period? Further work in genealogies may illuminate these historical dimensions in the study of Chinese kinship groups.

Ritual Aspects of Chinese Kinship and Marriage

MAURICE FREEDMAN

Rites are a variety of heightened behavior. In this essay I try to sum-
marize what we now know about Chinese rites in the contexts of ancestor worship and marriage, linking the poetry of symbolism and religious belief to the prose of social institutions. There are obviously many
ways and contexts in which Chinese family life and kinship can be seen
to be implicated in total systems of religion and rites; calendrical domestic rites alone form a vast panorama of activity, and the rites of birth,
sickness, and death are as theoretically interesting as those of marriage.
I have chosen to discuss ancestor worship and marriage mainly because
I know most about them and think myself more capable of raising important issues in those two fields than in any other.

I write as an anthropologist, drawing in the main on my own experience of Chinese life (in Singapore and Hong Kong) and on the experience of my colleagues.* I do not involve myself in complex historical
questions, nor can I, a non-sinologue, use extensive Chinese (and Japanese) documentation. Nevertheless, I assume that we may usefully generalize about key modes of behavior in Chinese society, huge though it is,
and I venture to speak as if I could support my general statements with
data from all parts of China and recorded at many points in time during
the last hundred years. This essay suggests models of ancestor worship

* Many of the ideas and formulations in this essay have been developed as a direct
result of my participation in seminars at the London School of Economics and at Cornell University; in that regard I have particularly to thank my colleagues (above all
Arthur Wolf) and the graduate students with whom I have worked. I am indebted to
Hugh Baker for his work for me on some of the Chinese sources, and to Stephan
Feuchtwang for his making available to me his notes from Chinese and Japanese published sources on marriage in Taiwan. Part of my research was made possible by the
London-Cornell Project for East and South-East Asian Studies, which is financed
jointly by the Carnegie Corporation of New York and the Nuffield Foundation. I owe
my wife a debt for her scrutiny of a draft of the essay.

and marriage rites. The models feed on the evidence as I know it; they are not intended to masquerade as substitutes for evidence. They may turn out to be bad models as we come to know more and more about China, but they are intended as hypotheses about some significant features of Chinese ritual life and about the connections between that life and characteristics of the institutions of family and kinship.

Ancestor Worship

Little was achieved in the study of Chinese ancestor worship until it was made clear that there are two distinct kinds of worshiped ancestors: domestic and extra-domestic. The universality of ancestor worship among the Chinese is the universality of the domestic cult, which, even when it dispenses with wooden tablets, always entails the representation of dead forebears and their ritual service. As we shall presently see, household ancestor worship is not the Chinese domestic religion par excellence, but from several points of view it is the more important half of the total cult of the ancestors. The part of the cult centering on lineage ancestors (the dramatic and awe-inspiring parade of ritualized piety) cannot be universal, for lineages are not everywhere found in China. Where they exist, and consequently both parts of the cult are present, the two parts differ in the ancestors they serve, the attitudes maintained toward them by the worshipers, the role ascribed to the ancestors, and the rites performed. The halves of the cult each belong to different phases of group life and have different implications for our understanding of Chinese social organization. This first formulation of the two classes of ancestors will, however, need to be modified a little later on, when we come to consider the possibility that ancestors are worshiped who are neither domestic (although they are in domestic shrines) nor the apical members of clearly structured lineages and their segments.

The domestic religion of the Chinese has many facets, but there is a sense in which the supreme domestic cult is that of the so-called Kitchen God, Tsao Chün, for in his worship each household (i.e., each unit defined in relation to its separate cooking place) stands out as a distinct religious entity.

In the village, the god, besides the ancestor spirits, who receives sacrifices most frequently is the kitchen god—his wife being sometimes included. The kitchen god ... is the supernatural inspector of the household, sent by the emperor of heaven. His duty is to watch the daily life of the house and to report to his superior at the end of each year.... Based on the report, the fortunes of the household will be decided. (Fei 1939: 99f.)

It is a picture familiar to anyone who knows Chinese home life. We can see that each Kitchen God shrine (which, however, need not be more than a place where incense sticks are put up) is the defining focus for a household in respect of its commensality. A separate household usually has a separate kitchen, and its Tsao Chün shrine is physically distant from those of related households; but two or more households may in some circumstances share a kitchen, and then the cooking place with its own shrine becomes the locus of differentiation. (It is clear that Stove God would be a better English name for Tsao Chün.) By the worship of this deity the domestic unit is linked into the hierarchy of groups with gods that gives Chinese bureaucracy its religious aspect.

This clear ritual segmentation of households does not coincide with the segmentation of units based on ancestor worship. Every house has an altar in its main hall (or at least in its main room when it cannot rise to the luxury of a hall); in it are set both the images of the gods that the household chooses to worship and its ancestor tablets (or substitutes). The household may be both wider and narrower than an ancestor-worshiping group. Not every member of a household is necessarily the descendant, or the wife of a descendant, of a dead forebear represented on the altar. The unit defined by a collection of ancestor tablets may include people distributed over several households. Imagine a house in which, by family partition, the immediate families of different brothers severally occupy distinct living quarters and yet maintain the hall of the house and its altar in common—by no means a rare pattern. Each household will keep a Tsao Chün shrine, for each eats separately; but the brothers, their wives, and their children will as a group collectively worship the ancestors on the altar.

Just as the household is tied into one religious hierarchy through Tsao Chün, so the family, whatever its precise constitution, is linked at least in principle to a ritual hierarchy of nearer and more distant ancestors. When each socially mature man or woman dies, a tablet is made for him and placed on the domestic altar. The qualification for being so treated is the attainment of parenthood, whether actual or merely potential, as when a man posthumously acquires an heir through an adoption; parenthood may also be only nominal in the sense that members of a junior generation accept the responsibility for caring for the tablet. A boy or girl of marriageable age dying single may be posthumously married—even perhaps to another dead mate—in order to establish a place on the altar. What the system rigidly excludes is the immediate entry of the tablets of dead children, for they are not considered potential ancestors and have committed an unfilial act by the mere fact of dying young. (Yet it may be possible after the lapse of a generation or more for the restless spirit of such an unfortunate and wicked child to be appeased by his being married off in a ghostly union so that he may join the ranks of the honored dead on the altar.) The tablet of a dead man rests (if for the moment we exclude the possibility of uxorilocal residence) on the altar that houses his father's, unless of course his family has by now moved from the place where that altar is kept. A married woman's tablet is installed in the altar belonging to her husband's family. A spinster is not supposed to die in her paternal house; if she is to stay unmarried even after death, then a nondomestic shrine must be found to accommodate her tablet, if indeed she is to have one.

As the generations unfold, new tablets are added automatically to the domestic stock, but old ones are being removed, for only some three or four generations are characteristically represented. A superannuated tablet is burnt or buried near the grave of the person for whom it stands. In principle, then, domestic ancestor worship works on a cycle in which the youngest living generation worships before an altar that houses the tablets of ancestors some four generations above it—a religious correlate of the Chinese abstraction that the core of agnatic kinship is formed by those related within the patrilineal *wu fu*, the five mourning grades. (See Freedman 1958: 41ff, 93ff.) But for several reasons a particular domestic altar may not present so orderly and self-limiting a set of tablets.

In the first place, the agnatic thread linking any set may be broken. If a man enters into that form of marriage in which he lives uxorilocally and fathers children to his wife's surname, both he and his wife come to rest as tablets on an altar that will now contain parents-in-law and son-in-law and parents and daughter. Moreover, it is possible for a set to include the tablet of a non-agnatic relative or even a non-relative when that person has been a member of the house and has nobody outside it ritually to serve him. This apparent anomaly raises a crucial question (that we shall examine later) about the nature of the ritual tie between living and dead.

Second, tablets cannot build up in a regular pattern when one or more of a group of brothers move out of the house. In a new house a fresh stock may begin when the most senior member dies off; his descendants there may worship him yet still go to the old house to take part in worship, within a wider group, of more senior generations. On the other hand, especially when a new house is set up at a distance from the old, the new stock may begin with a "general" tablet on which are recorded the details extracted from the individual tablets left behind; thus worship in the new house may be addressed to the same collection of ancestors as is worshiped in the old house.

Finally, by an extension of the principle that families resulting from a recent division may come together at the altar maintained by one of them, one such altar may continue over many generations—well beyond the "standard" four—to house tablets serving as the focus for a large group of agnates scattered over numerous houses. Such an altar is physically domestic, and it is ritually domestic for the people in whose house it stands; but, acting as a ritual center for a long line of agnates, it has become akin to the altar constructed in an ancestral hall.

Before we turn to the matter of ancestral halls, however, we ought to consider an aspect of the character of ancestor tablets and the manner of their keeping. An individual tablet is usually "dotted": it has a red dot (ink or blood) imposed on it to establish a *hun* (soul) of the dead person in it, or at least to provide the *hun* with a place to settle. That ritual act sets up one instrument and distinguishes it from all others that may come to be made for the same person. As far as domestic worship is concerned, the "dotted" tablet should act as the focus when all those who are the descendants of the person for whom it stands wish to serve it jointly. In theory, a stock of tablets passes down the generations by primogeniture, and it is in connection with his right-duty to maintain the stock that the oldest son may claim and get an extra share of property when a patrimony is divided up among brothers. It follows (again in theory) that when a domestic shrine serves as the ritual center for a large nondomestic group of agnates, that shrine will have been transmitted from oldest son to oldest son, younger sons having established their own domestic altars. In reality, however, the primogenitory rule may have been broken, and the chief altar may have passed down a line that excludes some oldest sons.

We may now make the transition to ancestral halls. When a domestic tablet is destroyed or buried, having served its tour of duty, that event may mark the end of the ritual memory of the person for whom the tablet was made. And indeed, most Chinese pass into oblivion in this fashion, a similar process of erosion taking place in the treatment of tombs, as we shall see. Appearances to the contrary, the Chinese have never overburdened themselves with ancestors. But another tablet may be made for the same person and installed in an ancestral hall; once in such an altar, the tablet will remain as long as the hall stands. Often, in the cities when a tablet is similarly deposited in a club building or temple for safe and ritual keeping, it escapes the annihilation to which a normal domestic life, so to speak, would have condemned it. But it cannot play the role in an agnatic community played by a tablet in an ancestral hall, except possibly where it has been placed in a shrine belonging to a clan association.

Ancestral halls must be clearly distinguished from temples and from domestic shrines. Temples are devoted to gods, even though some urban temples may accommodate ancestor tablets. An ancestral hall is a building put up and maintained by a patrilineal group to house their ancestor tablets and serve as the center of their ritual and secular activities. Though it may display one or more deities in side-shrines, it is dominated by the symbols of ancestors. It is physically quite distinct from any normal living accommodation. The commonest form of ancestral hall is that which belongs to a lineage, but any such lineage that is finely segmented may contain a hierarchy of halls, each of them the ritual center of a segment. A hall requires for its building and its maintenance and for the upkeep of its rites that it be endowed; hence, a hall is a mark of riches, and a segment that enjoys the ownership of a hall is a rich unit within a community of units.

The segments that form within a Chinese lineage are based on some sort of income-producing property, most commonly land. Some segments are not rich enough to build a hall, and so find their ritual foci in the tombs (they may in reality be cenotaphs) of the apical ancestors from whom they trace their origin or in the shrines incorporated in domestic altars. The segments lowest down in the hierarchy (that is to say, of the shallowest genealogical depth) are almost certain to own no ritual center other than such a tomb or shrine. It becomes clear, then, that whereas from the point of view of traditional Chinese, domestic ancestor worship is a necessity, ancestor worship in halls is a luxury, expressing and reinforcing the honor of a segment but not resting on an absolute religious obligation.

The segmentary order of a Chinese lineage, as we now know, is typically asymmetrical. Segments well enough endowed to own halls stand out against both coordinate segments that cannot afford halls and groups of agnates that lack the means even to be organized into segments. Social differentiation is given one of its ritual faces. The factors that will explain why deep lineages appear in some parts of China and not in others (Freedman 1966: 159–64; Potter, 130–38 above) will also explain why hall worship is found unevenly in the country. What accounts for differing degrees of genealogical elaboration will help us understand why nondomestic ancestor worship is differently elaborated.

The ancestral hall contains in the place of honor the tablet of the founding ancestor. Logically, if the segments tracing their origin to the sons of the founder also have their several halls, we should expect to find no other tablets in the main hall. But that situation we do not in fact find. The only lineage halls with a single tablet would appear to be those belonging to Hakka (or at any rate those in the southeastern part of the country) in which the solitary tablet is not that of the first ancestor but a general tablet for agnatic ancestors as a group (see, for example, Aijmer 1967: 57)—the hall equivalent of the general tablets we sometimes find in domestic shrines. It would seem that families will install a tablet for one of their dead members not only in the lowest segment hall to which they belong, but perhaps also in every higher segment hall of which they are members and in the lineage hall. In this way, one tablet becomes many. (The installation does not, however, have necessarily to wait upon a man's death; living men sometimes have their own tablets put on an altar where they will stand, for the time being, shrouded auspiciously in red, eventually to merge into the general company of the dead.) Indeed, if we reflect for a moment on the significance of hall tablets, we see that the duplication makes good sense. The installation of a tablet is the assertion of the prestige of those descended from the person represented or of the person himself if he installs his own. That prestige, though desirable enough in the lowest-level hall, is yet more desirable in the halls to which larger groups of agnates have recourse. Of course, in the old days when tablets could be entered in the lineage or some other high-level hall only when the descendants were titled scholars or were for some other reason thought worthy of the privilege (perhaps hard cash being paid for it), many tablets found in the lower halls were not duplicated in the halls at or near the summit of the system.

I think it is useful at this point in the argument to examine the best ethnography we have to date on the distribution of tablets in ancestral halls. The new information was collected in the early 1960's in one of the great lineages of Hsin-an county, Kwangtung—since 1899 living under British rule in the Hong Kong New Territories. The village of Sheung Shui (the Cantonese form of its name) is traditionally the settlement of a single lineage bearing the surname Liao. Numerous "trusts" or estates held jointly (Freedman 1966: 33ff) have evolved at various generation levels, but only three ancestral halls now result from them: the lineage hall, a hall in the fourth generation, and one in the seventh. (See Baker 1968: 114, fig. 7.) The main ancestral hall—the lineage hall —houses three groups of tablets, of which the most important (and centrally placed) consists of the tablets of certain ancestors senior to the lineage founder, of the founder and his wife, of his only son and that man's wives and three sons, and, in addition, six tablets of the fourth generation, four tablets of the fifth, and one of the fifteenth (this last something of a puzzle, unless the fact that it belongs to a man who was a "Battalion Second Captain" has something to do with his inclusion in the main group of ancestors). The next most important group is formed by the tablets of ancestors "of particularly high academic success": two tablets for *chü-jen*, provincial graduates. The final group is of 156 tablets belonging to men who subscribed money at various times to restore the hall; there are tablets for members of each generation from the sixth to the eighteenth, the latter generation flourishing about the beginning of the present century. It is interesting to note that when in 1932 the hall was last restored and partly converted into a school, an entirely different method of rewarding donors was resorted to: their framed photographs were put up, but not to be worshiped or tended—apart from anything else, it would be awkward to treat them ritually, for the photographs include two of men who are not members of the lineage (Baker 1968: 54–60).

The lineage has three primary segments, stemming from the three members of the third generation (the founder, we recall, had only one son). None of these segments, however, has a hall. The second hall in Sheung Shui defines the segment springing from a fourth-generation ancestor: the older of the sons of the founder of the second primary segment. In this hall there are again three groups of tablets. The central group (of 139) consists of a "composite" tablet for the first three generations of the lineage and individual tablets for the apical ancestor of the segment and his wife, the remainder being tablets each of which stands for a man and his wife or wives. These last include men from the fifth to seventeenth generations, several tablets being duplicated in the lineage hall; it is not at all clear why these tablets appear on the central altar. The second group is made up of three tablets of men of high honor. The final group is of 115 tablets for men who donated money for the building and the restoration of the hall; the men are drawn from the thirteenth to the nineteenth generations (Baker 1968: 103–8).

The third hall has as its apical ancestor a man of the seventh generation, a descendant of the brother of the apical ancestor of the second hall. Here there is only one group of tablets, 70 in all, some of them duplicated in the lineage hall. The group consists of individual tablets for the apical ancestor of the segment, his wife, and their sons and wives; for the ten men of the next generation, the ninth; and for various men of the tenth to fifteenth generations, some sort of merit having apparently decided their entry. All these tablets seem to have been installed when the hall was built in the early nineteenth century. Well endowed, the segment to which this hall belongs apparently has not needed to solicit donations against the privilege of setting up tablets (Baker 1968: 110f).

Few of these facts are in conflict with my earlier general statements; we see in Baker's admirably collated and analyzed data the duplication of tablets in halls and their roles as points of reference and markers of prestige. But Baker stresses in relation to my earliest treatment of the subject (Baker 1968: 61f; Freedman 1958: 82ff) that there is in his material on Sheung Shui no support whatever for the view that ancestors in their tablets can be promoted from domestic to hall shrines, "the only way of securing a place there being to be alive (and sufficiently wealthy) at the time the hall is restored" (Baker 1968: 62). As a matter of fact, this last statement can apply only to the groups of tablets that represent donors in the lineage and fourth-generation halls; the evidence shows that the tablets of the earliest generations in the main altars of all three halls must have been installed after death, and it seems to me that this may well have been the case with more recent tablets in the central altars of the lineage and fourth-generation halls. As for the domestic cult, Baker says (1968: 62) that ancestors are worshiped "for a much longer period" than is provided for in my model, "many homes having paper 'tablets' representing 'all the ancestors of the Liao surname,' while others have paper 'tablets' recording the names of individual ancestors of ten generations or more (wooden tablets have disappeared from the home)."

Now, men installing their own hall tablets (and leaving them auspiciously shrouded while they live) certainly will not have prevented their tablets being put up in the houses where they die; thus for some generations at any rate such men will be worshiped both in the hall and in a domestic shrine. But nobody lasts indefinitely in a domestic shrine (except in the vague sense that he is embraced in a "general" tablet of the kind Baker describes: "all the ancestors of the Liao surname"), and a man's only chance of a posthumous installation in a hall lies in his descendants procuring his admission, on some ground of eminence, to one or more of the central altars of the halls. Such an installation is no longer possible; but that may be because for the last generation at least the system has declined; certainly no new ancestral hall will now or in the future come into existence to make it possible for people to establish their ancestors in a permanent shrine belonging to a segment.

In Sheung Shui, as we have seen, individual tablets (in reality just sheets of red paper) may be kept in domestic altars for "ten generations or more." Two questions arise. First, has this lengthy retention something to do with the fact that eminent ancestors can no longer be put into hall shrines? Second, and more important, are some of the remoter ancestors kept in domestic shrines because they are in fact the foci of large and nondomestic groups of agnates? In connection with this second question I refer to other present-day evidence, drawn from a village study made in Taiwan. In Hsin Hsing there is a multiplicity of agnatic groups, none of which is very large. It would appear that only one of them has collective property and none an ancestral hall (Gallin 1966: 132–37). Yet the *tsu* (as they call themselves, using the term we normally translate as "lineage") participate in the common worship of ancestors on their death-dates, as do lesser groups within the *tsu*, the loci for such worship being domestic shrines (Gallin 1966: 247f). The relation between domestic worship proper and worship at a domestic shrine by some nondomestic group is indicated in Gallin's statement (1966: 248): "Generally, a single ancestor is worshipped for about two or three generations, or as long as someone remembers him in his lifetime. When no one remains who remembers him alive, he, together with other more or less forgotten ancestors . . . is worshipped only on one designated day of the year, and then perhaps by the *tsu*." In cases such as this we are witnessing the bringing together, within the context of a domestic shrine, of ritual attitudes and practices that are clearly segregated when hall and house worship are independently developed.*

Ancestor worship in China is not confined to shrines, the tablet being only one of two localizations of an ancestor. The other is the grave. Lineages and segments that maintain halls may, by means of their economic resources, keep up grand tombs for apical ancestors and may conduct periodic communal worship at them. Lacking ancestral halls, lineages and segments may fall back on tombs as the only places for their joint worship. Just as a distinction is to be made between worship at domestic shrines and worship in halls, so it can be made in the wor-

---

* In view of the clear differentiation between domestic and hall tablets, one might expect to find a vocabulary that reflects it. The common term for ancestral tablet is *p'ai* (*ling-p'ai*). Baker says that in Sheung Shui domestic tablets are *shen-wei* and hall tablets *shen-chu* (1968: 63). Shryock (1931: 170), on the other hand, gives *shen-wei* as the term for hall tablets, domestic tablets being *shen-chu*, although sometimes *shen-wei* in the case of great men. Addison (1925: 32) sets out a different use of the terminology: the front inner surface of the tablet bears the characters for *shen-chu*, the front outer surface those for *shen-wei*. There is, therefore, no consistent terminology, but the distinction between the two classes of tablet is often linguistically marked.

ship at graves: families cherish the tombs of their more recent fore-bears, gradually abandoning them as they recede in time; the graves of remoter ancestors are tended only when they serve as points of reference for lineages and their segments. As Baker puts it for Sheung Shui (1968: 62):

The most distant ancestor's grave known by me to be worshipped was that of a great-grandfather of the youngest agnatic descendant present. . . . Beyond this limit in generation depth graves are not worshipped by individual families, *but* grave-worshipped ancestors may be "promoted" to communal grave-worship and thus saved from extinction of memory, in much the same way as are the tablet-worshipped ancestors of Freedman's account.

Up to this point we have mapped out what might be called the general structural arrangements of Chinese ancestor worship. Now we must explore the nature of the ritual activity associated with those arrangements, beginning again with domestic worship. On any domestic altar there may be two kinds of tablet: individual and collective, the latter designating "all the ancestors." This possible combination helps us to see that domestic worship has two sides: on the one hand a family addresses itself on the major annual festivals to its ancestors and reports to them as a collectivity; on the other hand, individual ancestors are tended on their death-dates, perhaps with their favorite food being set before them and the family as a whole paying its respects. The distinction between the two classes of devotion does not, however, depend on there being two different kinds of tablet. Ancestors as a collectivity can be worshiped in the absence of any tablet that represents them as such, and individual ancestors do not require individual tablets to insure that they are worshiped on their death-dates. (Some families keep sheets of paper or boards on which important death-dates are recorded as a guide.) Yet, although these two aspects are present, it is the worship of individual ancestors that is the more distinctive of domestic worship. Indeed, it is the highly individualizing and personal character of ancestor worship in the house that marks it off sharply from worship conducted by nondomestic groups.

Although the head of a family should formally put himself in charge of the rites conducted before the ancestors, whether at the festivals or on the death-dates of particular ancestors, the routine tendance—the daily offering of incense and the special offerings made on the first and fifteenth days of every lunar month—is carried out by women. Everywhere in China, at least outside the families of the small Confucian elite, the routine care of ancestors falls essentially to women—as indeed does nearly every part of domestic religion. On their shoulders rests the responsibility for remembering the death-dates of the ancestors for whom the family is concerned; it is they who are likely to pray to the ancestors for well-being and peace; and, as I have argued elsewhere (Freedman 1967a: 97f), to the limited extent that ancestors can intervene detrimentally in the lives of their descendants, it is women who are probably the agents for the unfavorable interpretation of ancestral behavior. There are enough hints in the literature that in many places in China the most conspicuous role of men in domestic religion is in the conduct of the main rites for the Kitchen God. (See Freedman 1967a: 97; Eberhard 1958: 18; Maspero 1932: 292; Tun 1965: 64; Körner 1959: 35; and Bredon 1930: 13.) It may seem highly paradoxical that in the ritual sphere men should emerge as leaders of the household and women generally appear as prime agents in the rites of the family, but we might suggest that on the one side men are appropriately associated with the kind of domestic discipline for which Tsao Chün stands, and that on the other side they cannot be in too intimate a relationship with domestic ancestors because of the latter's potential power to inflict harm.

From the point of view of men, ancestors are essentially benign (Freedman 1967a: 93ff), their kindliness perhaps springing from the gradualness with which a son takes over responsibility from his father (for him the key domestic ancestor). Despite the ritual primacy of the oldest son (which we have already seen to be expressed in his custodianship of the family's stock of tablets and his right to an extra share of inheritance), there is, in real life, equality between brothers and no transfer from father to son of a power to control the other mature sons. The head of a family does not draw from his ancestors the capacity to punish by nonhuman means; he does not stand before the other members of the family with an array of disciplinary ancestors behind him. The ancestors represent protectiveness and solicitude. And yet they have rights—chiefly, to be served on their death-dates and provided with agnatic descendants—which, if they are denied, may lead them to cause sickness or some other discomfort to the living. The punitive element in ancestral behavior is a minor one, but (we may argue) it is of sufficient importance to make it difficult for men to deal closely with their dead forebears, that role being assumed by women. On marriage women are estranged from their own ancestors and placed under their husbands', to whom they now have special access and from whom they hope for protection and blessings even as they fear possible retribution.

The interpretation may well be wrong, but the evidence for the crucial place of women in domestic ancestor worship is accumulating. I was struck by the prominence of this womanly role in Singapore (Freedman 1957: 45); Gallin (1966: 148, 247) records it; and a Chinese writer has recently done the same in respect of another village in Taiwan, although he appears to treat what he has seen as a sign that men have abdicated their role in favor of women in recent times. He writes of the village of Chin Chiang Ts'o that he and his colleagues did not see a single case in which a male *chia-chang* (family head) led his sons and grandsons in domestic ancestor worship. Men (he goes on) have become indifferent, have neglected their responsibilities, and are now represented by women (Ch'en 1967: 174). I prefer to accept the observations and not draw any moral about modern social change.

We have seen that a collection of tablets in a domestic shrine may include a tablet of a non-ancestor, and the presence of such an out-sider, who will automatically share in the general offerings made at the altar, forces us to examine the implication of statements that Chinese worship their ancestors. Some Chinese writing about peasants (e.g., Yang 1948: 90) deny that "worship" is the right word, and it hardly needs to be said that Confucian agnosticism has made it possible for the educated elite to look upon (or at least to present) their reverential treatment of their ancestors as a form of decorous ceremony. I think that Yang (1948: 90) is unjustified in asserting that Chinese "do not worship their ancestors in the way the gods are worshiped," for it can be shown for the mass of Chinese that first, the same ritual elements enter into the approach to ancestors as in that to the gods (offerings, libations, incense, and so on), and second, both gods and ancestors fall into the category of *shen*, "spirit." (It does not follow, of course, that ancestors and gods are treated exactly alike. In an important paper entitled "Gods, Ghosts, and Ancestors," as yet unpublished, Arthur Wolf discusses the differences in ritual treatment on the basis of his Taiwan field data.) But a difficulty seems to arise from the fact that Chinese also speak of their actions for the dead as commemoration. In Singapore I found (Freedman 1957: 219) that Hokkien Chinese most commonly used the term *ki-liam* (Mandarin: *chi-nien*), "to commemorate," in the context of domestic ancestor worship, and it is clear that the desire to keep a person's memory green is a crucial element in the total system of ideas. The ancestral portraits of former times and the photographs of today are by themselves evidence of that notion: they are in no sense worshiped (except when photographs have been inserted into tablets or placed on altars as substitutes for them). As a Chinese, a person feels under an obligation to perpetuate the memory of somebody with whom he has lived. At the same time, the further obligation is incurred to prevent him from going unfed, whence his share in the offerings made in general at the altar. That is to say, the presence of outsiders on an altar highlights the fact that domestic ancestor worship is compounded of memorialism, devotion to the needs of the dead, and subjection to their vague authority.

Shifting our attention to the rites conducted in ancestral halls we see at once that we are dealing with a different kind of ancestor. There is a sense in which there are now no individual ancestors but rather a sort of ancestral collectivity, the common spiritual property of a corporate group. True, the names of key ancestors are picked out in the grand rites and people may decorate (and even perhaps pay private attention to) the tablet of some ancestor for whom they are specially concerned; but the atmosphere in the hall is overwhelmingly one in which a group of male agnates (or at least their elders and elite on their behalf) dramatize their existence by praising and sacrificing to a body of ancestors that they hold in distinction from other groups of like order. The twice-yearly rites and festivities are a manifestation, to both the worshipers and those from whom they are differentiated by those acts, of a claim to a special standing and distinction bound up with the reciprocal relationship of honor between living and dead. Men glorify their ancestors and parade them as the source of their being. For their part the ancestors bask in the glow of the solidarity and achievements of their descendants.

This is a world of men. Their wives enter the hall only as tablets— a dumb and wooden fate. And even then, they are rarely admitted in the same numbers as men, for as we have seen in the case of the Sheung Shui halls, the wives of the most senior ancestors are likely to be represented, but not those of the men who have been installed on account of their special honor or generosity. The ancestral hall is not merely the site of agnation; it is the locus of the political life of the agnatic community, and in that life women can have no public place. The contrast with domestic worship is sharp: that sphere belongs above all to women; the ancestors are capable of some immediate intervention in the lives of their descendants; it is a realm of personal relationships between living and dead. In the halls the ancestors are raised by men to a plane from which notions of punitive behavior are excluded, whence only pride and generalized benignity flow.

The very same systematic difference is to be seen between the rites performed at the graves of recent forebears and those at structurally significant tombs of remoter ancestors. When family parties go out to the graves (ideally sited in the hills) to care for and make offerings at them—which they do at least at Ch'ing Ming—they enter into the same kind of relationship with individual forebears as we find in domestic worship. The women are prominent; personal appeals to the dead may be made; the delicacies offered are likely to be adjusted to the tastes of the departed. But the rites at the great tombs of distant ancestors are all pomp and splendor, a kind of alfresco version of what (if a group has a hall) will have taken place indoors, perhaps with chants of praise and bursts of music.

Yet as soon as we begin to consider the role of tombs in ancestor worship, we are forced to recognize that the term "ancestor worship" cannot embrace all that the Chinese do ritually to make their ancestors significant in their lives. When they worship at the graves they address themselves to entities that are identical with, or at least of the same order as, those tended in domestic shrines. (The distinction depends on the analysis one makes of the *hun* elements of the nonphysical personality; see Freedman 1967a: 86.) But in this context the buried ancestor is presenting only one of two sides of his nature, for he is not merely a disembodied soul but also a mystified set of bones. As the former he is attached to a tablet and hovers above his grave; as the latter he is permanently in the earth, where his relationship to his "physical" surroundings has a direct bearing on the fate of his descendants. We are now in the realm of *feng-shui*, "geomancy," the mystical determination of fortune by the acts of men on their enviroment. (See Freedman 1966: 119–42; 1967a: 87ff; and 1969 *passim*.)

In the *feng-shui* of graves (that is, of *yin* habitations)—as distinct from that of buildings (*yang* habitations)—men seek to site their tombs where the "winds and waters" are most favorable; they look to this siting as a means of establishing or maintaining good fortune—riches, rank, and progeny—and they expect the ancestral bones to respond to the treatment to which they subject them. The worship of ancestors, which hinges on the moral duty of *hsiao* ("filial piety"), is counterbalanced by the "disrespect" of ancestors implied in the *feng-shui* of graves.

We have seen that tombs may be used as foci of lineages and their segments, either supplementing or replacing halls; and in the context of ancestor worship these graves are symbols of agnatic solidarity. But in geomancy the tombs mean something different, introducing fine points of differentiation among agnates. A man seeks to site a grave in such a way that the benefit it is designed to produce will flow to him alone or to him in the company of close patrilineal kinsmen. The benefit resulting from good siting ramifies along the lines of agnatic descent from the man or woman buried in the grave (a woman's agnatic descendants being her own children and the patrilineal issue of her sons); the remoter the buried ancestor, the wider will be the spread of beneficiaries, so that it becomes part of the strategy of choice in *feng-shui* to fasten onto a near ancestor in order to restrict the range of the people with whom one will be forced to share the benefits procured. The great tombs of apical ancestors yield geomantic profits of too general a character; agnates differentiate themselves by exploiting the *feng-shui* of their proximate forebears.

The point that in geomancy competition between agnates is of the essence is brought home most dramatically by the behavior of brothers, among whom in the Chinese system there is a built-in tendency to be rivalrous when they are adult. All brothers must of course benefit from the geomantically sited tomb of a common parent, but in fact the rules of *feng-shui* presuppose that they will not profit equally, for it is laid down that it is virtually impossible so to site and orient a tomb that all children will enjoy a like happiness. The evidence is abundant that brotherly squabbling attends the attempt to get agreement on precisely where, in which direction, and at what time to bury a parent. By *feng-shui* men seek to individualize their fate, pressing individualism to the point where each can strive to climb above his fellows, and at their expense, for one man's gain is seen as another's loss.

Ancestors in their tablets and as they receive offerings at their graves are *shen* and their affinities are with Heaven (*t'ien*). Men cannot expect them to pour out their blessings without reciprocity; the ancestors are moral beings. Ancestors as bones, on the contrary, partake of the nature of Earth (*ti*); they are morally neutral, and the benefits of which they are the vehicle are amoral. Men use their buried forebears for their selfish ends, manipulating in the context of *feng-shui* the ancestors whom they revere in the realm of worship. It is a remarkable feature of Chinese religion that the ancestors can be shown, in segregated spheres, to be symbols of authority and honor on the one hand and symbols of the satisfaction of greed on the other. That latter aspect of the treatment and conception of ancestors is poorly reflected in the literature. Is it because the *feng-shui* of graves is a kind of negative ancestor worship about which Chinese writers themselves are uncomfortable and which the foreign observers of China have been unable to see, partly perhaps by their being overpersuaded by the Confucian models set before them?

The brief excursion into geomancy in turn suggests the possibility that there remain much wider fields within which to inquire into the symbolic roles of Chinese ancestors. In this connection I may cite the pioneering work done in the last few years by Aijmer. In a recently published paper (1968; and see Aijmer 1964: esp. 84ff, 92ff) he has sketched out a set of ideas that explore the *yin* aspects (other than that revealed in *feng-shui*) of the ancestors, particularly in regard to their agricultural role in the underground, and has looked at the various key festivals of the Chinese year as forming a system of alternating visits between the living and their ancestors in both their *yin* and *yang* guises. He writes (1968: 96):

> During these festivals, *Qingming, Duanwu,* and *Zhongyang* [Ch'ing Ming, Tuan Wu, and Ch'ung Yang], there appears to be no particular concern about the ancestor tablets. New Year seems to be the big event for them. Thus *Qingming* implies a visit to the *yin* ancestors and *Duanwu* a return visit from the latter. *Zhongyang* implies a visit to the *yang* ancestors and New Year a return visit from them.

I leave the subject at this juncture. As with every other topic in the study of Chinese society, when we begin to systematize our understanding of it, the investigation branches off into directions—perhaps unforeseen at first—that lead to numerous points in the total system of Chinese social behavior and the total system of Chinese ideas. About these systems we have at the moment only general notions.

The Rites of Marriage

Ancestor worship and marriage rites form a balanced pair. They show the ritual treatment of the fixed bonds of agnatic kinship and the contractual ties of marriage. Marriage is an essential part of the making of kinship, but men are endowed with forebears and must choose affines. They are never relieved of the burden of dealing with their ancestors; they have only at irregular intervals to cope with the problem of taking in strange women. In the language of medicine, ancestor worship is chronic, marriage acute. The rites of marriage are, as I shall try very briefly to show, an extended commentary on the joy and trauma of forming new bonds of affinity. As in the case of ancestor worship, I shall assume that a general model of the rites can be constructed; in fact in this field we are on surer ground, for the descriptive literature is copious, and there is reason to suppose that there is a greater constancy over the whole of China in the institutions of primary marriage than there is in those of agnatic kinship. In view of the comparative richness of the sources I can afford to write more briefly in this part of the essay than in the first.[*]

[*] I list the most interesting of the sources I have used: Buxbaum 1968: 30–60; Cormack 1935: 41–58; Dols 1915–16: 467–86; Doolittle 1865: I, 65–98; Doré 1914: 29–39; Douglas 1901: 192–204; Egerod 1959: 50–53; Feng and Shryock 1950; Fielde 1885: 48–58; Fielde 1894: 35–47; Frick 1952; Gamble 1954: 379–85; Gray 1878: I,

The rites enshrine a single form of marriage, even though marriage is of different kinds, and it is to the one form that I shall confine the discussion: a man marries a virgin bride who is at that point brought into his paternal house as a primary wife. To Chinese, this is "marriage" in the abstract, and it is the norm from which all other forms of marital union are deviations, however significant they may be in real life. Men take secondary wives; widows marry; men marry into the houses of their fathers-in-law; girls are married in the houses to which they were given some years earlier in anticipation of marriage—sometimes these forms are statistically of great importance, but for the Chinese themselves their ritual expressions can never displace from its central position the set of rites that dramatize the movement of the virgin bride to her affinal family, there to occupy the status of her husband's major wife.

A marriage in this form transforms an immature girl under the authority of her agnates into a wife and potential mother within the control of her husband's kin. In moving from one family to another, a bride brings with her new sets of relationships for her affines, and in the transmutation of her own status from mere daughter to daughter-wife there begins a new traffic between two groups of agnates of which she is seen as the vehicle. For its continuity a family must have brides; the taking of them creates bonds of affinity that, from two points of view, provide uneasy benefits. To have affines is for a family to have potential friends and enemies. Especially when the status and rights of a married woman are at stake, the people who gave her in marriage may interfere intolerably in the affairs of those who received her. In the second place, the bride herself, the indispensable instrument for the perpetuation of the family and potentially an honored ancestress in it, is a menace to the very group she is summoned to serve, for she is an outsider who, in alliance with her husband, will form a nucleus from which will grow a new family pressing against the old—a new marriage in a new bedroom pointing toward a new stove. The doubtful profit from acquiring a bride and daughter-in-law and the relationships that adhere to her is a central preoccupation of the rites.

Before we turn to a brief summary of those rites (see Freedman 1967b for a fuller account and analysis) it may be worthwhile emphasizing one contrast between them and those associated with ancestor worship. The main dimension through which the ancestor rites move is

187–218; Grube 1901: 10–32; Highbaugh 1948: 46–51; Hsu 1949: 85–98; Hutson 1921: 14–21; Körner 1959: 8–14; Lin 1948: 39–49; Liu 1936; Lockhart 1890; Lynn 1928: 110–31; Osgood 1963: 277–84; Segers 1932: 91–117; Serruys 1944; Su 1966; Théry 1948; Wieger 1913: 451–87; Williams 1883: I, 785–91; Wolf 1964: 44–57; Yang 1948: 106–13. Also see Freedman 1957: 126–58.

time. Agnation is, so to say, a vertical extension; the rites look backward and forward in time, and with respect to place stress immobility. Families and lineages are conceptually anchored in space; they move forward along time. In the rites of marriage time recedes, for what is crucial is physical movement, symbolized above all in the transfer of the bride but realized also in the many comings and goings between the two houses that both precede and follow the central event. Space is now of the essence. It is no wonder, then, that in the People's Republic, in the face of fierce attacks against superstitious ceremonialism, people persist in practicing the central rite of the traditional wedding (the transfer of the bride in her sedan chair) by conveying her on a bicycle. Walking, even when practical, is just not good enough; a dramatic movement must be made.

The so-called "Six Rites" of marriage of the canonical *Li Chi, The Record of Rites*, lie at the base of the modern system, having been reworked at various times in dynastic codes and handbooks of rites and etiquette. The sequence of events laid down in the "Six Rites" is essentially the structure of all Chinese marriage in its preferential form, however modified and embellished by custom. Inquiries are made in a girl's family by a go-between sent by a family seeking a bride; genealogical and horoscopic data are sought by the go-between; the girl's horoscope is matched with the boy's; the betrothal is clinched by the transfer of gifts; the date of the wedding (that is, the transfer of the bride) is fixed; the bride is moved. (See, for example, Chiu 1966: 4ff.)

We need to fasten on one sociological feature of this sequence before considering its ritual expression. What for the sake of convenience we call "betrothal" is in reality the first step in the marriage itself, in the special sense that it establishes the bond of affinity between two families, the personal bond between the two parties most closely affected being fashioned later by the transfer of the bride. After betrothal a marriage exists that can be broken only by death or a negotiated rupture; but if one of the two parties dies, the marriage may still be carried to the second stage by the surviving girl proceeding as a widow to take her place in the boy's house or the surviving boy going through the final rites of marriage with the dead girl.

The "Six Rites" are not concerned with one essential feature of modern Chinese marriage: "initiation." The canonical rites keep that event quite distinct, but we know it as an intrinsic part of the rites immediately preceding the transfer of the bride. Each in his own house (usually the night before the day the bride is to be conveyed), the girl has her hair ritually put up, the boy is "capped" or given a courtesy name. By that solemn act the married pair are rendered fit to enter into the conjugal tie of marriage, both having been made ready for the circumscribed emancipation that the transfer of the bride will bring. Once placed side by side and installed in their bedroom (their private quarters), the couple form a unit endowed with its own economic personality and a promise of greater independence to come. It is one of the striking features of Chinese family organization that while a man has little in the way of individual property rights until he eventually takes out his share of the family property on division, when he marries he becomes part of a conjugal property-owning unit endowed with furnishings of the bedroom brought by the bride and paid for to a large extent out of the money earlier passed from the groom's family to the girl's. Within the conjugal unit the bride herself holds as her own property such personal wealth (jewelry and cash, but even sometimes rights to income from land) as she has acquired on her own as a maiden or been presented with by her family and friends. A new family has begun to grow within the bosom of the family that calls it into being.

The "Six Rites" begin with the tentative investigations preceding marriage and emphasize the exchange of genealogical and horoscopic details and the role of the go-between. The data on the two families are required for the proper matching of families of like social status and for determining the position of the boy and girl each in his own family; in real life they may be dispensed with. Horoscopes and go-betweens, on the other hand, are crucial, and we are able to see part of the reason why as soon as we realize what hopes are staked in marriage and what is feared from it. The Chinese say that marriages are made in Heaven, and the horoscopes are examined to discover who has been prematched with whom. Yet we know in fact that they are merely a ritual mechanism for confirming the matches already hit upon, even when the actors are unaware of procuring the supernatural confirmation of what they desire. (See Freedman 1967b: 10f, and Eberhard 1963.) Heaven must be made to speak, and yet people are bent on realizing the benefit of their careful calculations of social, economic, and political advantage. I think that Eberhard is wrong to suggest (1963: 55) that in this context people do not believe in "fate," the treatment of horoscopes seeming to be "a manipulation which normally is more or less playful or 'ceremonial,' but which can be used to call off marriage talks. . . ." The forms of divination used are far from playful; the belief in fate is, I suggest, genuine. Both the sanction of fate and the achievement of self-interest are sought; they can be reconciled by multiple divinations. The belief in the preordaining of a match (symbolized in the rites by using red threads to tie together documents, candlesticks, and cups) is part of a system of ideas that recognizes the appalling dangers and risks of marriage. As I have put the matter elsewhere (Freedman 1967b: 11), "the doctrine of predestined marriage relieves men of a frightening burden of responsibility. Fate does not force them to a course of action; it helps to reconcile them to its almost inevitable failure." More is hoped for from any marriage in the way of fruitfulness and peace than the system can produce. As for the go-between, whatever else his functions may include in the way of negotiating delicate transactions, if he is a matchmaker he stands as an external agent who can be blamed for disappointments and disasters that follow a marriage.

The main body of rites constituting a wedding segregate the girl from her ordinary life in her natal house, prepare her for the pains and duties of her married life, transfer her in a state of marginality to her new house, and begin the process by which she will be incorporated there. Consider as an illustration some of the data drawn from a study made in Tung-kuan, Kwangtung. A month before she is due to leave for her wedding, the girl is confined to one part of the house, where she is accompanied and comforted by girls of about her own age. They sleep with her at night and work with her in the day. "During the night she wails very loudly, and as she wails she cries one by one the names of her parents, her brothers and sisters, paternal uncles and aunts, and similarly close and intimate relatives and friends. The words she uses are like those of a sad song of parting." (Liu 1936: 85.) The texts of such songs are given in the source. There are also on record lamentations and songs sung for the girl by her relatives and friends that set out the duties she is about to assume and the tribulations of her new life. (See Frick 1952: 27f, 33ff; and see Yang 1963 and Highbaugh 1948: 47–49 for English translations of marriage songs.) The preparation, which in most cases culminates in the "initiation" rite of putting up the hair, is both a dour instruction in the domestic and marital discipline to come and a rupture of the relationship between the bride and those among whom she has grown up.

When at last the girl is dispatched to the husband's house we see in action the most complex set of symbols and ritual prescriptions and proscriptions, a very few of which we may note. To reach the sedan chair that awaits her (and which, coming from the other house to fetch her, has perhaps met with opposition and delay), the bride must either be borne out of the house or walk upon the covered ground. Again, when she leaves the sedan chair at her destination her feet must not touch the bare earth—between one house and the other she is, so to speak, in a state of suspense. The journey, a transition at once physical and social, must be lengthy; for this reason, if the two houses are close together (although that is unlikely to be the case in the countryside, since women usually marry out of their own villages), the procession with the sedan chair as its center must take a roundabout route. Sealed inside the chair, which has been inspected before her installation in it to insure its freedom from evil, the bride sits armed with instruments to ward off malign influences and with symbols of peace. The world of humans, spirits, animals, and things is replete with threats to her and her fertility.

Once in her new house, the bride is treated ritually (mirrors are flashed, for example) to cleanse her of the evil adhering to her before she is led for the first time to her bedroom. It is clear that in the period from her dispatch to her reception she has undergone a radical transformation as a person and as a vehicle of social relationships. When her family sends her off she becomes to them an outsider, moving from the status of cherished daughter to that of potential enemy: ritual acts are performed to prevent her taking away any of the prosperity of her natal house, and behind her the doors are shut to insure that its fortune does not follow her. In the new house, by the time she has been stripped of the malignities she may have brought with her and made by rites to express her promise to produce peace, she is on the point of being bonded to her husband by their joint worship of Heaven and Earth, the ancestors of the house, and the Kitchen God.

These religious acts are coupled with the grand feasting and "the disturbance of the room" to form the core of the rites that see the bride wedded and bedded. "The disturbance of the room" calls for some comment. It is the bride's last great public ordeal. She must submit herself to being exhibited in her bedroom in the company of her husband, exposing herself to boisterous and even obscene teasing from all comers, young and old. It is a climax in the rites in which the curtain of domestic discipline is temporarily raised to be decisively dropped forever. For during the rowdy display, and never again, the barriers between young and old are lowered and sexuality is given open expression.

If the rites so far described take place on the same day as the bride's transfer (and this is commonly the case), the next day sees her introduced formally to the seniors among her affines, and she is ritually inducted into her kitchen duties. A few days later, usually on the third day after the main wedding events, the couple go on a formal visit to the bride's natal house, where she is received as a guest. At this point, although further rites in the sequence may be found, we may say that the marriage is completed.

This is the barest sketch of a very few points in the sequence, which I now leave in order to explore some of its implications.[*] The rites of marriage demonstrate that the bride's body, fertility, domestic service, and loyalty are handed over by one family to another. To her natal family the loss is severe, both emotionally and economically: a member of the family is turned into a drain on its resources and a potential foe. On the other hand, the natural duty of marrying off a daughter is fulfilled and a bond of affinity is established with members of another family and community, a bond that, even as it leaves the girl's family ritually and socially in a relationship of inferiority with the boy's, provides it with a tie that in some circumstances may be worth exploiting. Economic and political relationships across communities may flow along the channels of affinity. For its part, the boy's family, while acquiring major rights in the girl and potential economic and political benefits parallel to those of the opposite family, must reckon with the possibility that the bride will become a focus of disruption within their own ranks and, never completely severed from her own kin, an occasion for unwanted interference in their affairs by their new affines. The rites presuppose what in reality may be quite untrue: that before "betrothal" the two families are unknown to each other. They emphasize the formality and distance between the families, mediating their relations through go-betweens, heightening their conflicting interests, and segregating them in the main events of the sequence from proposal to completion.

We may read the rites so openly, but they are not to be taken as simple statements capable of being given clear and unambiguous meanings by those who participate in them. Rites, as symbolic affirmations, are the opposite of jural rules. Jural rules rely for their value on their relative clarity; rites derive their strength from their poetic vagueness. Indeed, when the jural rules are themselves lacking in clear definition and are internally contradictory, then the rites exploit them by exaggerating their ambiguities and discrepancies. It seems to me that the Chinese rites of marriage above all stress the ambiguity of affinal relationships. Agnation has its problems, but both in ancestor worship and the rites of marriage clear enough leads are given to its ideal state; it remains for the rites of marriage to dramatize the indecisiveness of affinity.

The contrast between agnation and affinity leaves out of account the *tertium quid* of kinship through women. Yet it is precisely in this third category of relationships that we see at work the struggle between the first two. Affinity has a double aspect: from one point of view it is a bond

[*] Other points are dealt with in Freedman 1967b; I am planning a more comprehensive study of the subject.

between groups of agnates; from another, it is a tie between men and their mothers' agnates. As a man sees it, his mother having been incorporated into his family and placed in the company of his ancestors, is a member of his agnatic group; yet to her agnates he is both a kinsman and an affine—they are at once his matrilateral relatives and the group connected to his own by marriage. A man's wife and through her all her kin are his affines, but from the standpoint of the wife herself the relationships into which she was born are transmuted at the time of marriage into ties that take on the color of affinity; she is now a member of a group to which her natal group is linked by her marriage. (For the change made by marriage in a woman's mourning duties for her own kin, see Freedman 1958: 101.) It is in this ambivalence that we can detect uncertainties in the required behavior between affines and the playing out of the ambiguities in the rites of marriage.

The rites pose a problem and leave it unresolved. How is a woman to reconcile her duties as wife and daughter-in-law with those she has as sister and daughter? How are a group of agnates to reconcile their independence with the need to form ties by marriage? The bride's solemn send-off from her natal house is not a complete termination of her filial and sibling ties, for the rites also establish her as a married daughter with claims on her parents and brothers. (See Freedman 1967b: 23.) Her family retains an interest in her well-being, most dramatically stated in the rites at the end of her life, when her brothers arrive to insure that her death is natural and that her funeral is lavish enough to reflect their own standing. (See Freedman 1967b: 22.) These interfering men are affines to the bereaved family, and yet they are also mother's brothers, in which role they are affectionate protectors of their sororal nephews and often sought by them to act as mediators among themselves. They also occupy a chief place in the marriage rites, appearing in the rites performed in the bride's house and in the groom's; in the latter the maternal uncle is given the seat of honor at the feast. But the ritual involvement of ties through women does not end there, for the bride's younger brother (a mother's brother in the making) is usually given some special role to perform in the house to which the bride travels. (See Freedman 1967b: 21f.) Groom's mother's brother and bride's brother are ritual evidence of the non-agnatic links forged by a family in two generations—kindly matrilateral kinsmen on the one side, and troublemaking affines on the other.

This account of the marriage rites touches on the main line of the "argument" that runs through them; it ignores almost totally the rich symbolism—in word, action, and object—of which each significant step in the unfolding of the rites is composed. These symbols are of course not only related among themselves to form the "argument," but are each part of wider fields of symbolic discourse in Chinese culture. In the last analysis, then, we cannot fully understand what goes on at a Chinese wedding until we have studied all the realms of symbolic meaning that bring their significance to this one set of rites. Once again we have to end one study by saying that it is merely the beginning of another.

Chinese Kinship and Mourning Dress

ARTHUR P. WOLF

Seen from a distance, from the top of a building or one of the hills on which most graves are sited, the procession following a Chinese coffin is a colorful sight. The mourners wear long robelike gowns, some of rough dirty-brown sackcloth, others of gray flax or grass cloth, and still others of unbleached white linen or muslin; scattered among these are blue gowns, red gowns, and, on the rare occasion, a yellow gown. Female mourners cover their heads with a hood that almost hides the face and hangs down the back to the waist; men wear a hempen "helmet" over a short hood or one of two kinds of baglike hats of unbleached or dyed muslin.* A mourner's hood is sometimes of the same material as his gown, sometimes of a different material. The hood itself may be plain, or it may display a stripe or one or more patches of another material. A common combination is a tall spreading hat with a red stripe to which is sewn a smaller patch of grass cloth or blue muslin. I have never tried to count the number of mourning costumes in the Chinese repertoire, but there must be at least a hundred immediately recognizable variants. A funeral procession of fifty mourners usually includes twenty or more different combinations of textiles and colors.

This paper examines the meaning and social purpose of Chinese mourning dress, not to gain an understanding of mortuary customs, but as a means of studying Chinese symbolism and Chinese kinship. Mourning dress uses color and texture to distinguish among a number of categories or classes of kinsmen. In so doing it contrasts colors and textures and relates them to the social world, thereby defining the vocabulary of

---

* For further details on these and other costumes see De Groot (1894: II, chap. 6).

the symbolic system. It also contrasts kinsmen and expresses their relationships in terms of colors and textures, thereby defining another aspect of the kinship system. I say "another aspect" because the distinctions made at funerals are not the same as those drawn in other social contexts. The value of reviewing mourning dress is that it provides us with another view of a complex social landscape. This new perspective on familiar landmarks also gives us an opportunity to place other vantage points in social space.

I have already used the adjective Chinese several times, but the reader should be warned that what I say applies only to a part of China, a very small part. The funerals I observed all took place in or around the town of Sanhsia, an old river port in the southwestern corner of the Taipei basin in northern Taiwan; my informants—a geomancer, a seamstress, the proprietors of two small stores, and the mourners at several funerals —were all born and raised in the same town. In this area of Taiwan a widower who plans to remarry wraps his clothes in a bundle, ties the bundle to the end of an umbrella, slings the umbrella over his shoulder, and then jumps over his wife's coffin, as if to say, "You go your way and I'll go mine." In southern Taiwan a man would never declare his intention to remarry at his wife's funeral: "The wife's relatives would be furious." We must be careful not to let a part of China stand for the whole, or the whole for any one of the parts.

I will begin with the more obvious, less complicated aspects of the analysis and proceed, as gradually as the subject will allow, to the less obvious, more complex aspects. Consider first the way in which the deceased's lineal agnatic descendants are distinguished by generation. Sons wear a gown made of *muâ:-pò*, a rough, very coarse hempen material ordinarily used in making sacks; the grandsons, except for the eldest (to whom I will return later), wear gowns of *tĕ-â:-pò*, a yellowish-gray textile made of flax, finer in weave than mua:-po but still very rough; the gowns of the great-grandsons are usually made of muslin and are always dyed dark blue.* Despite marriage as early as twelve years of age, few people live long enough to see a fourth or fifth generation of descendents born, but for those few who do there are distinct mourning costumes for both generations. The appropriate mourning attire for the

---

* My romanization of Hokkien terms follows the orthography outlined in Nicholas C. Bodman's *Spoken Amoy Hokkien*. Chinese terms are italicized and marked for tone on first occurrence only. Where the original of a quotation uses Chinese characters or another romanization I have substituted Bodman's spelling. These substitutions are always given in brackets.

fourth generation is a red gown and a red hat; for the fifth generation, a yellow gown and a yellow hat.

These costumes do more than assign the generations to separate classes; they also order these classes along a continuum. Mua:-po is rougher and coarser than te-a-po, and te-a-po, which is too crude for daily wear, is rougher and coarser than muslin. The social use of colors in other contexts argues that the three colored gowns are also ordered. An imperial official of the first rank wore on the apex of his hat a dark red coral ball or button; an official of the second rank, a light red button. Officials of the third and fourth ranks were distinguished by dark blue and light blue buttons. The names of the emperor's lineal descendants were officially recorded on yellow paper; the names of his collateral agnates, on red paper (Gray, 1878: I, 22). Yellow, the imperial color, is of a higher order than red, and red in turn is of a higher order than blue. The overall order is from mua:-po gowns, at one end of the scale, through gowns of te-a-po, blue, and red, to yellow gowns at the opposite end of the scale.

The keys to the meaning of this scale are mua:-po and the color red. Mua:-po is to the Chinese what sackcloth was to the Old Testament Jews; it is the very essence of mourning, expressing sorrow and a complete abnegation of personal comfort. Red, on the other hand, is the color of joy, the color of firecrackers, good luck charms, and bridal gowns. And being the antithesis of sorrow, red is also opposed to mourning. When an emperor died shops all over China covered their red signs with black or white paper; during national mourning a bride had to travel in a black sedan chair rather than the usual red chair (Doolittle 1865: I, 371). The opposition between red and the emotions appropriate to mourning is displayed on doors all over Taiwan. On the first day of the lunar year every family pastes good luck charms or couplets on either side of the main door of its house; these are intended to renew the family's good fortune and are always painted on red paper. Should a death occur in the family during the year, these red charms are immediately pasted over with plain white paper.

Mua:-po and red stand in sharp opposition, but this opposition does not mark a break in the scale. There is rather a turning, by degrees, from sorrow and mourning to joy and renewal. Beyond red is the imperial color, yellow, expressing the intensified joy that comes with high attainment. Between red and mua:-po are te-a-po—which is like mua:-po only less so—and blue. Blue is the middle point on the scale, halfway between the extremes of joy and sorrow. The color of scholars' robes and the gowns of minor officials, it can express a dignified joy, a mild degree of attainment. But it is not inappropriate to sorrow and mourning. According to the Reverend Justus Doolittle (1865: I, 368), the official seal on a dispatch announcing an emperor's death was blue. Before electricity the lanterns people carried to light their way at night displayed either their surname or their official title; W. H. Medhurst (1873: 143–44) tells us that "the characters are always inscribed in red or black paint, save in time of mourning when blue is employed."

Contrary as it is to Western ideas of mourning, the expression of degrees of joy and sorrow at a funeral is entirely appropriate in China. A Chinese line of descent is essentially a chain of obligation in which every man's first duty is to perpetuate the chain. Each person receives from his father and grandfather a name, education, and property; in return for these he is obligated to respect and obey his parents and bear children to continue the line. There are therefore two emotions that are appropriate when a man dies. There must be grief and sorrow on the part of those who are most indebted to the deceased, but there can also be joy. If the man has lived to witness the birth of great-grandsons or even great-great-grandsons, he has repaid his parents and grandparents in full measure. His sons and grandsons must wear mua:-po and te-a-po to express their grief, but his great- and great-great-grandsons should wear joyful colors to announce this accomplishment to the world. The mournful degrees of our scale express the obligations of juniors to seniors; the joyful degrees, the happy fulfillment of these obligations.

An examination of the use of color in mourning adds to our understanding of the color's meaning as well as to our understanding of mourning attire. This is particularly true of the color red. When a death occurs, the bereaved family immediately pastes white over the red on their house; their neighbors hang a length of red cloth across the lintel of their front door. Red is inappropriate on the house in which death occurs, but it seems to be necessary on the homes of their neighbors. When I asked one of my informants why, he answered, "If you don't do something, someone in your family may die." This also seems to be why bereaved families often present a gift of red chopsticks and red silk to other families living in the same house. The Reverend Doolittle (1865: I, 209–10) explains: "As death is an inauspicious event, and the presence of the coffin containing the corpse in the common hall is an inauspicious circumstance, the Chinese have endeavored to dispel or prevent any unhappy results from reaching to the other family by the expedient of presenting red articles. These, under the circumstances, are emblematical of continued good fortune to the family, and are considered a surety that it will certainly have sufficient 'food and clothing,' the unlucky presence of the coffin, tending to the contrary, notwithstanding."

Red in China is more than an expression of joy; it is also a prophylactic color, a means of warding off evil. It has the same dual function as firecrackers, which announce happy events and at the same time disperse ghosts. In some contexts the emphasis is on one or the other of these meanings; in other contexts both are intended. When a friend or relative sends a wedding gift in a red envelope, or when a bereaved family's neighbors hang red cloth over their doors, only one meaning is emphasized, the positive idea of congratulation in the first case and the negative idea of protection from contamination in the second. As the color pasted on the doors of all houses at the New Year, the color of signs announcing the opening of a new shop, and the color of a bride's gown and chair, red has two meanings and two functions. The arrival of a new season, the opening of a new shop, and a marriage are all auspicious events, appropriately announced with red, but they are also fraught with danger. The new year may not bring good fortune; the business may fail; the bride may not bear sons. The house and shop are pasted with red and the bride dressed in red in an attempt to dispel misfortune and ensure success.

An appreciation of these two uses of the color red is necessary to interpret mourning dress. Although red is the prescribed color of mourning for the fourth descending generation, it would be unthinkable for other members of the deceased's household or any of his children or grandchildren to wear red. Yet an element of red appears in the mourning attire of everyone else who attends the funeral. Friends and hired helpers always attach a piece of red cloth to their costume if they choose to wear mourning; there is a red stripe on the hats worn by the deceased's wife's brothers and his daughters' and granddaughters' husbands. A daughter's fiancé, if he attends the funeral, wears a red sash across his chest. Sisters who have married out of the family display a patch of red on their headdress, and so do their children. Distant agnates such as a father's brothers' sons and grandsons wear a patch of red, and red may appear on the costumes of the deceased's brothers and their children. It all depends on whether or not they are members of the same household. If the deceased and his brothers belong to the same household, the brothers wear plain white; if they have established independent households, the brothers add a patch of red to their white headbands.

What appears to be a confusion of colors is actually only a confusion of the two meanings of the color red. When worn by the deceased's great-great-grandsons, red expresses joy; but this is not its meaning on all mourning attire. Asked why a friend of the deceased or his daughter's husband wears red, people in Sanhsia answer "Because there wasn't a death in his family." A few add "So he won't loss money," or "So his children won't get sick." Among some of the mourners red expresses joy; among others it performs its prophylactic function, protecting the wearer from the malignant influence of death. One sphere of meaning encompasses the deceased's lineal agnatic descendants and members of his household; the other, collateral agnates of other households, married sisters and their children, matrilateral kinsmen, affines, and friends. Take as test cases the deceased's son, his great-great-grandson, and his brothers. A son can never wear prophylactic red because he is always a descendant and usually a member of his father's household. The result is that he can never wear red at all without appearing to celebrate his father's death. A great-great-grandson is also a descendant and barred from wearing prophylactic red, but he can wear joyful red because his existence is cause for joy. A brother can never wear joyful red for the same reason that a son cannot, but this does not mean that he never wears red. He may be a member of another household, and in this case he should wear red as a prophylactic. What is significant is not the presence or absence of red on any particular mourning costume, but rather two spheres of meaning that define two classes of mourners.

Our analysis thus far suggests that red and mua:-po will never appear as elements of the same mourning costume. Those mourners who are eligible to wear red as a prophylactic are always outsiders who are not deeply obligated to the deceased. They may wear red, but they would never wear mua:-po. The only mourners whose obligations to the deceased are such as to require mua:-po are his own children, and they are barred from wearing either kind of red. Among the deceased's descendants the only mourners who can wear red are his great-great-grandsons, and it would be highly incongruous for them to wear mua:-po. The purpose of their costume is to celebrate the deceased's long line of descendants. As a color of joy, red stands in opposition to mua:-po as an expression of grief; as a prophylactic color, red is opposed to mua:-po as a symbol of obligation.

I arrived at this interpretation of red and mua:-po while still living in Sanhsia. The reader can imagine my discomfort when I later observed a funeral procession that included a young woman wearing a gown of red covered by a second gown of mua:-po. If she was the deceased's daughter why was she wearing a red gown? But if she wasn't the deceased's daughter, why was she wearing a gown of mua:-po? My analysis suggests that she must be a child who is also a stranger, and to my re-lief I discovered that this is exactly what she was. She was the deceased's second son's fiancée. As a member of another family and another line of descent, she did not share in the deceased's fortune and was entitled to the protection of prophylactic red. But as a person committed to be-coming a daughter of the deceased, she was obligated to express her sorrow and future debt by wearing a second gown of mua:-po.

The precision with which Chinese mourning dress uses its vocabulary impressed me again a few days later. Among the mourners attending a funeral a few miles from town was a girl of eight or nine wearing a gown and hood of mua:-po with the addition of a large patch of red muslin. Even at her age she could have been a son's fiancée, but I knew that all the deceased's sons were married. Who besides a son's fiancée could be a child and yet to some extent a stranger? I asked at the funeral but could not find anyone willing to identify the child. Not until a week later did a friend of the deceased tell me that he had lived for a number of years with a woman in town. The girl at the funeral was his daughter by his mistress. As she had taken her mother's surname rather than her father's, she was not obligated to the deceased as a child. But though she was not a member of his family or his line of descent, she was still his offspring and shared "his bones." Mua:-po and red do stand in oppo-sition to one another, but they can occur in combination when circum-stances merge opposed categories.

Although the means of making these distinctions is not the same for all classes of mourners, mourning dress in Sanhsia usually distinguishes the deceased's relatives by generation. The one exception is the eldest son's eldest son. In the procession to the grave this senior grandson rides in a chair hung in front with a length of te-a-po covered by a length of mua:-po. The boy himself wears a gown of te-a-po covered by a second gown of mua:-po. Outwardly at least, the senior grandson goes to the grave dressed as a son. At the grave the two lengths of cloth on the chair are reversed so that on the return trip the te-a-po covers the mua:-po. The boy either discards his gown of mua:-po or puts the gown of te-a-po on over the gown of mua:-po. Having gone to the grave dressed as a son, the senior grandson returns attired as a grandson.

Asked why the senior grandson wears mua:-po to the grave, people in Sanhsia answer "Because he is the smallest son." Some put it this way: "If a man has five sons when he dies, you can say that the senior grandson is the sixth son." The senior grandson shares with the de-ceased sons one important characteristic: he has the right to inherit a share of the family estate. Real property in China is held by the family as a corporate possession, with the eldest male or head of the family as trustee. Daughters receive small shares of this estate in the form of dowries; the remainder is divided between the sons and the senior grandson. Wealthy families sometimes allow the senior grandson a share of the estate equal to the shares taken out by the sons; among the poor the senior grandson usually gets at most "enough money to pay for a wife." The size of the senior grandson's share varies with the circumstances of the family, but it is generally recognized that he has a right to some share of the estate.

When the senior grandson receives a share of the estate in the form of real property, this land is registered in his name, not his father's name. The senior grandson is exactly what his mourning dress suggests: an heir in the same sense that a son is an heir. The property a son inherits is held by him as a corporate trust for his own sons and grandsons. Unless the family is forced to sell some part of this estate, it is not divided until the man's sons divide their natal household, usually not until after their father's death. The property taken out of an estate by a senior grandson has the same status. His share is not amalgamated with his father's share, but is held in trust for his own children. He adds to this estate when his father's household is divided, but the property he inherited as senior grandson is not shared with his brothers. This estate remains intact until his own sons divide their parental household.

The senior grandson goes to the grave dressed as a son because he inherits like a son, but why does he return dressed as a grandson? Again the answer is clearly related to the boy's rights in property. The senior grandson has a right to a share of the property inherited from his grandfather, but as senior grandson he does not have any right to property acquired by his father and his father's brothers. He is his grandfather's son, but not his father's brother. The senior grandson goes to the grave attired as a son because he inherits a share of the property inherited or acquired by his grandfather; he returns dressed as a grandson because he is only a grandson with respect to the property acquired after his grandfather's death.

The example of the senior grandson provides us with a clue to the general meaning and purpose of Chinese mourning dress. Mourning dress does not reflect generalized kinship statuses, but is rather a reflection or declaration of rights in property. This is clearly the social origin of the distinctions drawn by the two meanings of the color red. Among those mourners who share property rights with the deceased, his descendants and members of his household, red expresses joy; outside of the family among people who do not share property rights with the deceased, red is worn as a prophylactic. The most significant case is that of the mourning dress worn by brothers. Brothers who are members of the same family share property rights and do not wear red when one of their number dies; brothers who have divided their parental family do not share property rights and do wear red. The purpose of wearing red as a prophylactic is to protect one's fortune from the contamination of death. So long as brothers are members of the same family they share a common fortune and do not need such protection, but once their parental estate is divided they have independent prospects that can be adversely affected by attending a brother's funeral.

We must now return to the subject of the colors employed in mourning dress. Sinologists will already have asked themselves why I have proceeded so far without mentioning the color white. According to one eminent authority, J. J. M. De Groot, white should not be considered a Chinese mourning color. Writing on the basis of years of observation in Amoy, De Groot states (1894: II, 601): "From what has been adduced in the above pages it is perfectly evident that the opinion, generally prevailing among Europeans and pronounced by many an author on China, that white is the colour of mourning in the Middle Kingdom, is totally false. The truth is, that the mourning colour there consists in the absence of any artificial tint, in other words, it is the original colour which nature has lent to hempen and other textiles. Even the white colour produced by simply bleaching the material is, as the reader has seen, excluded from deep mourning and allowed only in slighter mourning; hence it takes the part of what we might call semi-mourning."

De Groot admits that the cloth worn by many mourners is white in color but insists that the Chinese do not regard it as white: "The term [*pěq-sâ:*], 'white dress,' is never used in China in any other sense than that of the dress of the laity, in contra-distinction to that of the Buddhist clergy, who wear no undyed garments." (*Ibid.*) He emphasizes his point by referring to the Chinese dislike of wearing as part of daily apparel any material used in mourning. "During the summer, nearly the whole of the higher and middle class in China dress in white; and this would certainly not be the case were white the colour of mourning, every Chinaman being thoroughly convinced that mourning clothes exercise a disastrous, nay, a deadly influence on whomsoever and whatsoever they come in contact with." (*Ibid.*)

Although I am reluctant to challenge a sinologist of De Groot's reputation on a linguistic point, he is surely mistaken in stating that the

Chinese do not regard the unbleached linen worn by many mourners as
white in color. On Taiwan the linen or muslin used in many mourning
gowns is called *pĕq-pò*, literally "white cloth," and it appears that the
same was true of Amoy in De Groot's time. After describing an under-
garment "called [*pĕq-pô-sâ*:], 'cloak of white linen or cotton cloth,'" De
Groot tells us that a man's paternal uncles and his wife's brothers and
sisters wear a mourning gown "of bleached cotton or linen, cut and made
exactly like the [peq-po-sa:]" (1894: II, 597, 600). But De Groot is nonetheless right in insisting that the Chinese dislike wearing mourning materials as part of their daily apparel. Perhaps not all Chinese today are
"thoroughly convinced that mourning clothes exercise . . . a deadly influence," but the fact remains that most are reluctant to wear such materials as mua:-po and te-a-po except as mourning dress. A Chinese student attending my class at Cornell was shocked when I put on a gown
of mua:-po as part of a classroom demonstration.

We are thus faced with a Chinese puzzle. Chinese mourners wear
white cloth as mourning and also as daily apparel, yet most Chinese dislike wearing mourning materials for ordinary dress. The first step toward
solving this puzzle is to identify the mourners who wear peq-po. Brothers and friends wear a gown or headband of peq-po; male affines, a
gown of peq-po and a distinctive hat with a broad red stripe. The only
other use of peq-po among male mourners occurs in the hats of children
related to the deceased as grandsons and brother's sons and grandsons,
but this use of the material does not have any social significance; peq-po
is used in such cases only because the appropriate mourning material is
not stiff enough to make hats of the proper style. What is intended is
made clear by the addition of a large patch of te-a-po to the front of the
hat. Adult kinsmen of this category wear a hood made entirely of te-a-po.

The presence of brothers, friends, and affines in one category may appear as much of a puzzle as the one we are trying to solve, but in this
case one puzzle helps us to solve another. Under no conditions would
a Chinese father or grandfather wear mourning for his son or grandson.
The wearing of mourning is a duty juniors owe seniors. We might accordingly expect men to wear mourning for their older brothers but not
their younger brothers, since in many social contexts younger brothers
are expected to defer to older brothers. But in fact brothers wear mourning for one another regardless of their relative age. The Chinese explain
this by saying that when a man dies he becomes senior to those of his
brothers who survive him. What may at first seem a trivial ethnographic
datum provides us with a significant clue to our puzzle: the seniority
enjoyed by an older brother over his younger siblings is so slight that it

can be inverted without offending basic kinship principles. Although younger brothers are expected to defer to their older brothers in many situations, the relationship is essentially one of equality. The same is true of affines. One family may be wealthier or more powerful than the other, but in the realm of kinship they stand on the same plane. Marriage does not create a hierarchy of wife-givers and wife-receivers.

We thus find that despite its apparent heterogeneity the category defined by white does have a common dimension. Affines and brothers share with friends the essential quality of being the deceased's peers. Together with the fact that mourning is only worn by juniors for seniors, this suggests that white is worn when the mourner's obligations to the deceased are minimal. White is essentially a neutral color that expresses little more than the form of mourning. It is worn more as a matter of courtesy that as an expression of grief. Although De Groot was wrong in insisting that unbleached muslin is not regarded as white, he caught the meaning of this material in speaking of it as "slight" or "semi-mourning."

The meaning of white in mourning can be further specified by placing it next to the other mourning materials. When people in Sanhsia lay a dead man in his coffin, they put a number of coins in his pocket. These are removed just before burial and distributed among his children and grandchildren, who tie the coins to their wrists with a piece of string. Children use white string, grandchildren blue string (except for the senior grandson, who uses one white string and one blue string). White appears in the Chinese mourning spectrum above blue but below te-a-po. Shortly after a person's death his family hangs mourning lanterns on either side of the main door to its house. Depending on the number of generations of descendants surviving the deceased, these lanterns are wrapped with one or more strips of mourning cloth. The order of the mourning materials is always the same. The first and highest strip is mua:-po, the second te-a-po, the third peq-po, followed in turn by strips of blue, red, and yellow muslin.

The use of white on mourning lanterns also reveals another facet of its meaning. The rule in Sanhsia is that a family is entitled to add one strip of cloth to the lantern for each generation of descendants, plus one more as a kind of genealogical bonus. By this rule the lanterns of a man who died with children and grandchildren should be wrapped with mua:-po, te-a-po, and peq-po; but in fact these lanterns always display these three materials plus blue. We have already seen that mua:-po is identified with sons, te-a-po with grandsons, and blue with great-grand-sons; the extra strip of material is obviously the white strip, peq-po. When the context refers to generations of descendants, white is the color that does not count. The dress worn at funerals refers to rights in property, and in this context friends, affines, and brothers do not count.

De Groot tried to resolve the apparent inconsistency between the wearing of white in daily apparel and the wearing of white funeral gowns by maintaining that the bleached muslin worn at funerals is not regarded as white. It makes more sense to argue that white mourning is not mournful. Mua:-po and te-a-po are associated with the death of a parent or grandparent. To wear these materials as ordinary clothing is to invite the kind of grief they express, but there is no equivalent reason to avoid the use of white materials. The white worn by mourners does not imply deep grief; it is a neutral color worn as a courtesy by those who owe the deceased nothing more than a show of respect. Chinese mourning white means the absence of positive, joyful colors. People who are not obligated to wear harsh materials like mua:-po and te-a-po but who nonetheless feel some obligation to the deceased remove all signs of joy by wearing white to his funeral.

We have already discussed the mourning costumes worn by the deceased's male descendants and his brothers. Of the men who usually attend a funeral, the most important remaining to be considered are the deceased's brothers' sons and grandsons. What they should wear can easily be deduced from what has already been said. They would not wear mua:-po because they do not inherit. Their mourning dress must be lower on the scale of obligation, but it cannot be blue, red, or yellow, since these are positive colors declaring the deceased's joy in perpetuating his own line of descent. Peq-po is in the appropriate range of the mourning scale, but would be unsuitable because white implies social equality and would appear to challenge the seniority of the elder members of the family and the lineage. The only suitable mourning material for a brother's descendants is te-a-po. A brother's adult sons wear a gown of te-a-po and a hood of te-a-po, with the addition of a red patch if they belong to an independent household. A brother's grandsons are distinguished from his sons by the further addition of a small patch of blue muslin.

The significance of these costumes is best seen in relation to the mourning attire of male affines. The deceased's wife's brothers and his daughter's and granddaughter's husbands all wear long white gowns and tall hats with a broad stripe of red muslin. The three generations are distinguished by the addition of a small patch of te-a-po to the hat of a daughter's husband and a small patch of blue to the hat of a granddaughter's husband. Where generation determines the material used in both the gowns and headdresses of the deceased's descendants, it appears as only a minor detail of the mourning attire of junior collateral agnates and affines. Regardless of their generation relative to the deceased, these mourners wear either gowns and hats of te-a-po or gowns and hats of peq-po. The important social fact about collateral agnates and affines is not their relative generation but the fact that they are collateral agnates and affines.

We can now sketch an outline of the distinctions drawn by the mourning attire of male mourners. Above the deceased in both generation and seniority are his father and grandfather, his mother's brothers, and the older men of his lineage. These men are in no way obligated to the deceased and wear no mourning. The remainder of his social world is divided into two parts by the positive and negative meanings of the color red. On one side are his descendants and members of his family; on the other, his friends and all remaining relatives. Brothers may be on either side of the line but are always on the same social plane. They are part of a category of peers that also includes affines of all generations and all agnates of the same generation. Below the deceased and obligated to him are his own descendants and collateral agnates of descending generations. As is also the case with affines, whose distinctive hats mark them as affines, junior collateral agnates belong to a class in which generation is recognized but not emphasized. Generation only becomes the significant aspect of mourning dress when we take the deceased's own point of view. We then see five ranks of descendants whose costumes turn from grief to joy as we move down the generations from sons to great-great-grandsons.

Our picture of mourning attire in Sanhsia still lacks one significant dimension. Although my informants are all native residents of the town, speak the same dialect, and share a common culture, there are certain classes of mourners for whom they prescribe different mourning attire. According to one elderly woman who had recently prepared the mourning costumes worn at her father-in-law's funeral, an unmarried daughter should wear a gown of mua:-po and a hood of the same material. The proprietors of two small stores that rent mourning materials agree, but a seamstress who makes her living sewing mourning gowns claims that an unmarried daughter must attach a piece of te-a-po to her hood "to show that she is not married." A geomancer who attends an average of three or four funerals a week disagrees with both prescriptions. In his view an unmarried daughter should wear a gown of te-a-po and a hood of peq-po "with just a patch of te-a-po." When I told him I was surprised to hear that an unmarried daughter did not wear mua:-po, he explained that daughters only wear mua:-po when their parents have no sons.

The same informants also disagree about the proper mourning attire for a married daughter. The old woman who had recently buried her father-in-law told me that his married daughters wore gowns of te-a-po and hoods of plain mua:-po. "A married daughter's body belongs to her husband, but her head still belongs to her parents." The seamstress agrees with this description and offers the same explanation of the combination of te-a-po and mua:-po, but my other three informants all prescribe different costumes. The proprietors of the two stores insist that a patch of te-a-po must be attached to the hood, and the geomancer claims that the hood itself is usually made of te-a-po. "Daughters who have married out always wear te-a-po on their heads. The only ones who wear mua:-po on their heads are those whose husbands have married into their wife's family."

Such a variety of mourning prescriptions suggests that the rules governing mourning attire are vague and open to personal preference, but this interpretation cannot be maintained. While there is disagreement about some classes of mourners, everyone is in agreement about other classes. All my informants agree about the essential details of the mourning costumes already described, and they also agree on the proper attire for wives of the deceased's male descendants. A daughter-in-law should wear a gown and hood of mua:-po; a grandson's wife, a gown and hood of te-a-po; and the wife of a great-grandson, a blue gown and a blue hood. There is even complete agreement on the mourning attire appropriate for the wife of the senior grandson. She should go to the grave wearing a gown of mua:-po over a gown of te-a-po and return wearing either a gown of te-a-po or a gown of te-a-po over a gown of mua:-po.

Where disagreements occur, they reflect conflict in the kinship system. The society insists that a married woman belongs to her husband. As one of these informants put it in explaining why a daughter-in-law should wear mua:-po "just like a son," "We pay money for our daughters-in-law, and the children they bear are ours." But the society also insists that parents have the right to expect loyalty and devotion from their children. It is easy to forget this precept with regard to daughters-in-law, but it is not so easy to forget with respect to daughters. The result is that people agree on the proper mourning attire for a son's wife but do not agree on what is proper for female children. Whereas some people are willing to accept the fact that a married daughter belongs to her husband and prescribe te-a-po as the proper mourning dress, others claim that a married daughter's head is still theirs and prescribe a headdress of mua:-po. Still others compromise by prescribing a head-dress of mua:-po with a patch of te-a-po "to show that the woman is married."

The same problem is reflected in the disagreement about the appropriate attire for unmarried daughters. Until a daughter is married only her parents have a claim on her, but everyone knows that she will eventually marry. Some people choose to emphasize the fact that she still belongs to her parents and prescribe a mourning gown of mua:-po. Others accept the inevitable and prescribe te-a-po. In their view a daughter should not be equated with a son unless her parents plan to retain her loyalty by means of an uxorilocal marriage. Were the vocabulary of Chinese mourning attire less precise, these disagreements would not be reflected in mourning dress. But because this vocabulary does define status with clarity, there is no way of avoiding inconsistencies. Disagreements between people are inevitable because there is ambiguity inherent in the kinship system. The only way to avoid variation in mourning dress without imposing an arbitrary code would be to resolve the conflicts that it reflects.

There are fewer ambiguities of status among male mourners, and hence fewer areas of disagreement about proper mourning dress. The most common subject of disagreement is men who marry uxorilocally. The old woman who talked to me a few days after her father-in-law's funeral says that a man who marries into his wife's family always wears a gown of mua:-po. The appropriate headdress depends on whether or not he changes his surname. If he takes his wife's surname and thus gives up his rights as a father, he wears a headdress of te-a-po and the same hempen helmet worn by sons. But if he does not change his name and retains the right to name some of the children to his line of descent, he wears a hat of peq-po with just a patch of te-a-po. In her view a man who marries uxorilocally never wears mua:-po on his head "because his head belongs to someone else."

My other four informants disagree. The seamstress and one of the two shopkeepers distinguish between men who change their names and men who do not, but they claim that a man who changes his name should wear the same mourning as the deceased's sons. The proper mourning attire for a man who retains his own surname is a gown of mua:-po and a headdress of te-a-po "to show that the head belongs to someone else." The proprietor of the other store and the geomancer prescribe the same mourning for all uxorilocally married sons-in-law whether or not they change their names, but disagree with one another on what this attire should be. Where the geomancer prescribes a gown of mua:-po and a

headdress of mua:-po, "the same as for sons," the shopkeeper insists on
a gown of mua:-po and a hat of peq-po with just a patch of mua:-po.

The source of the disagreement is again a conflict inherent in the
social situation. The assumption that women will leave their natal family makes it easy to ignore a daughter-in-law's ties with her parents, but
it is not so easy to discount an uxorilocally married son-in-law's par-
entage. Regardless of whether or not he changes his surname, an in-
marrying husband should accept the obligations of a son toward his
wife's parents. But because the society stresses the obligations of male
children to their own parents, these ties are not easily altered by contract. The result is an ambiguity that is reflected in mourning dress. If
one takes the cultural ideal of filial obligation as relevant, a man's head
always belongs to his parents. But if one refers to the ideals governing
uxorilocal marriages, the man who marries into his wife's family becomes
her parents' son. If one looks to the contract negotiated at the time of the
marriage, a distinction must be made between men who do and men
who do not change their surnames. But if one looks instead to the social
reality of a man living in his wife's home, this distinction is less significant.

The reader may feel that this explanation of disagreements about the
proper mourning attire for an in-marrying husband gives too little weight
to the fact that uxorilocal marriage is a departure from Chinese custom.
Might not the disagreement exist simply because uxorilocal marriage is
not the preferred form? One might think so were it not for the uniformity
with which other departures from the preferred pattern are treated. In
this area of Taiwan it is common for families to give away their daughters and raise in their places wives for their sons.* Although these arrangements are also a departure from the preferred pattern, everyone
agrees on the proper mourning dress for a girl in this status. If one of the
girl's foster parents dies while she is still a child, she must wear the same
mourning as an adult daughter-in-law. Should her intended husband die,
she is expected to wear the same mourning as his sisters. While the girl
acquires the status of a daughter-in-law on entering the family, she does
not enter into a conjugal relationship until a second ceremony is performed after puberty. There is obviously no lack of agreement about
what people should wear so long as there is agreement on who they are.

The orientation of Chinese mourning dress can be fixed by comparing
mourning categories with those defined by kinship terminology. Just

---

* This institution is described in further detail in Wolf 1966.

as mourning is worn by juniors for seniors, and never by seniors for juniors, so kinship terms are used by juniors addressing seniors, never the other way around. Mourning and address both express the respect a junior owes a senior, but they do not always divide seniors into the same classes. A man addresses his older brother with a kinship term and receives his personal name in return, but he wears the same mourning for both older and younger brothers. Father's brothers are also distinguished in address but are not distinguished in mourning dress. While they are alive a man addresses his father's older brother as *ā-pěq*, his younger brother as *ā-ciěk*; when they die he wears the same mourning costume to both funerals.

These divergencies between the two symbolic systems are clearly a function of the way they relate to the social world. Address terms reflect daily patterns of authority; mourning dress reflects rights in property. A man must display respect for his older brother, and his father must do the same for his older brother. Many men grow up in families headed by one of their father's older brothers, and many also live for a few years in a family headed by one of their own older brothers. Relative age is thus a significant aspect of precedence and authority, but it is not significant with respect to rights in property. The crucial question with regard to property rights is whether or not the mourners and the deceased share rights in the same estate. If they do not, the mourners add a patch of red muslin to their gowns; if they do, the red is omitted.

This difference in the intent of mourning dress and address can also be seen in behavior. A man who is on good terms with his wife's parents usually addresses them with the same terms used for his own parents, and many people use the same terms in addressing the parents of classmates and good friends. This usage is understood as a sign of respect and deference, but a similar extension of mourning attire would not be so interpreted. Anyone who comes to a funeral wearing the mourning dress of a son is understood as claiming a share of the estate. Indeed, conflicting claims to property are often displayed in just this fashion. A man who has left the family by marriage or adoption but who feels he still has a right to a share of his father's estate will press his claim by attending the funeral dressed as a son. This usually precipitates a bitter quarrel. The heirs cannot allow anyone to wear the mourning of a son without publicly admitting his right to a share of the property.

The usual anthropological picture of Chinese social life presents us with a drab terrain of rights and duties. One of the values of studying mourning dress is that it affords us another view of this familiar landscape. We see in the distinctive costumes of the deceased's descendants not only a hierarchy of generations, but also the grief of a son and the joy of a man who died knowing there were generations of grandsons to see him to his grave. The distinctions made in mourning dress add a dimension of meaning to our appreciation of Chinese family life. When a Chinese family divides and establishes separate households, they divide more than a house and an estate. They also divide their fortunes and their fate. Where the death of a brother would have previously been accepted as a common loss, it is now a source of malignant influences against which prophylactic measures must be taken.

The fresh vantage point afforded by the study of mourning dress also allows us to survey Chinese kinship from another angle. We sometimes see unexpected alignments of familiar landmarks. Were one to catalogue the rights and duties of kinsmen, no two would seem more unalike than brothers and affines. A man's brothers always appear at the center of his social world, his affines at the periphery. The fact that they both wear white to his funeral suggests that we have been seeing only one side of the relationship. With regard to what is expected of their relationship, brothers are the closest of relatives. But in terms of the extent to which they are obligated to one another, they are no closer than affines. Chinese mourning white is a neutral color that implies social equality. That this is the color a man wears to his brother's funeral reveals a structural weakness at the very center of the Chinese kinship system.

The use of textures and colors to spell out social statuses in visual detail also gives us an invaluable opportunity to study Chinese symbolism. We see that textures and colors are not isolated signs, but rather points on a scale. The relevant portion of the scale varies from one context to another, but the order of the items always remains the same. The deceased's children use white strings with the coins taken from their father's coffin. In this context white replaces mua:-po and te-a-po but retains its place relative to the blue used by grandchildren. The scale is not simple: although the items at either end remain positive and negative in all contexts, the meaning of the items toward the middle varies with context. Contrasted with red, blue carries negative connotations; compared with white, it is a positive color. The meaning of a color depends on its place in the Chinese spectrum *and* the use of color in a particular context.

This paper is incomplete, not only as an analysis but as a description of Chinese mourning attire, and even of the mourning customs of San-hsia. I have ignored some classes of mourners because my information is incomplete, and I have omitted some details of mourning dress to avoid confusing a complex subject. The reader must remember that what I have said of Sanhsia does not necessarily apply to other areas of China; he has only to look at De Groot's notes on Amoy or J. G. Cormack's description of mourning customs in Peking (1935: chaps. 8, 9) to find striking differences. There is also an important comparison to be made between popular mourning customs and the mourning obligations set out in the Ch'ing code (see Freedman 1958: chap. 5). This paper only recommends looking at Chinese society in the fresh light of mourning.

Chinese Kin Terms of Reference and Address

JOHN McCOY

This paper examines a set of Toishan kinship data in a framework constructed through componential analysis.* My primary purpose is to describe a different view of the Chinese material and not necessarily to develop concepts concerning the technique itself; the results are essentially practical, not theoretical.

Earlier work on the Chinese kinship system tends to be predominantly descriptive rather than analytic. Chen and Shryock (1932) refer to Morgan's pioneer work of 1871 but question the data and propose their own study as more accurate. They in turn use a rather mechanical listing that is based largely on dictionary material. Fêng (1948) presents a similar approach designed to improve on the historical materials used by Chen and Shryock, but no change in method is intended. Kroeber (1933) develops a somewhat more dynamic approach by isolating discrete items in the terminology and discussing their processes of combining, after which he uses an historical approach to associate the development of the nomenclature with cultural transition. Chao's paper (1956) is an excellent discussion of the social situations in which the various forms are used. He also devises a multiple chart-form layout that might well be categorized as the beginnings of a componential analysis. This essay, then, is offered to test the Chinese terminology in terms of recent developments in formal semantic analysis.

The data presented here were derived from a project of linguistic re-

* I want to thank Floyd G. Lounsbury who, as discussant at the original reading of this paper, made a number of valuable comments and observations, many of which have been incorporated into this revised version. Maurice Freedman also gave much advice that influenced all parts of this study. Arthur and Margery Wolf were extremely generous with their assistance and did much to improve both the form and the content of my paper.

search on Szeyap phonology of which Toishan dialects are one part. Mandarin terms have dominated much of the kinship material published so far; for contrast it is important to have records of the dialect forms. We find that the reference terms tend to be consistent through most of the studies made so far, but we can expect some variation to show up in the dialect forms of address terminology. The more complete our record of these variations throughout China, the more significant our general and specific statements about the Chinese kinship structure.

During the past ten years much has been written on the theory and use of componential analysis in anthropology, and it seems unnecessary for me to repeat here points that have been made elsewhere.* However, the greater part of the material written to date has been designed to probe the theoretical limits of formal analysis as applied to anthropological data. As the theory has become more refined and its application more complex, it has developed a distinctive vocabulary, method, and approach. As a result of this process, formal analysis has become a small subfield of anthropology, one not always accessible to students unless they have made a particular effort to follow all the specialized literature now appearing. This is unfortunate, for valuable insight may be derived from the technique even on a relatively simple level, and preliminary analysis of kin data early in a field research project might point out areas of potential interest, areas often overlooked until access to the informants has been lost. This paper is offered as an example of such an analysis and as a suggestion for more detailed investigation in later field work.

To explain the method of my study, I must duplicate to a degree earlier explanations by other authors; there are variations from author to author, but the basic steps are fairly uniform. First, a set of kin terms is defined. This process frequently involves a series of preliminary decisions that may be arbitrary and therefore may ultimately affect the final product. How broadly is the definition of kin term to be interpreted? Where does one draw the line to make the resultant body of data a homogeneous, consistent, and manageable set? Such general questions as homonymity, metaphor, and connotative versus denotative meaning have been discussed by other authors (e.g., Wallace and Atkins 1960), but in specific sets of data there may even be difficulties in determining what is a basic term. This last problem relates to my study and is also particularly apparent in Conant (1961), in which the analysis of Jarawa

---

* Following the pioneer works of Goodenough (1951; 1956) and Lounsbury (1956), dozens of articles have elaborated on the techniques of componential analysis and applied them to various kinds of ethnographic data. For a good picture of the status of the field, see Hammel (1965a), especially the bibliography, which lists most of the significant work done in componential analysis.

terms of address includes a number of forms that might more properly be defined as titles, personal names, and nicknames. Conant (1961: 21f) argues that their inclusion allows "analysis to proceed," and that otherwise the empty spaces in the kin-term structure would be proportionately too numerous to permit formation of a significant paradigm.

The Chinese address terms present a similar though less extreme problem, for which I propose another solution. A kin term must be understood and used by all equivalent members of the community in the same way, given the same relationship. The varying use of names or titles from person to person produces a separate and distinct set of terms for each member of the community, and results in a series of idiosyncratic structures that should not be thought of as kin-term paradigms. The empty spaces in a kin-term paradigm are significant in themselves and may reveal valuable information about the social structure of which kinship is a part. In the Toishan address system these empty spaces are here marked *Name*,* indicating that no general lexeme exists for this particular intersection of components and that the person is addressed simply by some form of his given name.

Once the kin terms are selected they are transcribed in an objective notational system. Most studies use a set of primitives and compounds of primitives (e.g., Fa, Mo, Br, FaMo, FaBr), although a number of more algebraic approaches have been employed with Boolean-type symbolization and more complex operations performed with the data. (For an example of the latter, see Hammel 1965b.) For this paper I use the more traditional set of primitives Fa, Mo, Br, Si, So, Da, Hu, Wi, O(lder), and Y(ounger), with a genitive relationship indicated by juxtaposition. This transcription results in a minimal description of the chain of kin through which ego can trace his relationship with any other kinsman (alter).†

In the final step this description of a kin chain is examined for criteria

* In Toishan the address name normally consists of a familiarizing prefix *ʔa* 2 plus all or part of the given name.

The romanization for Toishan used here was developed for my own work in the Szeyap dialects of Cantonese. It consists of: the consonants p, t, k, ʔ (glottal stop), m, n, ŋ, f, s, h, l, with the clusters ph, th, kh, ts, tsh, lh (lateral fricative); the vowels i, e, a, u, o; the tones 1 (high-level), 2 (mid-level), 3 (low-level), 4 (mid-falling), and 5 (low-falling). In addition, there are two morphophonemic "changed tones," which are here marked on the basic tone of a given syllable with the symbols ′ (high-rising) and ˋ (low-falling). The tone symbol will be written after the other elements in a given syllable.

† This description is minimal only if some rule of economy is set up by which the shortest of all possible chains is that chosen for the analysis. Thus, FaFaDaSo might be as good as FaSiSo to describe a cousin relationship, but the shorter will be preferred. Such a rule is not arbitrary, since the longer form frequently produces ambiguities of the type FaFaSoSo, which might be ego, a brother, or a cousin.

("components") that are minimal and unambiguous in distinguishing each kin term. Any criterion differentiating one kin term from another is a valid component, and the minimum number of these necessary to distinguish all terms in the given set can be the basis for a valid componential analysis. (These procedures and the theoretical foundations are discussed in much more detail in Goodenough 1964: 222–25.)

This last step may involve a number of arbitrary decisions, each of which suggests the possibility of extracting different minimal combinations of components for the same set of kin terms. The problem of these alternative solutions and the significance of this indeterminacy for any extrapolations concerning cognitive processes have been discussed elsewhere. (See esp. Goodenough 1965: 259.) Such theoretical aspects will not be treated here, but any solution satisfying Lounsbury's (1964) requirements of parsimony and sufficiency should be considered valid.

My data are restricted to those gathered from informants from the northern half of Toishan District in central Kwangtung Province. The Toishan reference terms closely agree with those outlined in Fêng (1948) and seem to reflect a consistency found throughout China. The Chinese address terms show more dialect variation than the reference terms, but much of this variation comes from a simple substitution of terms rather than a difference in system. All of my informants are males, between the ages of 35 and 60, residing in Hong Kong but born in Toishan District.

Toishan Components and Their Codes

In the following paragraphs I outline my system of codes for the Chinese data. If my selection differs from the more traditional analyses, I elaborate on the considerations involved.

Focus of system intersection (F). This subset of components is coded:

F_1 – Ego

F_2 – Spouse

System intersection develops the point that in the Chinese data ego's kin terms and spouse's kin terms form two separate, similar, but not necessarily equal systems that intersect at the conjugal union between ego and spouse. Only their common descendants represent a true convergence of potentially equivalent sets of kin types, and any analysis of the Chinese terminology must keep the two systems distinct. The socio-economic importance of the two systems is not equal, but this inequality is more likely to be reflected in the limitations of the address terms than in the structurally more complete set of reference terms.

Given the traditional Chinese emphasis on the male line and the almost total assimilation of a wife into her husband's kin group, it is not surprising that studies of the Chinese data would tend to reflect this emphasis. There is, of course, no question that traditionally the husband's kin group has been culturally more important than the wife's, and I would not propose that the kin terms be taken as contrary evidence. I merely suggest here that it is impossible to make any realistic analysis of the full set of Chinese reference terms without first dividing the terminology into ego's and spouse's domains. The importance of considering system intersection for componential analysis is immediately apparent if we postulate female ego and male spouse.

One effect of this reorientation might be to suggest the desirability of doing a follow-up study of the Chinese kin-term structure from the point of view of female ego both before and after marriage. Again, reference and address terms should be contrasted for any possible differential development after the marriage. If further coupled with a semantic differential test, such a study might turn up some details of the changing role played by the woman in her family of orientation and her family of procreation. (For discussions of semantic differential as a means of testing psychological reaction to linguistic signs—in this case the set of kin terms —see Osgood 1957 and 1961.)

Descent line within the systems (D). This subset is coded:

D_1 – Male line (through father, son, or brother)

D_2 – Female line (through mother, daughter, or sister)

These components divide each of the two intersecting systems of the previous section into two major lines. As defined for the purposes of this analysis these two lines are not symmetrical; the male line (D_1) is extended across generations only through the males (Fa, FaFa, FaFaFa, or So, SoSo, SoSoSo), whereas the female line (D_2), if extended, passes through one female to her male line (Mo, MoFa, MoFaFa, or Da, DaSo, DaSoSo). For my data this limited function of the bifurcation concept will handle all the terms. To be fully applicable to an extended form of the Chinese reference system the subset (D) would need to be repeatable at two or more points along the chain from ego to alter, creating multiple separations into male and female lines.

Bifurcation is in part a restatement on a smaller scale of the concept of system intersection. Each point at which bifurcation occurs marks the spot in a kin-term structure where a choice must be made between the kin of an individual and the kin of his spouse. The distinction between the components of system intersection and those of descent line is essentially one of degree rather than kind; the kin of ego's spouse represent a larger and more complete subset of ego's kinship terminology than do those of any other nonlineal female affine in ego's system.

Relationship of alter to ego's line (R). This subset is coded:

R₁ – Lineal

R₂ – Collateral

R₃ – Affinal

These three components are usually contrasted as elements in two binary separations of lineal versus collateral and consanguineal versus affinal, but the three components given here are adequate and neater for the Chinese kinship data without omitting elements or overlapping. Even as a mechanical device this step would have validity, but its chief merit appears when the three-way split also coincides with such secondary structuring of kin as are found in mourning grades, ceremonial participation, and inheritance. In general terms, and some restriction based on sex being ignored, it is those persons designated with component R₁ (lineal) whom ego worships or who will be chiefly responsible for taking care of ego during his old age and carrying out the proper ceremonies for ego after his death. From the persons designated with component R₂ (collateral) will come those who join ego in larger socioeconomic groupings such as those honoring common ancestors, but the relationship is looser and becomes more casual in proportion to the distance of the generation of common ancestor. Persons marked with component R₃ (affinal) are important to ego chiefly in terms of the point at which they marry into his kin system.

The category of consanguineal is thus interpreted strictly to include agnates subsumed under the lineal and collateral components. All other kin types will then be affines with the components (F and D) giving further information concerning details of the affinal relationship.

It may be of some value to restate the descriptions of these three components in different terms. For example, component R₁ applies to consanguineal kin with whom one shares ancestors and descendants;* R₂ applies to kin with whom one shares certain ancestors but no descendants; R₃ applies to those kin with whom there are no consanguineal ties, no ancestors in common, but possibly common descendants. Obviously a quite different set of reciprocal relationships is involved between ego and each of these three categories of kinsmen.

We should note that, with cousin marriages permissible in the Chinese case, a component R₃ would not necessarily rule out the possibility

---

* Strictly speaking, two persons in a lineal relationship share all the ancestors of the older but not all his descendants and all the descendants of the younger but not all his ancestors.

of a consanguineal relationship as well. The point must be that the relationship after marriage is the significant one, and at least terminologically the affinal relationship takes precedence over any earlier kin status; the kinship terminology provides us with no contrasts between cousin marriages and non-kin marriages.

   Generation of alter in relation to ego (G). This subset is coded:
   G_1 – Zero (ego's generation)
   G_2 – Plus one (first ascending generation)
   G_3 – Minus one (first descending generation)
   G_4 – Plus two
   G_5 – Minus two
Strictly speaking G_4 can be thought of as G_2 plus G_2, and G_5 as G_3 plus G_3. Any further extension of the generational levels is possible with the reduplication of G_2 and G_3. I have confined the Toishan data to two generations above and below ego, even though the Chinese terms of reference cover a wider range. Address terms exist only for those kin with whom ego has face-to-face contact and thus are restricted in the number of generations over which they might extend. Since my interest here is in a comparative analysis, I have limited the reference terms to the degree dictated by the address terms.

   Sex of alter (S). This subset is coded:
   S_1 – Male
   S_2 – Female
   Relative age (A). This subset is coded:
   A_1 – Older
   A_2 – Younger
These components have limited distribution in the Chinese data. They do not occur with the generation components G_3 (minus one generation) or G_5 (minus two generations). In conjunction with component G_1 (zero generation) they designate the relative age of alter to ego with component F_1 present, alter to spouse if component F_2 is present. With higher generations, relative age is functional only when contrasting alter or alter's spouse with a sibling who is a lineal kinsman of ego or ego's spouse.

   Sibling order by sex (O). This subset is coded:
   O_1 – First
   O_2 – nth
   O_3 – Last
These components function chiefly in the address system, although numerals may be found modifying reference terms when special distinctions are required. In the address system this ordering can be omitted

by the speaker when it is felt to be superfluous, and the term designating this numbering is then replaced by a familiarizing prefix *ʔa* 2 which is numerically neutral. In my lists of the address terms I have given only the form in *ʔa* 2, but I have added the component O_2 to mark those forms in which sibling order can be expressed.

This subset might be coded with only two components designating "order expressed" or "order not expressed." I have chosen to use a slightly different approach to clarify the details of the Toishan system. As a general rule, the numbering is used when two or more persons from the enumerable category are present. For example, if more than one FaFaBr are present, the address terms then would be *ʔai 4 kuŋ* 2 for the oldest, *ŋei 4 kuŋ* 2 for the second in order; then *lham* 2 "three," *lhei* 2 "four," *ŋ 1* "five," and so on will be prefixed down to the youngest who will be called *tseoŋ 5 kuŋ* 2. If only one FaFaBr is present, he would commonly be addressed simply as *ʔa 2 kuŋ* 2.

The neglect of these components in the study of Chinese kinship terminology can probably be traced to the fact that the earlier research was limited chiefly to the reference system; sibling order, however, is more typically a feature of the address system. Also, the importance of sibling order is frequently concealed because, as mentioned above, in a neutral situation the enumerating prefix may be replaced by the familiarizing *ʔa* 2. Relative age is operable in both the reference and the address systems, yet in cultural terms it does not appear to be as significant as sibling order. If there is any differential inheritance, any increased ceremonial responsibility, or any preferential treatment, these will likely go to the *oldest*, not simply to an *older* brother. Even if this preferential sequence is not actualized in this manner for every family, it is usually well internalized as an ideal. The expression of sibling order serves as a constant reminder to any individual about just how far he is out of first place. However, it is also operable for females in situations where the sociological importance of distance from first place is a little less clear.

The category of sibling order does not replace the category of relative age, and the two may appear simultaneously. If, for example, ego's father is the third of five brothers, ego would address paternal uncles as *ʔai 4 pak 2, ŋei 4 pak 2, lhei 2 suk 2,* and *ŋ 1 suk 2,* literally "oldest *older* (paternal) uncle," "number two *older* uncle," "number four *younger* uncle," and "number five *younger* uncle."

Generation of common ancestor (C). This subset is coded:

C_1 – Father's generation
C_2 – Grandfather's generation
C_3 – Great-grandfather's generation

Theoretically this subset could extend upward indefinitely, but in actual practice there need be only one generation above the last ascending generation having any collateral differentiation. It is interesting to note that this subset of components is necessary in my analysis only to distinguish male paternal parallel cousins from ego's brothers, a distinction made in the reference terms but not in the terms of address. The subset is not operative in other parts of the Toishan system.

Combining Processes for the Components

The codes for each kin term are selected and combined according to the sequence outlined in the sections above. It is important to realize that the codes in the table on pp. 218–19 are not necessarily bi-unique. That is, although for each kin term there is derived a unique code, one cannot always reverse the process and derive the same kin term from its code. This results chiefly from the fact that some codes could generate kin terms outside the set used in this study. Bi-uniqueness would be introduced here if all the applicable components were given in each code even at the expense of being redundant within the framework of kin terms used in this essay.

If none of the components of any subset is operable for a given kin term, no entry will be made from that subset. If two components are operable from a given subset, both subscripts will be recorded for the given code, yielding what I will term a "portmanteau component."

Evaluating the Method

Much of the analysis of these data derives from the process of selecting the components and is in effect expressed in my descriptions of the Toishan components and their codes. The mechanics of producing a coherent and useful set of components forces one to tear down and then rebuild the structure of the kinship terminology in a way not required in the more traditional descriptive approaches. The standard criteria of sex, generation, relative age, collaterality, consanguinity, and bifurcation taken as one-time operators are not adequate in a componential analysis of the complex Chinese data. Even the additional criteria proposed here are sufficient only for the restricted terminology of this study. An extension of one degree of collateral kin could easily be handled by the traditional Chinese reference system, but to satisfy a componential analysis this extension would require components in addition to those described. Such an extension could quickly take us outside the normal range of ego's socially significant kin, i.e. those kin ego is likely to meet in a face-to-face situation. This is demonstrated by the fact that the set of address terms would probably not expand beyond those recorded

THE TOISHAN KIN TERMS AND THEIR CODES

	Reference	Code	Address	Code
1. Fa	fu 4 thin 2	$F_1D_1R_1G_2S_1$	ʔa 2 pa 1	$F_1D_1R_1G_2S_1$
2. FaOBr[a]	pak 2 fu 4′	$F_1D_1R_2G_2S_1A_1$	ʔa 2 pak 2‵	$F_1D_1R_2G_2S_1A_1O_2$
3. FaYBr	suk 2 fu 4′	$F_1D_1R_2G_2S_1A_2$	ʔa 2 suk 2	$F_1D_1R_2G_2S_1A_2O_2$
4. FaOBrWi	pak 2 mu 5	$F_1D_1R_3G_2S_2A_1$	ʔa 2 mu 5	$F_1D_1R_3G_2S_2A_1O_2$
5. FaYBrWi	suk 2 mu 5	$F_1D_1R_3G_2S_2A_2$	ʔa 2 sim 1	$F_1D_1R_3G_{12}S_2A_2O_2$
6. FaSi	ku 2 mu 5′	$F_1D_1R_2G_2S_2$	ʔa 2 ku 2′	$F_1D_1R_2G_2S_2O_2$
7. FaSiHu	ku 2 fu 5	$F_1D_1R_3G_2S_1$	ʔa 2 tshiaŋ 5	$F_{12}D_{12}R_3G_{12}S_1O_2$
8. FaBrOSo	hoŋ 3 hen 2	$F_1D_1R_2G_1S_1A_1C_2$	ʔa 2 ko 2′	$F_{12}D_{12}R_{23}G_1S_1A_1O_2$
9. FaBrYSo	hoŋ 3 ʔai 4′	$F_1D_1R_2G_1S_1A_2C_2$	Name	
10. FaBrODa	hoŋ 3 tei 1	$F_1D_1R_2G_1S_2A_1$	ʔa 2 tei 1	$F_1D_{12}R_2G_1S_2A_1O_2$
11. FaBrYDa	hoŋ 3 moi 1′	$F_1D_1R_2G_1S_2A_2$	Name	
12. FaSiOSo	piau 1 hen 2	$F_1D_{12}R_{23}G_1S_1A_1$	piau 1 ko 2′	$F_1D_{12}R_2G_1S_1A_1$
13. FaSiYSo	piau 1 ʔai 4′	$F_1D_{12}R_{23}G_1S_1A_2$	Name	
14. FaSiODa	piau 1 tei 1	$F_1D_{12}R_{23}G_1S_2A_1$	piau 1 tei 1	$F_1D_{12}R_2G_1S_2A_1$
15. FaSiYDa	piau 1 moi 1‵	$F_1D_{12}R_{23}G_1S_2A_2$	Name	
16. FaFa	tu 1 fu 4	$F_1D_1R_1G_4S_1$	ʔa 2 ie 3	$F_1D_1R_1G_4S_1$
17. FaMo	tu 1 mu 5′	$F_1D_1R_2G_4S_2$	ʔa 2 ŋin 3	$F_1D_1R_1G_4S_2$
18. FaFaOBr[b]	pak 2 tu 1 fu 4	$F_1D_1R_2G_4S_1A_1$	ʔa 2 kuŋ 2	$F_{12}D_{12}R_{123}G_{24}S_1O_2$
19. FaFaYBr	suk 2 tu 1 fu 4	$F_1D_1R_2G_4S_1A_2$	ʔa 2 kuŋ 2	$F_{12}D_{12}R_{123}G_{24}S_1O_2$
20. FaFaOBrWi	pak 2 tu 1 mu 5′	$F_1D_1R_3G_4S_2A_1$	ʔa 2 pho 3	$F_{12}D_{12}R_{123}G_{24}S_2O_2$
21. FaFaYBrWi	suk 2 tu 1 mu 5′	$F_1D_1R_3G_4S_2A_2$	ʔa 2 pho 3	$F_{12}D_{12}R_{123}G_{24}S_2O_2$
22. FaFaSi	ku 2 tu 1 mu 5′	$F_1D_1R_2G_4S_2$	ku 2 pho 3	$F_1D_{12}R_2G_4S_2$
23. FaFaSiHu	ku 2 tu 1 fu 4	$F_1D_1R_3G_4S_1$	tshiaŋ 5 kuŋ 2	$F_1D_{12}R_3G_4S_1$
24. Mo	mu 5 thin 2	$F_1D_2R_1G_2S_2$	ʔa 2 ma 1	$F_1D_2R_1G_2S_2$
25. MoBr	khiu 5 fu 4	$F_1D_2R_2G_2S_1$	ʔa 2 khiu 5	$F_1D_2R_2G_2S_1O_2$
26. MoBrWi	khim 5 mu 5′	$F_1D_2R_3G_2S_2$	ʔa 2 khim 5	$F_1D_2R_3G_{12}S_2O_2$
27. MoOSi	i 3 mu 5′	$F_1D_2R_2G_2S_2A_{12}$	ʔa 2 i 3	$F_{12}D_2R_2G_{12}S_2A_1O_2$
28. MoYSi	i 3 mu 5′	$F_1D_2R_2G_2S_2A_{12}$	ʔa 2 i 3‵	$F_{12}D_2R_2G_{12}S_2A_2O_2$
29. MoSiHu	i 3 fu 4	$F_1D_2R_3G_2S_1$	ʔa 2 tshiaŋ 5	$F_{12}D_{12}R_3G_{12}S_1O_2$
30. MoBrOSo	piau 1 hen 2	$F_1D_{12}R_{23}G_1S_1A_1$	piau 1 ko 2′	$F_1D_{12}R_2G_1S_1A_1$
31. MoBrYSo	piau 1 ʔai 4′	$F_1D_{12}R_{23}G_1S_1A_2$	Name	
32. MoBrODa	piau 1 tei 1	$F_1D_{12}R_{23}G_1S_2A_1$	piau 1 tei 1	$F_1D_{12}R_2G_1S_2A_1$
33. MoBrYDa	piau 1 moi 1‵	$F_1D_{12}R_{23}G_1S_2A_2$	Name	
34. MoSiOSo	piau 1 hen 2	$F_1D_{12}R_{23}G_1S_1A_1$	piau 1 ko 2′	$F_1D_{12}R_2G_1S_1A_1$
35. MoSiYSo	piau 1 ʔai 4′	$F_1D_{12}R_{23}G_1S_1A_2$	Name	
36. MoSiODa	piau 1 tei 1	$F_1D_{12}R_{23}G_1S_2A_1$	piau 1 tei 1	$F_1D_{12}R_2G_1S_2A_1$
37. MoSiYDa	piau 1 moi 1‵	$F_1D_{12}R_{23}G_1S_2A_2$	Name	
38. MoFa	ŋoi 4 tu 1 fu 2	$F_1D_2R_1G_4S_1$	ʔa 2 kuŋ 2	$F_{12}D_{12}R_{123}G_{24}S_1O_2$
39. MoMo	ŋoi 4 tu 1 mu 5	$F_1D_2R_1G_4S_2$	ʔa 2 pho 3	$F_{12}D_{12}R_{123}G_{24}S_2O_2$

[a] Normally one might not expect a "changed tone" on this and other reference terms, but a number of my informants alternated between changed and basic tones in this position. I assume the variation to be optional here.

[b] In some of the mergings represented by the address codes a component of sibling order is included, although some of the kin types involved may not be enumerable; e.g., $F_{12}D_{12}R_{123}G_{24}S_1O_2$ is the code for FaFaBr, MoFaBr, WiFa, and MoFa, of which the first two can be enumerated but the last two cannot. In all such cases it will be clear when only one of a given kin type exists, as in MoFa.

THE TOISHAN KIN TERMS AND THEIR CODES (*continued*)

	Reference	Code	Address	Code
40. MoFaOBr	ŋoi 4 pak 2 tu 1 fu 2	$F_1D_2R_2G_4S_1A_1$	ʔa 2 kuŋ 2	$F_{12}D_{12}R_{123}G_{24}S_1O_2$
41. MoFaYBr	ŋoi 4 suk 2 tu 1 fu 2	$F_1D_2R_2G_4S_1A_2$	ʔa 2 kuŋ 2	$F_{12}D_{12}R_{123}G_{24}S_1O_2$
42. MoFaOBrWi	ŋoi 4 pak 2 tu 1 mu 5′	$F_1D_2R_3G_4S_2A_1$	ʔa 2 pho 3	$F_{12}D_{12}R_{123}G_{24}S_2O_2$
43. MoFaYBrWi	ŋoi 4 pak 2 tu 1 mu 5′	$F_1D_2R_3G_4S_2A_2$	ʔa 2 pho 3	$F_{12}D_{12}R_{123}G_{24}S_2O_2$
44. MoFaSi	ŋoi 4 ku 2 tu 1 mu 5′	$F_1D_2R_2G_4S_2$	ku 2 pho 3	$F_1D_{12}R_2G_4S_2$
45. MoFaSiHu	ŋoi 4 ku 2 tu 1 fu 4	$F_1D_2R_3G_4S_1$	tshiaŋ 5 kuŋ 2	$F_1D_{12}R_3G_4S_1$
46. OBr	ka 2 hen 2	$F_1D_1R_2G_1S_1A_1C_1$	ʔa 2 ko 2′	$F_{12}D_{12}R_{23}G_1S_1A_1O_2$
47. YBr	pou 2 ʔai 4′	$F_1D_1R_2G_1S_1A_2C_1$	Name	
48. OBrWi	lhou 1	$F_1D_1R_3G_1S_2A_1$	ʔa 2 lhou 1	$F_1D_1R_3G_{13}S_2O_2$
49. YBrWi	ʔai 4 fu 5	$F_1D_1R_3G_1S_2A_2$	ʔa 2 sim 1	$F_1D_1R_3G_{12}S_2A_2O_2$
50. BrSo	cit 4	$F_1D_1R_2G_3S_1$	Name	
51. BrDa	cit 4 nui 1	$F_1D_1R_2G_3S_2$	Name	
52. OSi	ka 2 tei 1	$F_1D_2R_2G_1S_2A_1$	ʔa 2 tei 1	$F_1D_{12}R_2G_1S_2A_1O_2$
53. YSi	pou 2 moi 1′	$F_1D_2R_2G_1S_2A_2$	Name	
54. OSiHu	tei 1 fu 5	$F_1D_2R_3G_1S_1A_1$	ʔa 2 tshiaŋ 5	$F_{12}D_{12}R_3G_{12}S_1O_2$
55. YSiHu	moi 1 fu 5	$F_1D_2R_3G_1S_1A_2$	Name	
56. SiSo	saŋ 2 tu 1	$F_1D_2R_2G_3S_1$	Name	
57. SiDa	saŋ 2 nui 1	$F_1D_2R_2G_3S_2$	Name	
58. So	tu 1	$F_1D_1R_1G_3S_1$	Name	
59. SoWi	lhet 2 fu 5′	$F_1D_1R_3G_3S_2$	ʔa 2 lhou 1	$F_1D_1R_3G_{13}S_2O_2$
60. SoSo	lhun 2 ŋei 5′	$F_1D_1R_1G_5S_1$	Name	
61. SoDa	lhun 2 nui 1	$F_1D_1R_1G_5S_2$	Name	
62. Da	nui 1	$F_1D_2R_1G_3S_2$	Name	
63. DaHu	nui 1 lhai 4	$F_1D_2R_3G_3S_1$	Name	
64. DaSo	ŋoi 4 lhun 2	$F_1D_2R_1G_5S_1$	Name	
65. DaDa	ŋoi 4 lhun 2 nui 1	$F_1D_2R_1G_5S_2$	Name	
66. Wi	nui 1 tu 1	$F_2R_3G_3S_2$	Name[c]	
67. WiFa	ŋok 4 fu 4	$F_2D_1R_1G_2S_1$	ʔa 2 kuŋ 2	$F_{12}D_{12}R_{123}G_{24}S_1O_2$
68. WiMo	ŋok 4 mu 5′	$F_2D_1R_1G_2S_2$	ʔa 2 pho 3	$F_{12}D_{12}R_{123}G_{24}S_2O_2$
69. WiOBr	nui 4 hen 2′	$F_2D_1R_2G_1S_1A_1$	ʔa 2 ko 2′	$F_{12}D_{12}R_{23}G_1S_1A_1O_2$
70. WiYBr	nui 4 ʔai 4′	$F_2D_1R_2G_1S_1A_2$	Name	
71. WiOBrWi	khiu 5 lhou 1	$F_2D_1R_3G_1S_1A_1$	ʔa 2 khim 5	$F_{12}D_1R_3G_{12}S_2O_2$
72. WiYBrWi	khiu 5 ʔai 4 fu 5	$F_2D_1R_3G_1S_2A_2$	ʔa 2 khim 5	$F_{12}D_1R_3G_{12}S_2O_2$
73. WiOSi	i 3 tei 1	$F_2D_2R_2G_1S_2A_1$	ʔa 2 i 3	$F_{12}D_2R_2G_{12}S_2A_1O_2$
74. WiYSi	i 3 moi 1′	$F_2D_2R_2G_1S_2A_2$	ʔa 2 i 3`	$F_{12}D_2R_2G_{12}S_2A_2O_2$
75. WiSiHu	i 3 fu 5	$F_2D_2R_3G_1S_1$	ʔa 2 tshiaŋ 5	$F_{12}D_{12}R_3G_{12}S_1O_2$
76. WiBrSo	nui 4 cit 4	$F_2D_1R_2G_3S_1$	Name	
77. WiBrDa	nui 4 cit 4 nui 1	$F_2D_1R_2G_3S_2$	Name	
78. WiSiSo	i 3 saŋ 2	$F_2D_2R_2G_3S_1$	Name	
79. WiSiDa	i 3 saŋ 2 nui 1	$F_2D_2R_2G_3S_2$	Name	

[c] Here and in a few other address terms a number of possible circumlocutions will be found used about as often as given names. This includes such devices as referring to Wi as "mother of (son's) name."

This listing conforms to the numbering of the kin terms in the table immediately preceding. The reference term comes first, the address term next, if there is one.

1. 父親, 阿爸
2. 伯父, 阿伯
3. 叔父, 阿叔
4. 伯母, 阿母
5. 叔母, 阿嬸
6. 姑母, 阿姑
7. 姑夫, 阿丈
8. 堂兄, 阿哥
9. 堂弟
10. 堂姉, 阿姉
11. 堂妹
12. 表兄, 表哥
13. 表弟
14. 表姉, 表姉
15. 表妹
16. 祖父, 阿爺
17. 祖母, 阿人
18. 伯祖父, 阿公
19. 叔祖父, 阿公
20. 伯祖母, 阿婆
21. 叔祖母, 阿婆
22. 姑祖母, 姑婆
23. 姑祖父, 丈公
24. 母親, 阿媽
25. 舅父, 阿舅
26. 妗母, 阿妗

27. 姨母, 阿姨
28. 姨母, 阿姨
29. 姨父, 阿丈
30. 表兄, 表哥
31. 表弟
32. 表姉, 表姉
33. 表妹
34. 表兄, 表哥
35. 表弟
36. 表姉, 表姉
37. 表妹
38. 外祖父, 阿公
39. 外祖母, 阿婆
40. 外伯祖父, 阿公
41. 外叔祖父, 阿公
42. 外伯祖母, 阿婆
43. 外叔祖母, 阿婆
44. 外姑祖母, 姑婆
45. 外姑祖父, 丈公
46. 家兄, 阿哥
47. 胞弟
48. 嫂, 阿嫂
49. 弟婦, 阿嬸
50. 姪
51. 姪女
52. 家姉, 阿姉

53. 胞妹
54. 姉夫, 阿丈
55. 妹夫
56. 甥子
57. 甥女
58. 子
59. 媳婦, 阿嫂
60. 孫兒
61. 孫女
62. 女
63. 女婿
64. 外孫
65. 外孫女
66. 女子
67. 岳父, 阿公
68. 岳母, 阿婆
69. 內兄, 阿哥
70. 內弟
71. 舅嫂, 阿妗
72. 舅弟婦, 阿妗
73. 姨姉, 阿姨
74. 姨妹, 阿姨
75. 姨夫, 阿丈
76. 內姪
77. 內姪女
78. 姨甥
79. 姨甥女

here, but the reference terms could be increased considerably by adding generations or degrees of collaterality. Any such expansion must be matched by an increase in the categories of components.

My data, for example, include MoFaOBrWi, which is coded $F_1D_2R_3$-$G_4S_2A_1$. This coding is translatable into: female affine, two generations above ego in ego's female line, and connected through a lineal who is younger than the spouse of alter. This description would also fit MoMoOBrWi except for the fact that ego's female line (i.e. component D_2) is here defined as progressing through Mo, MoFa, MoFaFa, etc. To take care of MoMo, MoMoMo, MoFaMo, and similar combinations in all parts of the system, additional components would be needed that could chart the line from male to female, female to male, and female to female. Such components would need to be repeatable with the final value of their subset expressed as a product or total. This might suggest a generative approach using a number of simple repeating operators to map a course through the maze from ego to alter, a practical method of taking care of the data but one that runs the danger of becoming mechanical and less explanatory than the componential approach.

Contrasts in size and completeness. A glance at the codes for the Toishan kin terms shows that the reference terms are more complete than the address terms. Part of this difference is expressed by the use of alter's name, showing that no address terms exist for a given component intersection. Every intersection of the reference system is filled, not only for the data in this study but also for a considerably extended list of kin terms. With only a few special exceptions, each of the reference terms is a distinctive and unique marker for a specific individual as defined by the primitives and their compounds. In the address system larger numbers of unfilled intersections exist, even in the restricted data presented here, and any extension of the range of these terms would merely increase the ratio of empty to filled intersections. It should be assumed that the address terms here represent almost the total of any significantly patterned system, and that an extension of this system to include more distant kin, unlike an extension of the reference system, would not produce new unique terms for each intersection but would turn up more empty intersections and more portmanteau components.

The difference between the reference and address systems is also apparent as a function of the larger number of portmanteau components in the address codes. These portmanteau components are significant because they represent mergers, points at which a given code refers to more than one basic kin type. The bulk of these are kin that the reference system differentiates but the address system does not. In the reference

system these portmanteau components appear only in the codes for ego's cousins (except paternal parallel) and in those for mother's sisters.*
Out of a total of 79 primitives in my reference terms only fourteen are coded with portmanteau components.

On the other hand, the address system has only nine codes which do *not* have one or more portmanteau components. These cluster in father's family of orientation plus mother and her brothers; this has the effect of giving special distinction to all members of the older generations who might be resident with ego and the group of mother's kin frequently having formal responsibilities vis-à-vis ego. The remainder of the address system is covered either by personal name or by portmanteau components. Obviously the address terms represent a considerable simplification of the total kin-term system, accomplished by eliminating a number of terms and by combining others.

Breaks in the pattern of address by given name. It is important to note in the address system the patterning of the gaps where no kin terms are available. By checking the coding of the corresponding reference term we see that the address system uses the given name of an individual when the generational components G_3 (minus one) or G_5 (minus two) appear, or when G_1 (zero generation) appears in conjunction with the relative age component A_2 (younger). This means that persons in descending generations or those younger than ego in his own generation are addressed by name only.

However, there are some interesting exceptions. These are YBrWi, SoWi, WiBrWi, and WiYSi. Here we have an obvious requirement for special treatment of female affines. This is not an incest taboo in a general sense, since this list includes no kin types coded with components F_1 plus either R_1 or R_2; in other words, no lineal or collateral females of male ego's system are included. Perhaps then, the phenomenon is more a politeness observance to guard against the disruptive influence of intra-familial adultery rather than of incest, since the latter could be expected to apply to female lineals and collaterals.

Differential use of subsets of components. Another significant contrast between the reference and the address codings is found in the difference of type of components used by each. The subset of sibling order by sex

---

* This irregularity in the address terms for MoSi may be unique in the Szeyap dialects. In the other Chinese dialects for which I have data the term for MoYSi and MoOSi are the same. In Toishan, as well as in some of the other Szeyap forms I worked with, these two terms are distinguished by the use of a "changed tone" form *ʔa 2 i 3′* for MoYSi in contrast to the basic tone form *ʔa 2 i 3* for MoOSi. This corresponds to a general use of the "changed tone" to give endearing or diminutive force.

is used in the address system but generally neglected in the reference; the subset of generation of common ancestor is used in the reference system but not in the address. When viewed together with the contrasts in size and completeness referred to above, these differences may well be great enough to require a separate analysis of the address system, defining a distinct set of components that apply only to the address terms without any attempt to consider the address system as an abbreviated form of the reference system. Such an analysis would be entirely valid, but without the contrasts of the present approach it might be less useful. Here my goal has been to preserve the maximum number of like features for the specific purpose of highlighting similarities as well as differences between the two systems.

Concrete and abstract components. It is possible to distinguish between components that are spelled out in the kin terms themselves and those derived either by investigation of the primitives and their compounds or by intuitive selection in terms of the needs of the analysis as a whole.

As an example of a concrete component we have the criterion of sibling order, which is clearly an isolable part of the Toishan address system and is openly expressed in it. A simple translation of the kin term would uncover this component for us.

At the first level of abstraction are the components derived in a fairly straightforward fashion but only through an investigation of the primitives and their compounds. Older and younger are easily isolated, but probably only because the primitive terms used here originated in English and not some other language such as Chinese. Generation, sex, and other components are inherent in the primitives but at least require a preliminary analysis of the basic referent of each primitive.

At the second level of abstraction are those components not derived either from the kin terms or the primitives but from the patterning of the total system. These components are selected or even invented by the analyst in order to complete a neat and functioning whole that will handle all the data and, hopefully, add insight in the process. For example, the criterion of generation of common ancestor is difficult to support in any concrete sense. There are no such concepts openly expressed in the kin terms or in their primitives. It would also be difficult to support the selection of this subset by any reference to cognitive processes of the native informants. The choice was made here chiefly on the grounds that it handled the material in a satisfactory way and also had a certain degree of explanatory power because it could be correlated with other data from outside the kinship terminology.

When I asked my informants to define their kin in terms of primitives, they would in fact count back only to the generation of common siblings, one generation short of the common ancestor, then down the collateral line. Although this detail merits further study, its importance here lies in pointing out how the informants conceptualize the kin structure in chart form; it is only suggestive as a guide in selecting categories of components for total analysis. Of equal value in the selection is that co-operation on the lineage level in ceremonial observances and certain larger economic activities is based on a structure of collateral kin lines deriving their relationship from a focus on the common ancestor. This particular problem in the analysis might also be handled as in Good-enough (1965: 273) with components of degree of collateral distance between ego and alter, a direct solution cutting straight across the genealogical space in a manner suitable for his data, but probably not so useful for the Chinese data as would be some statement of common ancestor.

As the components become more abstract, the indeterminacy becomes more a part of the selection process. It is at the second level of abstraction that alternative solutions are most likely to be born.

Contrasts in function. Murdock (1949: 98) thinks that the reference system is more useful in kinship analysis because it is more complete and has fewer duplications and overlaps. Conant (1961: 29) cites the Jarawa evidence to support his view that the address system is a better guide to "socio-structural reality." The Chinese data given here force me in part to agree and in part to take issue with both these points of view. The reference system here is certainly more complete, but usefulness is a quality to be defined in terms of specific goals. For deriving universals applicable to the greatest number of individual sets of kinship terminology and for the construction of general theory, it is doubtless more productive and more convenient to work with the fuller material of the average reference system. On the other hand, for analyzing the data of a single culture, where completeness more than general applicability is the prime concern, it would be unwise to neglect either system. If there is a contrast between the reference and address systems of any given culture, that contrast itself is a significant fact and should be recorded.

Conant, generalizing on the basis of specific data, states (1961: 29) that "the system of address, more so than the system of reference, appears to provide a guide for personal behavior with respect to consanguineal kin." This is in agreement with Murdock's earlier statement (1949: 106–7) that the "terms of address form an integral part of the culturally patterned relationships between kinsmen, even though they are an aspect of habitual verbal rather than gross muscular behavior."

However, Murdock (1949: 107) adds, "since any status is defined in terms of the culturally expected behavior in the relationship in which it is embedded, there are *a priori* reasons for assuming a close functional congruity between terms of reference and the relationships in which the denoted kinsmen interact."

If the Toishan data contribute to this discussion, it is because the Toishan reference system is essentially a classification device that spells out in great detail the entire set of kin relationships. The system is highly internalized by most Chinese and serves as an easy guide for ego to orient himself in relation to all others who might call on his kin responsibilities to any degree. It is a complex paradigm probably over-differentiated when compared with behavioral patterns—there is certainly more sociocultural realism in the merging process and in the use of personal names in the address system at the first and second descending generations, in spite of the fact that at these levels the reference terms methodically distinguish basic kin types.

If the Chinese reference system can be considered a classification device, then the address system might well be thought of as a behavioral guide that demands not so much an understanding of the kin structure as a grasp of the interpersonal commitments existing between ego and his more important kin types. The address system assures ego of at least the basic proprieties in his dealings with kinsmen, providing for him protection from overfamiliarity and a built-in deference. The many mergings of the address system do not necessarily suggest that these merged kin types are equals in the behavioral requirements of ego. It is more probable that the address terms indicate only the minimum requirements of the personal relationship, and the maximum requirements are reflected in the reference system. The behavior expected toward oldest brother, oldest paternal parallel cousin, and wife's oldest brother can hardly be equal, yet all three are addressed as *?ai 4 ko 2'*, i.e. "oldest older brother." The merging may be better interpreted as a grouping together of clearly distinct kin who share much (as with brother and cousin) or little (as with brother and wife's brother), but who all have a common nucleus of similarity that makes it possible to address them with a single term. It is not a question of their "enjoying all the same privileges or exercising the same functions" as Lowie (1917: 100, quoted in Murdock 1949: 108) indicates. It is rather a matter of getting the task of daily contact taken care of within certain vague guidelines of economy. The supposition that this may be in the nature of serving a minimum politeness requirement is reinforced by the fact that the term *?ai 4 ko 2'*, as well as others such as *?a 2 kuŋ 2* and *?a 2 pho 3*, move beyond the kinship system to apply as mild honorifics to persons who have no consanguineal or affinal relationship to ego.

Conclusions

The claim will not be made here that the componential approach to anthropological data will uncover information that cannot be discovered through other techniques. There is no reason why the substance of this paper could not have been derived from any sort of structural analysis of the Chinese kinship terminology or, more specifically, of the terminology in conjunction with certain anthropological data. However, a componential analysis does necessitate a process of systematization that often produces a new approach to known data. The ability to quantify and simplify large sets of information increases the probability of insights and represents a refinement in research equipment.

It is axiomatic that at no time can the analysis be divorced from specific data outside the kinship terminology. At any stage in the selection process it would be possible to choose components that have less connection with the realities of the Chinese scene, but such a choice would decrease the overall value of the final product. As the analysis becomes more abstract and symbolic it may become less in harmony with other anthropological data. This development may be useful in terms of formulating a general theory of kinship terminology, but it may actually conceal information within a specific limited set of data. We are not searching simply for a means of deriving a translation of kin terms from one language to another. Of course, this is one result of our work, but it is more important that we be able to thread our way through any analytic process and note at each turn the correlation between the analysis and reality. In this light, componential analysis can supply the area specialist with a very useful new kind of organization of the material, a different kind of rigor, and an increased facility for handling sets of related data.

Japanese Kinship: A Comparison

JOHN C. PELZEL

This paper is part of an attempt to interpret and to compare Japanese and Chinese kinship, but since space is limited, and my audience is familiar with the Chinese example, most of my discussion will concern the Japanese case.* Though no attempt has been made to avoid speaking of similarities, this essay reflects my view that the two systems are in essence radically different. My formulation is, of course, ideal-typical and usually refers to the kinship systems that met modernization during the nineteenth and early twentieth centuries.

Terms of Reference

Japanese terms for nuclear statuses are virtually identical in nature to those used in Chinese. For example, both languages characteristically distinguish between older and younger sibling of the same sex. There is presumptive evidence, moreover, that this similarity owes nothing to borrowing; it is present in the earliest materials from both cultures, and it occurs in all cognate languages of the Sinitic group, and in the Korean and Altaic groups to which Japanese is sometimes seen to be related.

For statuses beyond the nuclear, however, usages differ markedly in the two societies. It is true that all of the characters for kin terms used in literary Chinese were borrowed in earliest historic times and given Sino-Japanese pronunciations. Sinophiles using these readings sometimes have produced texts that make the two systems appear identical. Never-

* This paper was originally presented before the appearance of Professor Nakane Chie's book on Japanese kinship (Nakane 1967), surely the most cogent statement and interpretation especially of corporate groups involved in kinship in any language. The main justification for the publication of this paper even after the appearance of Professor Nakane's book is that we say some of the same things differently.

theless, there are native Japanese pronunciations for only a very few of these characters, and as Smith (1962) has shown, only these few have had any general usage in Japan for the period of more than a thousand years for which we have good evidence. The differences between the two systems must therefore be taken as fundamental and comprehensive.

Chinese kinship terminology allows explicit recognition of many attributes of the relation with ego, such as sex, generation, lineality, relative age, and collaterality, for a circle of kinsmen that includes even quite distant relatives. Japanese terminology, on the other hand, is even more niggardly than American English in its identification of particular statuses and its description of their attributes. In Japanese as in English there are terms for parent's sibling (*oji* and *oba*) and for ego's sibling's child (*oi* and *mei*), terms that recognize collaterality, generation, and sex; there are also terms for parent's parent (*ojī* and *obā*), which specify lineality, generation, and sex. Parent's grandparent and grandparent's sibling are distinguished by the addition of a generation prefix (*hi-* and *ō-*, respectively) to the terms for parent's parent and parent's sibling, but Japanese speakers generally find as little occasion to employ these designations as do Americans. The term for ego's grandchild (*mago*) does not specify the sex of the kinsman. No other consanguineal relatives are identified, except by the kind of generic term used in English for collaterals ("cousin," i.e., *itoko*). Step-relatives and affines are usually referred to in nuclear terms, though both can be set apart, as in English, by the addition of an agglutinative element (*mama-* and *giri no-*, respectively).

The statuses that in Japanese have particularizing terms share one characteristic: all such kinsmen may be expected under one or another common condition to share a household with ego, if they are patrilateral relatives, and, since this is a bilateral terminological system, matrilateral relatives are assimilated to those through the father's line. The clearest feature of the system, therefore, is the separation off and the individual identification of co-residential statuses, in contrast with the melding of all other kin as "cousins." Among the identified kinsmen, moreover, Japanese terminology specifies only the attributes of sex, generation, very close degrees of collaterality, and, among first-degree collaterals, relative age.

Insofar as kin terms are signs that guide behavior, therefore, Japanese usage alerts ego only to those closest kinsmen with whom he might, for household reasons, be expected to interact intensively, leaving behavior toward others to be prompted by other kinds of cues. Chinese terminology, on the other hand, guides ego to recognize a larger number of particular relationships and a wider range of behavioral duties, from the intense to the relatively weak, and in a set of categories (e.g., patrilineal and affinal). In actual practice, relations of kinsmen beyond those of the nuclear family are on the whole congruent with these emphases, though in spite of the close resemblance between the Japanese and English terminological systems, behavior patterns in these two cultures probably differ as much from each other as either does from Chinese.

Household and House

In common usage, the Japanese term *ie* has traditionally meant both the household at a given point in time and a more durable entity, the "house," which exists over time and is composed of only one household in each generation—that household headed by the male who is the legal successor to the former household head. It is this succession of households down through the generations that is the basic and ideal meaning of the term *ie*; the extant household is merely the concrete but transient form of the latter. Assets, whether tangible or not, are always the assets of the *ie*, and a current household controls them for its time as a trustee. Organizational statuses in the contemporary household are subsumed in, and secondary to, similar statuses in the durable house.

In theory, nonsucceeding sons set up neolocal households at marriage, and daughters of course marry out; the succeeding male, on the other hand, remains with his own wife and family of procreation in the household of the older head, whose post he will in time acquire. The composition of the ideal household is thus stem, rather than joint, as in China: it should consist of the family of procreation of only one male—the successor to the headship—in each living generation. It may also include the remnants of previous households in the succession line (e.g., the retired head of the former generation or his widow) as well as those members of any household of orientation in the line who are not incorporated into a different house (the unmarried sons and daughters of any generation, or those who, though once married, are widowed without issue).

The ideal form of household seems to be found a good deal more frequently in Japan than in China. As many writers have noted (Freedman 1958: 19), the ideal joint family of China is statistically rare. Even in 1960, however, 36.7 per cent of all Japanese households included at least the residue of the nuclear families of two or more generations, and this rate for families in agriculture was 62.3 per cent (Koyama 1962: 51).

Considering the normal household cycle over time, and the fact that in 1960 another 56.9 per cent of all Japanese households were composed of a conjugal family that could be expected in a considerable proportion of cases to turn into a stem unit, this seems a very high degree of approximation to the ideal.

Since failure to achieve joint families in China usually produces stem households, real residence units in the two countries are very similar in size and composition. In Japan, of course, the ideal household form is more modest and requires fewer economic assets than does the joint family. Assets that do exist are preserved more readily in the Japanese system of one-male inheritance than in the Chinese system of equal property division among all sons. Also, a variety of institutions in China, both inside and outside the kinship system (equal inheritance itself, socialization of brothers to be competitive for the parents' favors and for opportunities, the system of free property alienation and economic mobility, the educational and bureaucratic encouragement of merit, etc.), all but negate the hierarchical significance of the terminological distinction between elder and younger brother and tend to produce egalitarian relations between them. Thus, in most cases they take up separate residences when the parents' centralizing authority is gone, for social and psychological as well as for economic reasons. By way of contrast, there is in Japanese society nearly complete support of a hierarchical distinction between succeeding and nonsucceeding brothers, a situation that allows the prescribed inheritance and residence patterns to be easily followed. (Even today, the values behind these institutions remain strong; it is widely reported that, undeterred by express provisions of the new Civil Code allowing for equal inheritance, other siblings regularly sign away their rights to the brother chosen by the parents to succeed.) Social ideals relating to household composition thus seem more homogeneous and pragmatic (in general socioeconomic terms) and so more supportive of the ideal in the Japanese than in the Chinese case.

The assets of a house are various. They include its economic and political resources, of course, but in addition they comprise intangibles of great importance: the myth that the house has endured, and will persist, throughout significant time, and the genealogy that substantiates this claim for time past; the house name and insignia; the constitution, laying down the precepts of the ancestors; the spirits of the ancestors and of the guardian god, together with the paraphernalia and ceremonies of their commemoration; its membership in a given Buddhist sect and temple, and its grave in that temple's yard; its general social class status; the house's membership in other organizations and the right to be represented in them by its own members, as well as its right to permit its members to take part in external social relations only as its delegates; its particular style of action and reputation in its own community. Control of these assets is vested in the house (and household) head (*kachō*). With respect to his own household members he holds formal powers over the assets that are undivided. No other member except his apparent successor (the *ato-tori*) has a formal status in the organization, but the status of *ato-tori* is so crucial that the eldest brother, as heir presumptive, is normally designated by the special title *chōnan* to distinguish his potential leadership role from the purely relational role termed *ani*, i.e., any elder brother in contrast to a younger. On the other hand, if the actions of the head are relevant to the well-being of the *ie* rather than to that of the contemporary household alone, he may be guided and judged by the house council, an *ad hoc* organization composed of his patrilateral seniors and peers of both sexes. (On occasion, matrilateral relatives of the same statuses may also take part.) The council may be called by any of its members to advise the head or to ratify, veto, or direct his actions. The council is in theory the trustee of the generations of the house, and the contemporary head is the executive trustee; in Japan the law and the courts act to enforce this interpretation.

The ideal pattern for continuation of the house, usually called primogeniture, is more properly described as succession by one male. The eldest son is normally the successor, but this is neither required nor under certain common conditions allowed. When the headship cannot be taken over by an eldest son competent to do the job, the post is given to another male able to do so, and law and custom strongly institutionalize any arrangements necessary to ensure this result. A widowed wife of a head, during the minority of her son or in the absence of a male heir apparent, may fully exercise the authority of the headship, but though surveys show that at any given time in recent generations 10–20 per cent of households may be headed by women for the sake of expedience, the permanent house head must ideally be a male.

In conformity with these requirements, any of a great variety of dispensations may be made. An eldest son may be disinherited (*kandō*) at the decision of senior house authorities, and the post given to another qualified male (normally, but not necessarily, one of the younger sons). All studies have shown that the practice of disinheritance is quite common. One representative national sample of farm households, for example, revealed that over the three generations prior to 1948 a son other than the eldest had in fact succeeded in about 25 per cent of all the relevant cases. (Raper *et al.* 1950; unpublished data in author's posses-

continued in of house

sion.) Other studies have shown that another person was made successor
in an even higher proportion of cases. In virtually every case that can
be investigated, moreover, this action was taken for the convenience of
the house—i.e., because of the eldest son's incompetence or because it
was agreed that he could do better for the house in an urban occupation
than by inheriting the traditional assets and responsibilities. In the
absence of a qualified direct-line descendant, a close or a distant kinsman, or with great frequency even a male with no genetic link whatsoever to the house, may be adopted as the successor to the head. If there
are daughters but no son, it is usual for the adopted successor to be
brought in simultaneously as the husband of the eldest daughter. Whatever the successor's origin, once adopted he takes the family name, and
in all formal and legal respects he becomes the authorized head of the
household and house he has entered and is incorporated into its genealogy. These practices are by no means limited to farm families or to
those with extensive properties: the mystique of the durable house is
itself sufficient to require such arrangements.

The keeping of genealogies and the myth of the durability of the
house over time should not mislead us. Genealogies are kept only for
houses, as we have defined the *ie*, not for genetic relationships; they
might therefore be called the historic tables of organization of the house
to distinguish them from the more genetically oriented Chinese homo-
logue. The myth of house durability, moreover, does not in any sense
imply that the house has endured eternally or that there is unusual concern with long lines of relatedness. For the Japanese, genetic legitimacy
is racial or ethnic, not subsocietal, and is ensured by the myth that all
Japanese alike are descended from the gods. The idea essential to the
emphasis on the house's durability is the "significant time" covered since
the genealogy in fact began.

Only the family name and (in earlier times) the formal legal class
status descend patrilineally to all male issue. Nonsucceeding sons, like
daughters, have no right to any of the other assets of the house (though
either may receive gifts that have no connotations of formal inheritance
from their father during his lifetime, and a son will normally enter an
occupation, a Buddhist temple, and communal organizations similar to
those of the senior household). A nonsucceeding son who sets up an independent household thus is potentially starting a house other than that
of his father and his father's successor. Without the interjection of
another principle, that of the "lineage," a house consists of one and only
one household in each generation, and cadet branches create entirely
new house lines.

It is clear that although the house is an impersonal corporation organized in kinship terms and serving a number of purely kin ends, it is primarily an institution concerned with external task performance. Genetic links across the generations are provided for, but not at the expense of an inadequate adjustment within society—as we have seen, able nonrelated males can be adopted into the line. The household group is larger than the nuclear family and can furnish enough labor for the family farm and a suitable climate for an extensive kind of socialization, but it is not so large as to overtax the group's resources. As we shall note later, in the relations of co-residential kinsmen emotions are institutionalized to a much greater degree than within the Chinese household, but in a manner that makes these relations secondary to the requirements of a successful task performance. Thus, dyadic bonds must remain subordinate to corporate bonds. To this end, household and house are provided with a head who has undivided authority and is chosen in terms of his ability to perform in the role. Designated heir apparent at birth, the first son can usually be adequately socialized to the demands that will be made upon him, demands that emphasize his obligations as executive and trustee rather than his rights as a wielder of power. When this socialization is ineffective, or when other adaptive requirements of the household and house make such a course desirable, the apparent successor is disinherited in favor of another male among the acquaintances of the current authorities who can perform according to the impersonal demands of the role. The possibility of inadequate performance is guarded against through the rights of the house council over the head, and the politico-legal system supports these emphases through Civil Codes and the action of the courts.

The house is fundamental to the ideology of kinship. Such concepts as *shinrui* or *shinseki* (i.e., "relatives") designate the members of ego's bilateral kindred plus affines, and though of great behavioral importance, they are of relatively little ideological significance. What is called the "lineage" is, like the house itself, responsive to impulses other than those of kinship, and it exists within limits convenient to the prior requirements of the house and therefore is secondary to that corporation.

The "Lineage"

The Japanese organization to which the term "lineage" is applied is less understood than is its apparent counterpart in China, only partly because it has taken different forms in different periods and situations or because only some of the more attentuated of these have survived into the era when modern scholars could study them. Even Japanese terminology confuses the issue, for organizations that we must take as examples of "lineage" are known by a variety of special terms—*uji* in antiquity; *maki, jirui,* etc., in more recent centuries—and a single generic designation exists only in the modern technical term *dōzoku,* manufactured by sociologists. But the main reason the Japanese "lineage" is difficult to understand is that, like the house itself, it is not essentially a kin group, but rather, as Nagai (1953) suggests, a locality group. I would add that it can be viewed as a locality group existing for the organization of power.

A "lineage" potentially comes into being when independent households of procreation are established by two or more brothers. If they do not in fact sever all but kindred relations with one another, they remain together in a corporate relationship that, at its simplest, might be called a "compound house," composed of a main household with cadet lines in some manner dependent on it. The household of the one who succeeds their father to the headship of the *ie* is thereafter, for as long as this arrangement endures, known as the "main family" (*honke*), and the households of the other brothers are, with equal durability, known as "branch families" (*bunke*). In subsequent generations, all sons who do not succeed to extant household headships but nevertheless remain within the compound *ie* establish still other, new, branch families. There is thus at any given time only one main family household, no matter how numerous or how distantly related to it or to one another its branches may be, just as there can be only one succeeding household across the generations in the simple *ie*.

In keeping with the principles of house succession and headship, this single main family inherits in each generation all the assets, rights and obligations of the original parental household; and in conformity with the genetic bond between senior and cadet siblings, the branch families are related to the main household in a strict hierarchy that involves the assets—both tangible and intangible—of the house. The head of the main family alone, for example, can permit or prohibit any son within the compound house to marry and set up a new household. Likewise, the main family assumes the duty of supporting dependent members, most importantly by granting a new branch the use of some part of the house property and giving it an appropriately prestigious position within local society, both under main household direction. If membership in the compound *ie* were mandatory and economy and society static, all non-succeeding sons would remain entirely dependent on the lands and businesses of the main family for a livelihood and on its assignment to them of desired roles within the community. In fact, this situation did

obtain in some recorded cases in which a considerable number of genetically related branch households were heavily dependent on an often
genealogically distant main family.

Nevertheless, "lineage" relations take a great variety of other forms.
At one extreme from the model just described is the organization to
which one or another of the native terms for "lineage" has been applied.
Prior to the eighth century, for example, Japan was divided into territorial communities known as *uji* (usually translated as "clan") in which
the entire local political population was formally organized through
kinship ties with the ruling head family of the unit. There is good evidence, however, that many, if not most, of the households in the territory
were affiliated to the family of the rulers on a fictitious and purely
genealogical rather than genetic basis. Later and throughout Japanese
history (though best reported for rural regions only after the mid-
Tokugawa) rich and powerful main families often controlled adopted
branches in addition to, or even rather than, genetically related branches.
Toward the other extreme, there are units of compound *ie* status that
were often subdivided internally, some of the branches having by their
own efforts gained control of such considerable assets that they were able
to assume the status of main families vis-à-vis their own genealogical
descendants, even though they retained the nominal status of branches
with regard to the original main family. A really old and extensive "lineage" of this sort thus might in effect be a maximal "lineage," composed
of numerous minimal, and even intermediate, components, some of which
might dispose of more resources than the nominal head household. In
another variant, a "lineage" was frequently composed of branches whose
dependence on the main family was relatively slight; in such a case
their ties might involve only a mere recognition of relatedness, and their
cooperation accordingly might be effective for only part-societal purposes—for ritual or local political purposes, for example. But though such
variations did occur, it seems likely that at any given time in Japanese
history many, if not most, households have not been organized on the
basis here being discussed at all.

The "lineage" in Japanese usage, therefore, is an organization of certain households into a kind of expanded or compound *ie*. The component
branches may be related to their main family genetically, but many
genetically related households may not so associate themselves, and
extant households of this sort may be excluded and replaced by units
bound only by the ties of fictitious kinship. Kinship is the nominal basis
for the bonds between senior and junior members, and where the factors
that make it proper to form the "lineage" at all do not disqualify real

kinsmen, they are used to man the organization. But these factors are not predominantly related to kinship and may even involve eliminating kinsmen; in such cases related families can be dropped from the genealogy and unrelated tenants or other dependents can as easily be adopted into it, just as a successor can be adopted as head of the house.

The thesis that the "lineage" is in function more a community than a kinship organization is perfectly true, but this organization is not necessarily limited to a single territorial community, nor does it perform functions that are necessarily seen to be of community-wide use. Since it is always based on an unequal distribution of power resources it seems appropriate to suggest that the "lineage" is primarily an instrument for the organization of power. Its functions seem usually to involve gaining power advantages not otherwise procurable by the members of a hierarchically organized community. For the senior member, a "lineage" means dependable labor and support to use capital or communal resources too large to be worked by the household alone. For the junior member, it means the assured use of capital goods he does not himself own, and a role he would not otherwise acquire in communal affairs controlled by others.

The key to the formal variability of the organization lies in the fact that the Japanese economy and society have not, after all, been static. An agricultural frontier, the growth of cities, and new occupational opportunities helped the social class system to change steadily. In consequence, nonsucceeding sons have often been able to take independent economic and social positions; they have not needed to remain dependent on senior kinsmen, and seniors have not had to fulfill their duties to their juniors. Thus too, many successors have been deprived of the resources with which to support even the pretense of a "lineage," or if they have retained "lineages," they have discovered it more advantageous to adopt non-kin rather than cadet branches into their genealogies.

In China, the lineage also performed certain general socioeconomic and political functions. Through it seniors might gain control of collective economic resources and political tools in the local community, and juniors might acquire access to lands, educational and welfare opportunities, and a role in village affairs. But the advantage to seniors was less than in Japan because of the necessity of collegiate leadership of the clan and the rapid socioeconomic mobility of individual households. Perhaps the principal gain in China was the local political security the lineage provided to all its members, a function that was much less often needed, or possible, in a Japan where local communities were more controlled and protected by higher governmental bodies.

In any event, though the Chinese lineage performed these external functions, it was unable (at least after the destruction of de facto feudalism with the T'ang) to escape a constitution in which pure kin factors were determinative. The lineage was formed only on the basis of genetic relationships, true or assumed, and there was no inclusion or exclusion of households for reasons of general socioeconomic performance. Popular Chinese ideology extolled the virtues of the lineage, and law and bureaucratic practice supported its priorities; thus, much of the advantage its members derived lay in the prestige they gained by fulfilling ideal kin expectations. In Japan, in contrast, kinship ideology focuses on the simple *ie,* and little in either civil law or popular thought praises wide extensions of genetic relationship. Terminology does not counter this emphasis, for it lumps distant collaterals together and sharply distinguishes them from near kin. Even where a "lineage" already existed, the main family head and house council had almost absolute authority over juniors, and they exercised it with a devotion to the interests of the main house that would be inexplicable if "lineage" rather than the house were indeed, and covertly, the more valued institution. Thus, neither succeeding sons nor their younger brothers needed to be impelled by considerations of kinship alone to enter into so extensive an association; on the contrary, the emphasis on the *ie* made it more attractive to remain apart, the one to cultivate his trusteeship, the other to start a new *ie.* Most important, the house ideal kept alive the pattern of an organization in which kin provides the form but, in time of conflict, task performance regulates its process.

We see, then, that what we call the Japanese "kinship" system has traditionally had at its core a set of corporate groupings—household, house, and "lineage"—institutionalized to a striking degree for the performance of general socioeconomic tasks. Insofar as certain tasks in any society can be seen to be more nearly of a "pure" kinship sort—to establish genetic filiation, to provide general socialization, to provide for the expressive needs of, and support to, the individual personality, etc.— these too have been performed within these corporate institutions, but as secondary matters. The ranking of priorities is, very generally, the reverse of that found in Chinese kinship units.

Japanese society in general is organized in terms of solidary communities (at every level) that perform specific adaptive tasks. Kin corporations are only the more diffuse of these associations, which also include economic, religious, neighborhood, village-political, regional-political, and national-political units. The Japanese myths picture the gods as already so organized; on the "High Plain of Heaven" kinship goals do not compete with adaptive goals, and kin units perform as parts of the wider community. History does not suggest that Japanese society has ever departed fundamentally from this model. The conflict between the purposes of kin and non-kin that Confucius failed to resolve for Chinese ideology therefore is clearly resolved from the beginning for the Japanese, and task-oriented organizations that fall somewhere between family and nation, while rare in China, are relatively numerous in Japan. By values, and by the nature of the institutional framework in which they live, therefore, Japanese are used to formal association with more, rather than fewer, members of their communities, and to the justification of links with kinsmen—as with non-kinsmen—in non-kin terms.

The symbols of organization in the Japanese household, house, and "lineage" have been those of kinship, though it is not for this reason alone that we call them "kin" units; they do after all also perform more nearly "pure" kin functions. But kinship forms are also used by the Japanese to structure most other organizations, and these relationships, because they are not founded on a genetic basis, we call "secondary." We have mentioned that the first political states bound rulers and subjects to one another in a fictitious genealogical relation, and historic "lineages" have typically included dependents to whom a simulated kinship has been extended. In general, any relationship, entered into for whatever reason, that is expected to be long lasting and in some way intimate, may be said to be automatically structured in the forms of nuclear kinship. Age-senior neighbors are called "aunt" or "uncle"; a power senior is called *oyakata* ("*patronus*"); seniors in brotherhoods (or sisterhoods) are called "elder brothers (or sisters)"—all as in many another society. But the pattern is far more pervasive than in China or than in the West. In Japan a girl also calls her lover "elder brother"; workmen, students, officials, call their seniors "elder brother" and their boss "*patronus*," and so on. Although household and "lineage" are somewhat less oriented to kin ends than in China, secondary bonds are structured more in terms of kin forms than in China.

One result of this structuring should be to invest secondary bonds with the role and relational expectations of the household, a subject we shall touch on in a later section. But the kind of society we are speaking of is one in which the choice of the object of a relationship is to a high degree conscious and deliberate, and instrumental to perceived socioeconomic interests. On the whole, Japanese society has been characterized by the degree to which the choice is made by the agent of the corporation, acting in terms of his organization's group interest. The decision

Kinship secondary not genetic

of a household to enter into relations with other households, whether bound by "lineage" ties or not, is primarily a matter of the interests of the group, pursued by its head, rather than of the wills and wishes of individual members. But there is also a wide area within which the choice is made by individuals, sometimes for individual, and sometimes for corporate, purposes.

The Kindred

At first sight, the basic units of Japanese kinship seem to be strongly patrilineal. Moreover, as the Japanese borrowed the Chinese vocabulary, with its sharp distinction between patrilineal and non-patrilineal relations and its emphasis in the ideal on the former, Japanese in their law codes and formal writings give the impression that the patriline was the only important kinship channel. Yet we have suggested that in none of the units of this basically corporate system do the requirements of kinship itself have the overwhelming, or perhaps even the most important, part to play. The actor is concerned with the world, and his solutions must reach a compromise between kin and, to put it briefly, success calculations.

Such an outlook inevitably leads a Japanese to consider the advantages that may accrue from relations with his bilateral kindred. In fact terminology presents no block, and evidence suggests that bilateral kinsmen may be quite significant to ego. At least among the aristocracy of the Heian Period (tenth to twelfth centuries), residence seems to have been often uxorilocal or duolocal and never virilocal; women inherited and disposed of properties without regard to the patriline; and close ties with matrilateral kinsmen were in clear evidence. (See McCullough 1967. Similar, more general, illustrations appear in Ariga 1947 and are summarized for English readers by Befu 1963.)

In the village a Japanese will maintain warm personal ties with matrilateral kinsmen as often as with patrilateral relatives. Again, on occasions such as the New Year, Japanese pay ritual visits and by the exchange of gifts and salutations symbolize the structure of their important continued interactions. Such rituals are enacted not only with house or "lineage" members, but with close kindred on both sides, as well as with co-members of non-kin groups and organizations. Most important, Japanese communal life includes numerous institutionalized and often mandatory relationships for the exchange of aid and labor, both at the life crises and in a variety of economic and political contexts—for moneylending, in the fields at the busy seasons of transplanting and harvesting, in house-building, etc. Depending on the circumstances, these relationships include kinsmen on either side, neighbors, and households with which ego is linked through other non-kin ties, as much as, or more than, they include patrilateral kin.

Marriage and the Dyadic Relationships

In few other areas of kinship were Chinese influences so direct and so obtrusive as in the propagation of marriage ideals and the dyadic concept of kin ties; and in few others was this influence so at variance with what seem to have been the basic Japanese ways.

In early times filial piety was taken over as the main conscious principle governing the relations between parents and children, as were Chinese ideas about the subordinate status of women as daughters, sisters, and wives, and about the arranged marriage. Significantly, however, the other kin dyads stressed in the Chinese ideal—e.g., the tie between brother and brother—were hardly noted in Japan, then or thereafter, and the borrowed ideas about even the arranged marriage, the filial relation, or the subordination of women had little practical significance until the Tokugawa period gave cachet to philosophical Confucianism. It is true that if one reads only the didactic, philosophical, and historicizing literature of the years from mid-Tokugawa through early Meiji, one is impressed by the prominence given these Chinese conceptions. Yet the *Twenty-Four Examples of Filial Piety* and similar homilies, as well as the *School for Women*, a book of precepts for the demure female, were widely disseminated for the first time only in the late seventeenth century.

Moreover, even at that later time, these borrowings were stressed only in the formal and legal mode of ideology, effective primarily among the upper classes, in a society that legislated different ways of life for different levels. The jurists who wrote the Meiji Civil Code (promulgated in 1898) had been educated to such conceptions at the very end of the Tokugawa. They began their work by compiling data on kin customs from all regions and classes in Japan, and were amazed at the enormous diversity their survey revealed. They expressed horror at the slight degree to which their fellow countrymen shared, or practiced, their own partly Confucian ideals—at the finding, for example, that the "lower classes" (who on any definition may have formed over 90 per cent of the population at the time) "make no distinction between husband and wife." The code they wrote reflected their own ideals, rather than the "anomalies" their survey revealed, and so put the Chinese model forward. In subsequent generations, the development of a national culture, and of mass education, literacy, and communications transmitting its standards, as well as widespread social climbing in terms of its symbols, gave greater currency and realization to that model than it had ever had before, even as in most other ways the Japanese were sprinting ever faster away from traditional Chinese prototypes. Of course, the same post-Meiji generations saw other cultural developments that diluted the Confucian orientation, and the post-1945 Civil Code and its attendant ideologies have already swept away much of the temporary Chinese veneer. Nevertheless, it is ironic that the clearest kinship influences from China gained status at only that time when Western ideas were also beginning to enter Japan, and achieved wide currency only after Japan had committed herself fully to modernization.

Both before and during the period when these Chinese patterns were important, the durable house and its attendant institutions continued to occupy the central place in Japanese kin ideology; all legal codes, including that of Meiji, gave them first prominence. Because of the paucity of historical materials, it is harder to show that prior to the Tokugawa formal ideology, let alone behavior, having to do with marriage and interpersonal kin relations was of an entirely un-Chinese character. Nonetheless, that is my thesis.

The standards of Japanese exogamy are minimal, and less restrictive even than those of the United States. Marriage within the Japanese "lineage," as defined above, not only was allowed as it was not within the apparent Chinese counterpart, but enjoyed some degree of preference, as one would expect to observe within a power-interest group. Moreover, from at least the tenth century on (McCullough 1967: 136) marriage with aunts or uncles, nieces or nephews, has been freely permitted, as have unions between either parallel or cross-cousins on either side; in recent centuries cousin marriage at least has been entered into in a higher proportion of cases than is true in the modern West (Neel *et al.* 1949). Furthermore, there is in the Japanese tradition a far more permissive attitude toward even sibling unions than is true in the West— let alone in China, so quickly outraged by any association between the family and sexual aberration. The Japanese myths frankly pictured brother-sister marriage among the gods, and only as Chinese influence came to bear was the sanction restricted to the union of half-siblings; finally historic law and custom forbade mention of any form of sexual relation between members of the same nuclear family. It is not suggested that brother-sister incest, let alone marriage, has ever taken place with more frequency in Japan than in other societies, but the popular Japanese attitude toward incest is distinctive. The dirty joke, assumed here to be a device for expressing a positive interest in a subject only moderately tabooed, is a sound piece of evidence. A dirty joke that does no more than celebrate the sexual or the scatological seems of interest to Westerners but thoroughly dull to Japanese. The Japanese dirty joke, on the other hand, very frequently hilariously treats of incest, a subject on the whole so unacceptable to Westerners that it is not allowed even this mode of expression.

The Chinese brand of puritanism, with its ideal of female chastity except in the marriage bond and its admiration for the *chün-tzu* celibate except in the performance of his procreative duties, is at some distance from the Japanese view. It is not merely that extra-marital intercourse seems to have been relatively free of condemnation in Japan: the myths and popular literature romanticize the sexual act as a mode of individual expression very much as is done in the West. This idealization of free sexual choice seems radically un-Chinese, since it conflicts with the idea of the arranged marriage. Moreover, during recent centuries when arranged marriages have been more common, the Japanese have developed a number of devices that permit the principals still to take a more or less active part in the choice of their partners—the *miai*, a formal meeting to allow the girl and boy to register their personal reactions to one another, and the *naien*, or common-law marriage, a union that is officially unregistered but that has been entered into in an extraordinarily high proportion of cases. It is true that the *naien* was often used by the arranging parents to test the bride's fertility and compatibility with the groom's family before they should be obligated to her, but it was also very frequently used by principals intent on escaping the limitations of the arranged match.

There is no evidence that marriage as free from parental initiative as in the contemporary United States has ever been accepted or common in Japan, but parents and principals have been expected to work jointly toward a compromise of their respective interests to a degree much greater than under the formal Chinese system. Contemporary attitude studies show that most (70–80 per cent) of both parents and children say that spouses should be selected either by the principals alone, or by the two generations in intimate consultation with one another (Watanabe 1963: 392). If my thesis is correct, this result is to be seen, not as a new departure in response to modernization, but as a post-Confucian reemphasis of a traditionally freer system of marriage choice.

Many of the formal restrictions imposed by kinship in China have thus been absent in Japan, and relations can be entered into more freely with existing or prospective kinsmen. People are less often stereotyped into generic roles of the "male-female," "parent-child" sorts, and certain individual interests, including the interest in intimate ties that will allow emotional expression, have been given more freedom. Nevertheless, the individual element should not be overemphasized. The Chinese faith in the patriline, the dyadic bond, and the universal moral principle are in Japan matched by faith in the corporate group, through which individual freedom is sometimes negated more effectively than it is in China.

Structure and Principles of the Kin Group

The Japanese household and "lineage" have been spoken of as solidary corporations, because each is organized to operate as an entity under the centralizing direction of the head, and in a web of wider relations in which the group is treated as an indivisible unit. Larger organizations require the participation not of individuals, but of households, each represented by a member appropriate to the situation—the wife in a religious group, a mature son in a work group, the head at a meeting to discuss governmental demands, etc. Conversely, individuals as such find virtually no serious and continuing social roles open to them outside the household. Perhaps there is little difference in ideology in this regard between the demands made on Chinese and Japanese groups. Nevertheless, the Japanese community has been filled with organizations and institutionalized interactions among households that did not exist in China; though higher echelons of Chinese government seldom came into contact with the household, throughout most of Japanese history, manorial, fief, or national governments impinged bureaucratically —through village headmen and neighborhood association leaders—on the smallest residential unit. Practice in Japan thus reinforced theory.

The internal organization of the small group was also quite different in the Chinese and Japanese cases. It has already been pointed out that no roles other than those of the house head and his heir-apparent are given any real definition in Japan. It is true that after the seventeenth century, borrowed Chinese ideas emphasizing filial piety and the subordination of women laid the groundwork for the emergence of a theory of roles and inter-role relations for the parent and child, the husband and wife. Thus, by the time of the Meiji Civil Code, there was a body of opinion that, reinforced by Western thought, gave some prominence to the statuses of individual kin members and to their dyadic relations with one another. This view lost out in the writing of the Code, however, it being the majority view that the important facts about a body of kinsmen living together were not their genetic ties, but the manifestation in them of the durable *ie*, not the attributes of their separate roles and relations, but the unity with which they operate. At no time has there been the kind of Japanese attention to these matters that the Chinese have traditionally devoted to the Five, or the Six, Relationships. We must conclude that Japanese theory has seen the household—and indeed any small face-to-face group—as internally all but unstructured save in terms of its leadership, in contrast with the Chinese predilection for seeing it as a network of statuses in essentially dyadic relations with one another.

So too we must expect a person's view of himself, and his preference for individualized or corporate behavior, to differ in the two cultures. In China, for example, an individual can gain a sense of self as most importantly a parent, a child, a husband, etc., independent of other roles that involve him as part of the corporate household. Thus the Chinese much more often than the Japanese may respond in particularizing, rather than corporate, roles. Furthermore, though little formal philosophy may have penetrated the mind of the average Chinese, he is of a culture built on the Confucian affirmation of the existence and value of the individual moral soul, responsive to universal ethical rules. In this basic sense, Confucianism never took root in Japan, and no other strain of thought has ever, prior to modern times, offered the Japanese a faith in the existence of an individual temporal personality. A Japanese has therefore never been able to justify the view of himself as a valuable social entity distinct from his culturally expected behavior and apart from the largely group-representative and group-organic roles provided for him. Much of the great beauty and (from the Western and Chinese point of view) pathology of literature and art, and of the excruciatingly sensitive individual personality in Japan, stems from this background. Thus, an individualized social personality failed to emerge in Japan—or what did emerge was a social personality immersed in the solidary corporation.

In my discussion so far I have implied that the nature of the Japanese organization with which we are concerned is as much a matter of the form of personality brought to it by its members as it is of the manner in which the corporation itself is institutionalized. From either standpoint, then, it seems misleading to try to delineate independent statuses and relations among them within the household group in Japan, and essential to do so for China. Guides to and limits on what it is proper to ask of a member of a Japanese household of course exist, set superficially by age and sex attributes and more deeply by what is understood of the experience and ability of the individuals. But most fundamentally they are set by the requirements of the group, and any member may legitimately be called upon to perform any action appropriate to the group's situation. What is good for the corporation is indeed in this context good for its members. The status of the head is fixed and definite, but, as we have seen, is assignable to persons ultimately on the basis of achievable attributes, and the overriding expectations of the role are simply that it maintain the group in society. All other members can perhaps most appropriately be said to perform only behaviors rather than permanent roles.

Both the Chinese and the Japanese household heads are in theory given complete authority. They must make all decisions and direct all activities for their organizations, and they control the assets and the powers of reward, punishment, expulsion, and disinheritance that can enforce their will on their members. Yet in practice the authority of the Japanese role is on the one hand less personal and more predictable, and on the other hand more nearly absolute.

In part, the greater ease with which the Japanese head can enforce his wishes results from the structure of his group. As noted earlier, its internal role system presents fewer crosscurrents. For some of the same reasons, he is constrained to be less arbitrary in the exercise of his authority. The head is after all usually also the father, and it is distinctly less important to be the father than the head in Japan, whereas the reverse is true in China. In addition, the father status in China is invested with a personal authority that even ideologically has only tentative and unclear limits, with the result that idiosyncratic departures from any ideal statement of the role could occur there and in effect disrupt the behavior of the person as head; such a departure from the ideal could far less easily occur in Japan. Though in theory certain limitations on the role were in both countries laid down by public law and community opinion, these could in fact lead to fewer and weaker sanctions in China than in Japan. We have already seen that the Japanese house council, and within a "lineage" the main family, could impose a counterweight to the authority of the head, something that no external kin agency could do so well in China. Equally or more important, the aloofness of the government and the isolation of the kin group within the community in China meant that law and opinion could not so easily influence the household head. In both countries, for example, rules forbade actions by the household head that would drive brides to suicide, lead to the murder of a kinswoman for unchasteness, or bring about the death of a son for insubordination. Nevertheless, when these things did happen, it was far more difficult to bring the responsible head to book in China than in Japan, and there seems good evidence that such behavior occurred in a shocking number of cases in China but in very few cases in Japan.

Arbitrariness was no doubt prevented most effectively, however, by the manner in which persons were recruited into the role and by its definition. We have already spoken of the procedures that tend to ensure that a Japanese head is in a high proportion of cases selected for competence, and Ruth Benedict has established so well that group roles are in Japan defined in terms of the incumbent's obligations and only slightly in terms of his rights that there is no need to recapitulate her argument here. The one point at which the Chinese role structure places a similar emphasis on obligation is, of course, in the behavior of the child vis-à-vis his parent. It is curious and instructive that the heaviest load of duty is with the junior in the Chinese household; in Japan it is with the head, responsible for the welfare of a corporation of which juniors are as much the beneficiaries as they are the obligated.

So far we have stressed the corporate nature of the household—a kin group that is on the whole oriented toward socioeconomic adjustment to the world around it—as well as the congruent molding of the roles of its individual members. The corporate nature of the group is its most important characteristic, ideologically, and by custom. Nevertheless, the Japanese household was also responsive to a more complex roster of orientations, of which I shall give only two examples here.

Though formal authority resides in the headship, however one may wish to argue the logic of the result, real authority is diffused throughout the group, all the members of which are expected to take part in the decision-making process if it is to be truly effective in mobilizing them. The formal statement of a decision and of orders must be made by the head, without credit given to others. But such a statement is typically preceded by quiet interchanges between the head and the other leading members of the group, and eventually, directly or indirectly, every member who can reasonably be expected to be concerned by either interest or competence. Members are expected thus to introduce any subject about which they are properly concerned and propose their solution—though within so complex and indirect a fugue of communications that only the person sensitive to the tradition of Japanese cues would be aware of the full import of the remarks. It is the duty of anyone to report such remarks back to the head, and it is his responsibility to sound all members for their knowledge, preferred solution, and the limits within which they will acquiesce to a decision, on any problem that comes to his attention. A decision made formally has thus been pretested, and represents a consensus of the wills of the members of the group. Conversely, if it has not been arrived at in this manner, it will be passively disobeyed or will not motivate the members. The tolerance for authoritarianism is perhaps higher in the Japanese than in many Western or Chinese situations, but in Japan no head can expect well-motivated action on any decision that has not been deliberately accepted by members who have the right by interest or competence to be heard.

Another example of the response of the household to various orientations may be understood if one realizes that the formal mode of the household, as it has been described, leaves no room for the gratification of the individuality of members. Indeed, I argue that no attention is in fact paid to what may be called the social personality of the individual member. It is the emotional aspects of the personality that are instead given outlet in the procedures of the Japanese small group, and a wealth of standard behavior patterns can only be interpreted in this light. The same head who reaches decisions with an authoritarian concern for the welfare of the household will at other times pet his children in extreme attempts to give them physical pleasure, will amuse his family with his drunken inanities, and will spend time and money on a clearly compulsive search for amusements that he has learned give special pleasure to each member of his family. The person who is defensively proud of those competences that benefit his group in the serious business of life will at another point, and with apparent masochistic delight, reveal to the others his failures and incompetence. Such behavior is, moreover, in every sense mutual and clearly deeply appreciated by all.

To interpret this pattern of behavior as an outlet for the tensions of Japanese life has something to recommend it, but this sort of action is, after all, not without its own history and philosophy. It can be interpreted culturally as the institutionalization of a set of values having to do with *ninjō* (literally, "human feeling").* The most direct ancestry of the doctrine of *ninjō* seems to be twofold, and in neither aspect specifically Chinese—namely, a tendency apparent even in the myths to define the individual in terms of his emotions, and the Buddhist concept of compassion. In any event, *ninjō* does not demand that persons "love" one another, but it does perceive the individual as a bundle of emotional sensibilities that require gratification and must not be exposed to avoidable pain. It is a moral rule, as it is also a psychological evaluation, for it is wrong to give the other person unnecessary pain and laudable to

---

* One may wish to see this idea gaining something from the statement of Mencius that men cannot bear to see the suffering of others and so will not act to harm them, but the fact is that Confucianism did not on this basis develop a psychology or a doctrine of behavior at all similar. The key Confucian concept *jen* is clearly ethical love—humanitarianism if you will, or attention to the moral rights of another person. The Japanese doctrine of *ninjō* likewise differs profoundly from the popular Chinese concept of *kan-ch'ing*, with its instrumental use of the emotional ties between two people to develop relations of common social, economic, and other such interests.

please his emotional needs. Certainly most of Japanese literature embodies the perception of the emotional composition of the individual, and for this reason, as Kroeber has pointed out, differs fundamentally from Chinese literature, and almost alone in the world closely parallels Western writing. The institutions that give expression to this humanism in the small group have thus as secure a base in the ethos of Japan as Confucian humanitarianism has in China.

The satisfaction of the demands of *ninjō*, and of collegiate decision making, produces procedures in the small Japanese group at variance with those we have discussed earlier. It thus seems appropriate to see the group as being institutionalized to express a variety of principles. Some of these—those expressing corporateness, hierarchy, solidarity, etc. —we may wish to call "formal" because they are cued to public patterns of behavior, or "primary" because in any situation of conflict they have a clear priority. The others—those expressing collegiateness, *ninjō*, and others we have not discussed here—we may wish to call "informal," or "secondary." But the trick of successful group dynamics, and the mark of the able leader, is behavior that will maximize the cultural demands to be satisfied in a given situation. If we are to keep track of the link between principle and behavior, we must predicate (as Ruth Benedict saw so well) that Japanese cognitive categories for the small group stress situationalism and cue the actor to the set that is to govern a particular sequence of actions.

References

Introduction

Aijmer, Göran. 1967. "Expansion and Extension in Hakka Society," *Journal of the Hong Kong Branch of the Royal Asiatic Society*, vol. 7.

Baker, Hugh D. R. 1968. A Chinese Lineage Village: Sheung Shui. London.

Baller, F. W. 1892. The Sacred Edict, with a Translation of the Colloquial Rendering. . . . Shanghai.

Cohen, Myron L. 1969. "Agnatic Kinship in South Taiwan," *Ethnology*, vol. 8, no. 2, April.

Fei Hsiao-tung. 1936–37. "The Problem of Chinese Relationship System," *Monumenta Serica* (Journal of Oriental Studies of the Catholic University of Peking), vol. 2.

Fêng Han-yi. 1948. The Chinese Kinship System. Harvard-Yenching Institute, Cambridge, Mass. (Originally published in 1937, *Harvard Journal of Asiatic Studies*, vol. 2, no. 2.)

Freedman, Maurice. 1958. Lineage Organization in Southeastern China. London School of Economics Monographs on Social Anthropology, 18.

———— 1966. Chinese Lineage and Society: Fukien and Kwangtung. London School of Economics Monographs on Social Anthropology, 33.

———— 1967. "Ancestor Worship: Two Facets of the Chinese Case," in Maurice Freedman, ed., Social Organization, Essays Presented to Raymond Firth (London).

Gallin, Bernard. 1960. "Matrilateral and Affinal Relationships of a Taiwanese Village," *American Anthropologist*, vol. 62, no. 4, Aug.

Gamble, Sidney D. 1954. Ting Hsien: A North China Rural Community. Institute of Pacific Relations, New York. (Reissued in 1968 by Stanford University Press.)

Han Suyin. 1965. The Crippled Tree. London.

Hsu, Francis L. K. 1942. "The Differential Functions of Relationship Terms," *American Anthropologist*, vol. 44, no. 2, April–June.

———— 1947. "On a Technique for Studying Relationship Terms," *American Anthropologist*, vol. 49, no. 4, pt. 1, Oct.–Dec.

———— 1963. Clan, Caste and Club. Princeton, N.J.

Jacobs, Norman. 1958. The Origin of Modern Capitalism and Eastern Asia. Hong Kong.

Lang, Olga. 1946. Chinese Family and Society. New Haven.

Lebra, William P. 1966. Okinawan Religion—Belief, Ritual, and Social Structure. Honolulu.

Levy, Marion J. 1953. "Contrasting Factors in the Modernization of China and Japan," *Economic Development and Cultural Change*, vol. 2, no. 3, Oct.

Pasternak, Burton. 1968a. "Agnatic Atrophy in a Formosan Village," *American Anthropologist*, vol. 70, no. 1, Feb.

———— 1968b. "Atrophy of Patrilineal Bonds in a Chinese Village in Historical Perspective," *Ethnohistory*, vol. 15, no. 3, Summer.

———— 1969. "The Role of the Frontier in Chinese Lineage Development," *The Journal of Asian Studies*, vol. 27, no. 3, May.

Pratt, Jean A. 1960. "Emigration and Unilineal Descent Groups: A Study of Marriage in a Hakka Village in the New Territories," *The Eastern Anthropologist* (Lucknow), vol. 13, no. 4, June–Aug.

Yang, C. K. 1959. The Chinese Family in the Communist Revolution. Cambridge, Mass.

Developmental Process in the Chinese Domestic Group

Ch'en Ta. 1938. Nan-yang Hua-ch'iao yü Min-Yüeh she-hui. Shanghai.

————. 1940. Emigrant Communities in South China. Institute of Pacific Relations, New York.

Chow Yung-teh. 1966. Social Mobility in China. New York.

Cohen, Myron L. 1967. "Variations in Complexity among Chinese Family Groups: The Impact of Modernization," *Transactions of the New York Academy of Sciences*, Ser. 2, vol. 29, no. 5.

———— 1968. "A Case Study of Chinese Family Economy and Development," *Journal of Asian and African Studies*, vol. 3, no. 3.

Fei Hsiao-tung. 1939. Peasant Life in China. London.

Fei Hsiao-tung and Chang Chih-i. 1949. Earthbound China. London.

Freedman, Maurice. 1958. Lineage Organization in Southeastern China. London School of Economics Monographs on Social Anthropology, 18.

———— 1961–62. "The Family in China, Past and Present," *Pacific Affairs*, vol. 34, no. 4.

Fried, Morton H. 1953. Fabric of Chinese Society. New York.

Ho Ping-ti. 1962. The Ladder of Success in Imperial China. New York.

Hu Hsien-chin. 1948. The Common Descent Group in China and Its Functions. Viking Fund Publications in Anthropology, 10, New York.

Kulp, Daniel H. 1925. Country Life in South China. New York.

Lang, Olga. 1946. Chinese Family and Society. New Haven.

Levy, Marion J. 1949. The Family Revolution in Modern China. Cambridge, Mass.

Lin Yueh-hwa. 1948. The Golden Wing: A Sociological Study of Chinese Familism. New York.

McAleavy, Henry. 1955. "Certain Aspects of Chinese Customary Law in the Light of Japanese Scholarship," *Bulletin of the School of Oriental and African Studies*, vol. 17.

Moench, Richard U. 1963. Economic Relations of the Chinese in the Society Islands. Unpublished doctoral dissertation, Harvard University.

Osgood, Cornelius. 1963. Village Life in Old China: A Community Study of Kao Yao, Yünnan. New York.

Simon, G. E. 1887. China: Its Social, Political, and Religious Life. London.

Smith, Arthur H. 1900. Village Life in China: A Study in Sociology. Edinburgh and London.

Tawney, R. H. 1932. Land and Labour in China. London.

Yang, C. K. 1959a. The Chinese Family in the Communist Revolution. Cambridge, Mass.

———— 1959b. A Chinese Village in Early Communist Transition. Cambridge, Mass.

Yang, Martin C. 1945. A Chinese Village: Taitou, Shantung Province, New York.

Child Training and the Chinese Family

Lang, Olga. 1946. Chinese Family and Society. New Haven.

Whiting, John W. M., Irvin L. Child, and William W. Lambert. 1966. Field Guide for a Study of Socialization. New York.

Wolf, Margery. 1968. The House of Lim. New York.

The Families of Chinese Farmers

Buck, John L. 1930. "The Farm Family and Population," Chap. 9 in Chinese Farm Economy: A Study of 2,866 Farms in Seventeen Localities and Seven Provinces in China (Institute of Pacific Relations, Chicago).

———— 1937a. Land Utilization in China: A Study of 16,786 Farms in 168 Localities, and 38,256 Farm Families in Twenty-two Provinces in China, 1929–33. Nanking. Reproduced by The Council on Economic and Cultural Affairs, New York, 1956.

———— 1937b. Land Utilization in China, Atlas. Nanking.

———— 1937c. Land Utilization in China, Statistics. Nanking.

Chiao Chi-ming. 1933–34. "A Study of the Chinese Population," *Milbank Memorial Fund Quarterly (Bulletin)*, vol. 11, no. 4, Oct. 1933, vol. 12, nos. 1–3, Jan., April, July, 1934.

Notestein, Frank W. 1937. "Population," chap. 13 in Buck 1937a.

———— 1938. "A Demographic Study of 38,256 Rural Families in China," *Milbank Memorial Fund Quarterly*, vol. 16, no. 1, Jan.

Family Relations in Modern Chinese Fiction

Borowitz, Albert. 1954. Fiction in Communist China 1949–1953. Dittoed monograph, Center for International Studies, M.I.T., Cambridge, Mass.

Chen, A. S. 1964. "The Ideal Local Party Secretary and the 'Model' Man," *The China Quarterly*, Jan.–March.

Chen, Lucy H. 1963. "Literary Formosa," *The China Quarterly*, July–Dec.

Chin, Ai-li S. 1951. Interdependence of Roles in Transitional China: A Structural Analysis of Attitudes in Contemporary Chinese Literature. Unpublished dissertation, Radcliffe College.

The China Quarterly. 1963. Special Survey of Chinese Communist Literature, Jan.–March.

Chow Tse-tsung. 1960. The May Fourth Movement: Intellectual Revolution in Modern China. Cambridge, Mass.

Hsia, C. T. 1961. A History of Modern Chinese Fiction. New Haven.

———— 1963. "Residual Femininity: Women in Chinese Communist Fiction," *The China Quarterly,* Jan.–March.

Hsia Tsi-an. 1961. "Taiwan," in C. T. Hsia, 1961.

Land and Lineage in Traditional China

Buck, John L. 1930. Chinese Farm Economy. Chicago.

Cressey, George. 1934. China's Geographic Foundations. New York.

Crook, Isabel, and David Crook. 1959. Revolution in a Chinese Village: Ten Mile Inn. London.

Fei Hsiao-tung and Chang Chih-i. 1945. Earthbound China. Chicago.

Freedman, Maurice. 1958. Lineage Organization in Southeastern China. London School of Economics Monographs on Social Anthropology, 18.

———— 1966. Chinese Lineage and Society: Fukien and Kwangtung. London School of Economics Monographs on Social Anthropology, 33.

Gamble, Sidney D. 1954. Ting Hsien, A North China Rural Community. Institute of Pacific Relations, New York. (Reissued in 1968 by Stanford University Press.)

———— 1963. North China Villages: Social, Political, and Economic Activities before 1933. Berkeley and Los Angeles.

Hsiao Kung-chuan. 1960. Rural China: Imperial Control in the Nineteenth Century. Seattle, Wash.

Hsu, Francis L. K. 1948. Under the Ancestors' Shadow: Chinese Culture and Personality. New York.

Hu Hsien-chin. 1948. The Common Descent Group in China and Its Functions. Viking Fund Publications in Anthropology, 10, New York.

Lang, Olga. 1946. Chinese Family and Society. New Haven.

Liu Hui-chen Wang. 1959. The Traditional Chinese Clan Rules. Association for Asian Studies Monographs, 7, Locust Valley, N.Y.

Potter, Jack M. 1968. Capitalism and the Chinese Peasant: Social and Economic Change in a Hong Kong Village. Berkeley and Los Angeles.

Sahlins, Marshall D. 1961. "The Segmentary Lineage, an Organization of Predatory Expansion," *American Anthropologist,* vol. 63.

Wiens, Herold J. 1954. China's March Toward the Tropics. Hamden, Conn.

Yang, Martin C. 1945. A Chinese Village: Taitou, Shantung Province. New York.

The Chinese Genealogy as a Research Source

Eberhard, Wolfram. 1954–56. "The Leading Families of Ancient Tun-huang," *Sinologica,* vol. 4.

———— 1962. Social Mobility in Traditional China. Leiden.

Fairbank, John K., and Masatake Banno. 1955. Japanese Studies of Modern China: A Bibliographical Guide. Rutland, Vt.

Fei Hsiao-tung. 1939. Peasant Life in China. London.

Freedman, Maurice. 1957. Chinese Family and Marriage in Singapore. Colonial Research Studies, 20, London.

───── 1958. Lineage Organization in Southeastern China. London School of Economics Monographs on Social Anthropology, 18.

───── 1966. Chinese Lineage and Society: Fukien and Kwangtung. London School of Economics Monographs on Social Anthropology, 33.

Fried, Morton H. 1966. "Some Political Aspects of Clanship in a Modern Chinese City," in Marc J. Swartz, Victor W. Turner, and Arthur Tuden, eds., Political Anthropology (Chicago).

Gallin, Bernard. 1960. "Matrilateral and Affinal Relationships in a Taiwanese Village," *American Anthropologist*, vol. 62, no. 4, Aug.

Hsu, Francis L. K. 1948. Under the Ancestors' Shadow: Chinese Culture and Personality. New York.

Hu Hsien-chin. 1948. The Common Descent Group in China and Its Functions. Viking Fund Publications in Anthropology, 10, New York.

Lin Hsien-t'ang et al., eds. 1935. Hsi-he Lin-shih tsu-p'u. Taichung.

Lin-shih tsu-p'u pien-chi wei-yüan-hui, ed. 1963. Lin-shih tsu-p'u. 3d ed. Taichung.

Liu Hui-chen Wang. 1959. The Traditional Chinese Clan Rules. Association for Asian Studies Monographs, 7, Locust Valley, N.Y.

Makino Tatsumi. 1936. "Mei-Shin zokufu kenkyu josetsu" (A Preface to the Study of Chinese Genealogy in the Ming and Ch'ing Dynasties), *Toho Gakuho*, vol. 6.

───── 1949. Kinsei Chugoku sozoku kenkyu (A Study of the Clan in Modern China). Tokyo.

P'an Kuang-tan. 1933. "Chung-kuo chia-p'u-hsüeh lüeh-shih" (A Brief History of Chinese Genealogical Studies), *Tung-fang tsa-chih*, vol. 26, no. 1.

Sheng Ch'ing-yi. 1963. "T'ai-wan chia-p'u pien-tsuan chih yen-chiu" (A Study of the Compilation of Taiwanese Genealogies), *T'ai-wan wen-hsien*, vol. 14, no. 3, Sept.

Su Hsün. 1698. Su Lao-ch'üan hsien-sheng ch'üan-chi, 20 chüan.

Taga Akigoro. 1960a. Sofu no kenkyu (An Analytical Study of Chinese Genealogical Books). Toyo Bunko, Tokyo.

───── 1960b. "Kei-fu" (Descent Line), in Ajia Rekishi Jiten, vol. 3, Tokyo.

Twitchett, Denis. 1959. "The Fan Clan's Charitable Estate, 1050–1760," in David Nivison and Arthur Wright, eds., Confucianism in Action (Stanford, Calif.).

Yang, Martin C. 1948. A Chinese Village: Taitou, Shantung Province. London.

Yuan I-chin. 1931. "Life Tables for a Southern Chinese Family from 1365 to 1849," *Human Biology*, vol. 3.

Ritual Aspects of Chinese Kinship and Marriage

Addison, James T. 1925. Chinese Ancestor Worship: A Study of Its Meaning and Relations with Christianity. Shanghai.

Aijmer, Göran. 1964. The Dragon Boat Festival on the Hupeh-Hunan Plain, Central China: A Study in the Ceremonialism of the Transplantation of Rice. The Ethnographical Museum of Sweden Monograph Series, 9, Stockholm.

———— 1967. "Expansion and Extension in Hakka Society," *Journal of the Hong Kong Branch of the Royal Asiatic Society*, vol. 7.

———— 1968. "A Structural Approach to Chinese Ancestor Worship," *Bijdragen tot de Taal-, Land- en Volkenkunde*, pt. 124.

Baker, Hugh D. R. 1968. A Chinese Lineage Village: Sheung Shui. London.

Bredon, Juliet. 1930. Chinese New Year Festivals. Shanghai.

Buxbaum, David C. 1968. Some Aspects of Substantive Family Law and Social Change in Rural China (1896–1967): with a Case Study of a North Taiwan Village. Unpublished Ph.D. thesis, University of Washington.

Ch'en Chung-min. 1967. "Ancestor Worship and Lineage Organization in Chin Chiang Ts'o" (in Chinese), *The Bulletin of the Institute of Ethnology, Academia Sinica*, no. 23.

Chiu, Vermier Y. 1966. Marriage Laws and Customs of China. Hong Kong Institute of Advanced Chinese Studies and Research, The Chinese University of Hong Kong.

Cormack, J. G. (Anne). 1935. Everyday Customs in China. Edinburgh and London.

Dols, P. J. 1915–16. "La vie chinoise dans la province de Kan-sou (Chine)," *Anthropos*, vols. 10–11.

Doolittle, Justus. 1865. Social Life of the Chinese. New York.

Doré, Henry. 1914. Researches into Chinese Superstitions. M. Kennelly, trans. and ed. 1st pt., vol. 1. Shanghai.

Douglas, Robert K. 1901. Society in China. London.

Eberhard, Wolfram. 1958. Chinese Festivals. London and New York.

———— 1963. "Auspicious Marriages: A Statistical Study of a Chinese Custom," *Sociologus*, n.s., vol. 13, no. 1.

Egerod, Søren. 1959. "A Sampling of Chungshan Hakka," in Søren Egerod and Elsa Glahn, eds., Studia Serica Bernhard Karlgren Dedicata (Copenhagen).

Fei Hsiao-tung. 1939. Peasant Life in China: A Field Study of Country Life in the Yangtze Valley. London.

Fêng Han-yi and J. K. Shryock. 1950. "Marriage Customs in the Vicinity of I-Ch'ang," *Harvard Journal of Asiatic Studies*, vol. 13, nos. 3 and 4.

Fielde, Adele M. 1885. Pagoda Shadows: Studies from Life in China. 4th ed. Boston.

———— 1894. A Corner of Cathay: Studies from Life among the Chinese. New York.

Freedman, Maurice. 1957. Chinese Family and Marriage in Singapore. Colonial Research Studies, 20, H.M.S.O., London.

———— 1958. Lineage Organization in Southeastern China. London School of Economics Monographs on Social Anthropology, 18.

———— 1966. Chinese Lineage and Society: Fukien and Kwangtung. London School of Economics Monographs on Social Anthropology, 33.

———— 1967a. "Ancestor Worship: Two Facets of the Chinese Case," in Maurice Freedman, ed., Social Organization, Essays Presented to Raymond Firth (London).

———— 1967b. "Rites and Duties, or Chinese Marriage." An Inaugural Lecture, London.

———— 1969. "Geomancy," *Proceedings of the Royal Anthropological Institute of Great Britain and Ireland for 1968* (London).

Frick, Johann. 1952. "Hochzeitssitten von Hei-tsui-tzu in der Provinz Ch'ing-hai (China)," *Folklore Studies*, Supplement no. 1, Ethnographische Beiträge aus der Ch'inghai Provinz (China), Peking (printed in Japan).

Gallin, Bernard. 1966. Hsin Hsing, Taiwan: A Chinese Village in Change. Berkeley and Los Angeles.

Gamble, Sidney D. 1954. Ting Hsien: A North China Rural Community. Institute of Pacific Relations. New York. (Reissued in 1968 by Stanford University Press.)

Gray, John Henry. 1878. China: A History of the Laws, Manners, and Customs of the People. W. G. Gregor, ed. 2 vols. London.

Grube, Wilhelm. 1901. Zur Pekinger Volkskunde, *Veröffentlichungen aus dem Königlichen Museum für Völkerkunde*, vol. 7, pts. 1–4, Berlin.

Highbaugh, Irma. 1948. Family Life in West China. New York.

Hsu, Francis L. K. 1949. Under the Ancestors' Shadow: Chinese Culture and Personality. London.

Hutson, James. 1921. Chinese Life in the Tibetan Foothills. Shanghai.

Körner, Brunhild. 1959. Die religiöse Welt der Bäuerin in Nordchina. Statens Etnografiska Museum, Stockholm.

Lin Yueh-hwa. 1948. The Golden Wing: A Sociological Study of Chinese Familism. London.

Liu Wei-min. 1936. "An Account and Analysis of the Marriage Customs of Tung-kuan" (in Chinese), *Min-su*, National Sun Yat-sen University Research Institute, vol. 1, no. 1.

Lockhart, J. H. Stewart. 1890. "The Marriage Ceremonies of the Manchus," *Folk-Lore*, vol. 1, no. 4.

Lynn, Jermyn Chi-hung. 1928. Social Life of the Chinese (in Peking). Peking, Tientsin.

Maspero, Henri. 1932. "The Mythology of Modern China," in J. Hackin *et al.*, Asiatic Mythology (London).

Osgood, Cornelius. 1963. Village Life in Old China: A Community Study of Kao Yao, Yünnan. New York.

Segers, Arthur. 1932. La Chine, le peuple, sa vie quotidienne et ses cérémonies. Antwerp.

Serruys, Paul. 1944. "Les cérémonies du mariage: Usages populaires et textes dialectaux du sud de la préfecture de Ta-t'oung (Chansi)," *Folklore Studies* (Peking), vol. 3, no. 1.

Shryock, John. 1931. The Temples of Anking and Their Cults: A Study of Modern Chinese Religion. Paris.

Su, Tina Han. 1966. A Thematic Study of Chinese Marriage Ritual and Symbolism. Unpublished B.A. Hons. thesis, Cornell University.

Théry, François. 1948–49. "Les coutumes chinoises relatives au mariage," *Bulletin de l'université l'Aurore*, 3d. series, vols. 9 and 10, nos. 36, 37, 38.

Tun Li-ch'en. 1965. Annual Customs and Festivals in Peking. 2d ed. Derk Bodde, trans. and annot. Hong Kong.

Wieger, L. 1913. Moral Tenets and Customs in China. L. Davrout, trans. and annot. Ho-Kien-fu.

Williams, S. Wells. 1883. The Middle Kingdom. Rev. ed. London.

Wolf, Arthur P. 1964. Marriage and Adoption in a Hokkien Village. Unpublished Ph.D. thesis, Cornell University.

Yang, Martin C. 1948. A Chinese Village: Taitou, Shantung Province. London.
Yang Pi-wang. 1963. "Ancient Bridal Laments," *China Reconstructs*, vol. 12, no. 4, Oct.

Chinese Kinship and Mourning Dress

Bodman, Nicholas C. 1955. Spoken Amoy Hokkien. 2 vols. Kuala Lumpur.
Cormack, J. G. 1935. Everyday Customs in China. Edinburgh and London.
De Groot, J. J. M. 1892–1910. The Religious System of China. 6 vols. Leyden.
Doolittle, Justus. 1865. Social Life of the Chinese. 2 vols. New York.
Freedman, Maurice. 1958. Lineage Organization in Southeastern China. London School of Economics Monographs in Social Anthropology, 18.
Gray, John Henry. 1878. China. 2 vols. London.
Medhurst, W. H. 1873. The Foreigner in Far Cathay. New York.
Wolf, Arthur P. 1966. "Childhood Association, Sexual Attraction, and the Incest Taboo," *American Anthropologist*, vol. 68.

Chinese Kin Terms of Reference and Address

Chao Yuen Ren. 1956. "Chinese Terms of Address," *Language*, vol. 32.
Chen, T. S., and J. K. Shryock. 1932. "Chinese Relationship Terms," *American Anthropologist*, vol. 34.
Conant, Francis P. 1961. "Jarawa Kin Systems of Reference and Address: A Componential Comparison," *Anthropological Linguistics*, vol. 3.
Fêng Han-yi. 1948. The Chinese Kinship System. Cambridge, Mass. (Originally published in *Harvard Journal of Asiatic Studies*, vol. 2, no. 2, 1937.)
Goodenough, Ward H. 1951. Property, Kin, and Community on Truk. Yale University Publications in Anthropology, 46, New Haven.
———— 1956. "Componential Analysis and the Study of Meaning," *Language*, vol. 32.
———— 1964. "Componential Analysis of Könkämä Lapp Kinship Terminology," in Ward H. Goodenough, ed., Explorations in Cultural Anthropology (New York).
———— 1965. "Yankee Kinship Terminology: A Problem in Componential Analysis," in E. A. Hammel, ed. 1965a.
Hammel, E. A., ed. 1965a. Formal Semantic Analysis. A special publication of *American Anthropologist*, vol. 67, no. 5, pt. 2.
———— 1965b. "A Transformational Analysis of Comanche Kinship Terminology," in E. A. Hammel, ed. 1965a.
Kroeber, A. L. 1933. "Process in the Chinese Kinship System," *American Anthropologist*, vol. 35.
Lounsbury, Floyd G. 1956. "A Semantic Analysis of the Pawnee Kinship Usage," *Language*, vol. 32.
———— 1964. "A Formal Account of the Crow- and Omaha-type Kinship Terminologies," in Ward H. Goodenough, ed., Explorations in Cultural Anthropology (New York).
Lowie, Robert H. 1917. Culture and Ethnology. New York.
Morgan, Lewis H. 1871. Systems of Consanguinity and Affinity of the Human Family. Smithsonian Contributions to Knowledge, 17, Washington, D.C.

Murdock, George P. 1949. Social Structure. New York.

Osgood, C. E. 1957. The Measurement of Meaning. Urbana, Ill.

———— 1961. "The Logic of Semantic Differentiation," in Sol Saporta, ed., Psycholinguistics: A Book of Readings (New York).

Wallace, Anthony F. C., and J. Atkins. 1960. "The Meaning of Kinship Terms," *American Anthropologist*, vol. 62.

Japanese Kinship: A Comparison

Ariga Kizaemon. 1947. "Dōzoku to shinzoku," in Origuchi Shinobu, ed., Nihon minzokugaku no tame ni (For Japanese Ethnology), vol. 2 (Tokyo).

Befu Harumi. 1963. "Patrilineal Descent and Personal Kindred in Japan," *American Anthropologist*, vol. 65.

Freedman, Maurice. 1958. Lineage Organization in Southeastern China. London School of Economics Monographs on Social Anthropology, 18.

Koyama Takeshi. 1962. "Changing Family Structure in Japan," in Robert J. Smith and Richard K. Beardsley, eds. Japanese Culture, Its Development and Characteristics (Chicago).

McCullough, William H. 1967. "Japanese Marriage Institutions in the Heian Period," *Harvard Journal of Asiatic Studies*, vol. 27.

Nagai Michio. 1953. Dōzoku: A Preliminary Study of the Japanese "Extended Family" Group and Its Social and Economic Functions. Columbus, Ohio.

Nakane Chie. 1967. Kinship and Economic Organization in Rural Japan. London School of Economics Monographs on Social Anthropology, 32.

Neel, James V., et al. 1949. "The Incidence of Consanguineous Matings in Japan," *American Journal of Human Genetics*, vol. 1, no. 2.

Raper, Arthur F., et al. 1950. The Japanese Village in Transition. Tokyo.

Smith, Robert J. 1962. "Stability in Japanese Kinship Terminology: The Historical Evidence," in Robert J. Smith and Richard K. Beardsley, eds., Japanese Culture, Its Development and Characteristics (Chicago).

Watanabe Yōzō. 1963. "The Family and the Law: The Individualist Premise and Japanese Family Law," in Arthur von Mehren, ed., Law in Japan: The Legal Order in Changing Society (Cambridge, Mass.).

Character List

All Chinese terms and names are in their Mandarin form unless followed by C for Cantonese or H for Hokkien. Japanese terms are marked J.

a-ciek H 阿叔
ani J 兄
a-peq H 阿伯
ato-tori J 跡取り

bunke J 分家

Chang-chou-fu 漳州府
Chap Ng Tsoh C (Chi-wu-tsu) 輯五祖
chen 鎮
cheng 正
chia 家
chia-chang 家長
chia-p'u 家譜
chih 支
Ch'ing Ming 清明
chi-shu-yuan 技術員
chiu-mu 九牧
chōnan J 長男
Chou Wu Wang 周武王
chü-jen 舉人
Ch'ung Yang 重陽
chün-tzu 君子

dōzoku J 同族

erh-shen 二嬸

fang 房
fen-chia 分家
feng-shui 風水
Fui Sha Wai C (Hui-sha-wei) 灰沙圍
fu-pi 副妣

giri no- J 義理の

Han 漢
Hang Mei C (K'eng-wei) 坑尾
Hang Tau C (K'eng-t'ou) 坑頭
Ha Tsuen C (Hsia-ts'un) 厦村
hi- J 會
honke J 本家
hsiao 孝
hsien 縣
Hsien-tai Wen-hsüeh 現代文學
hsi-p'u 系譜
hsiu-ts'ai 秀才
hu 戶
hui-kuan 會館
hun 魂

ie J 家
itoko J 從兄弟

jen 仁
Jen-min Wen-hsüeh 人民文學
jirui J じるい

kachō J 家長
Kam Tin C (Chin–t'ien) 錦田
kan-ch'ing 感情
kandō J 勘當
k'ao 靠
Kaohsiung 高雄
kao-tsu 高祖
kao tui-hsiang 搞對象
ki-liam H (chi-nien) 記念
kuan-t'a kuan-te chin 管她管得緊
kung-p'u 公譜
kuo-fang-tzu 過房子

lao-pai-hsing 老百姓
liang-t'ou-chia chih-tu 兩頭家制度
liao-chieh 了解
Lin 林
ling-p'ai 靈牌

mago J 孫
maki J まき
mama- J 繼
Matsu 媽祖
mei J 姪
Mei-nung 美濃
miai J 見合い
ming-ling-tzu 螟蛉子
mow (mu) 畝
mua:-po H 麻布

naien J 內緣
Nan-yang Hua-ch'iao yü Min-Yüeh
she-hui 南洋華僑與閩粵社會
ninjō J 人情

ō- J 大
oba J 伯母（叔母）
obā J 祖母
oi 甥
oji J 伯父（叔父）
ojī J 祖父

p'ai 牌
p'ang 傍
peq-po H 白布
peq-po-sa: H 白布衫
peq-sa: H 白衫
Ping Shan C (P'ing-shan) 屏山
p'u-chü 譜局
p'u-tieh 譜牒

Sanhsia 三峽
shen 神
shen-chu 神主
shen-wei 神位
shih 氏
shih-fu 師父
shih-lu 世錄
shih-piao 世表
shinrui J 親類
shinseki J 親戚
shu-tzu-chiao 樹仔脚
sim-pua H 新婦子
szu-p'u 私譜
szu-tzu 嗣子

ta-fang 大方
T'ai-p'ing 太平
Ta-li 大里
t'a-ma 他媽
Tang C (Teng) 鄧
t'a-tieh 他爹
te-a-po H 袋仔布
ti 地
t'ien 天
Ting Hsien 定縣

Tsao Chün　竈君

tsu　族

tsung-p'u　宗譜

tsu-p'u　族譜

Tuan Wu　端午

T'u-ch'eng　堥城

tui-hsiang　對象

t'ung-chia jen　(Hakka : t'oung-
　ka ngin)　同家人

t'ung-hsing　同姓

tung-shih　懂事

t'u-ti　徒弟

uji <u>J</u>　氏

Wai Shan <u>C</u> (Wei-hsin)　維新

wan-t'an　餛飩

Wen-hsüeh Tsa-chih　文學雜誌

Wu　伍

Wu-feng　霧峯

wu fu　五服

yang　陽

Yat T'ai <u>C</u> (I-t'i)　一體

yen　嚴

yin　陰

Zunn Tak <u>C</u> (Ch'ung-te)　崇德

Index